Galatians as Examined by Diverse Academics in 2012 (St. Andrews, Scotland)

Hermit Kingdom Studies in Christianity and Judaism, 3

Galatians as Examined by Diverse Academics in 2012 (St. Andrews, Scotland)

Edited

by

Heerak Christian Kim

ASIA EVANGELICAL COLLEGE AND SEMINARY

The Hermit Kingdom Press
Newark * Seoul * Bangalore * Cebu

Galatians as Examined by Diverse Academics in 2012 (St. Andrews, Scotland)
(Hermit Kingdom Studies in Christianity and Judaism, 3)

Copyright ©2013 The Hermit Kingdom Press

All rights reserved. No part of this book may be reproduced in any form or by any means, electronic or mechanical, including photocopying, recording, or by any information storage and retrieval system (including computer files in any form), without permission in writing from the publisher.

Paperback ISBN13: 978-1-59689-117-3

ISSN: 1932-6718

Write To Address:
The Hermit Kingdom Press
P. O. Box 9062
Newark, DE 19714
The United States of America

Library of Congress Cataloging-in-Publication Data

Galatians as examined by diverse academics in 2012 (St. Andrews, Scotland) / edited by Heerak Christian Kim.
    pages cm. -- (Hermit Kingdom studies in Christianity and Judaism, ISSN 1932-6718 ; 3)
  Includes bibliographical references.
  ISBN 978-1-59689-117-3 (pbk. : alk. paper)
  1. Bible. Galatians--Criticism, interpretation, etc.--Congresses. I. Kim, H. C. (Heerak Christian)
  BS2685.52.G34 2013
  227'.406--dc23
                            2013014326

Dedicated
to the Church of Scotland
and John Knox, an alumnus of
the University of St. Andrews, Scotland

Contents

Foreword
Page 9

Contributors
Page 11

Inscribing Abraham: Apocalyptic, the Akedah, and 'Abba! Father' in Galatians
/ Sigve K. Tonstad / *page 15*

Jesus Christ: Victim or Victor? Revisiting Galatians 3:13 in conversation with Karl Barth and Scripture
/ Matthias Grebe / *page 28*

Apocalyptic Allegory: Paul's Use of Genesis and Isaiah in Galatians 4:19–5:1
/ Joseph Hyung S. Lee / *page 42*

Promise, Law, Faith: Covenant-Historical Reasoning in Galatians
/ T. David Gordon / page 57

Contents

A Cinderella Story: The Role of Galatians within a Gospel Canon
/ Paul David Landgraf / *page 135*

Sola Scriptura and Galatians 1:8-9: Galatians' Prejudice against Alternative Interpretation
/ Heerak Christian Kim / *page 164*

FOREWORD

"Paul's Letter to the Galatians & Christian Theology" conference was held at the University of St. Andrews in Scotland from July 10-13, 2012. The University of St. Andrews was founded in 1413, fully one hundred years before the Protestant Reformation. It is Scotland's first university and the third oldest in the English speaking world.

Since the very beginning, the University of St. Andrews has played an instrumental role in providing leadership for the academic study of theology and for the Christian church. John Knox, the founder of the Presbyterian church, is among the luminaries who studied at the University of St. Andrews. As an ordained Presbyterian clergy, the University of St. Andrews, thus, holds a very special place in my heart.

It is most appropriate that the most important conference on Galatians in recent memory was held at this esteemed university. For several days, the greatest minds in the world, researching and teaching Galatians in universities, seminaries, and churches, gathered in the most illustrious city of St. Andrews, Scotland, to discuss and learn from each other.

I am glad that this volume provides a taste of the theological research and discussions enjoyed at the important conference on Galatians. As an editor of the volume, I feel honoured that such illustrious scholars and theologians and pastors have contributed to this book.

I hope that this book will provide helpful resources for theologians, scholars, pastors, and students of theology and ancient studies. This volume has relevance for correlative fields, such as Jewish Studies, Old Testament studies, comparative literature, and philosophy.

This book can serve as a valuable resource, or text book, for university classes, seminary seminars, research, and for church Bible study classes. May this book help in encouraging bright discourse and creative thinking. And may those who search for truth find in this book a beacon of light to guide them toward their goal.

All of the contributors of the book thank the kind hosts of the University of St. Andrews. I would like, in particular, to thank Dr. Mark Elliott and Prof. N. T. Wright, scholar-theologians at the University of St. Andrews, for their kindness and erudition.

Heerak Christian Kim
Ludwig Maximilian University of Munich, Germany
International Organization for the Study of the Old Testament 2013
August 9, 2013

CONTRIBUTORS

T. David Gordon is Professor of Religion and Greek at Grove City College, where since 1999 he has taught courses in Religion, Greek, Humanities, and Media Ecology. Prior to that, he taught for thirteen years at Gordon-Conwell Theological Seminary in S. Hamilton, MA; and for nine years he was pastor of Christ Presbyterian Church in Nashua, NH. He is an ordained minister in the Presbyterian Church in America.

Dr. Gordon has contributed to a number of books and study Bibles (his notes on John's gospel appear in the New Geneva Study Bible and the Reformation Study Bible), and has published scholarly reviews and articles in journals such as *New Testament Studies*, *The Westminster Theological Journal*, *Interpretation*, and *Journal for the Evangelical Theological Society*. His popular articles have appeared in periodicals such as *Modern Reformation, Tabletalk, Decision*, and *Lay Leadership*. He has written *Why Johnny Can't Preach: The Media Have Shaped the Messengers* and *Why Johnny Can't Sing Hymns: How Pop Culture Re-Wrote the Hymnal*. He maintains a webpage at www.tdgordon.net

Dr. Gordon is a graduate of Roanoke College (B.L.A.), Westminster Theological Seminary (M.A.R., Th.M.), and Union Theological Seminary in Virginia (Ph.D.). He lives in Grove City, PA, with his wife Dianne, and daughters Grace and Dabney (and innumerable cats). The Gordons attend Grace Anglican Fellowship in Slippery Rock, PA.

Galatians as Examined by Diverse Academics

Matthias Grebe completed his undergraduate degree in theology, philosophy and rhetoric at the University of Tübingen before coming to the University of Cambridge to undertake an M.Phil in New Testament studies, working with Dr. Simon Gathercole on Paul's cultic background to the doctrine of reconciliation. He then began his Ph.D. at Christ's College, Cambridge, working with Professor David Ford on Karl Barth and his use of Scripture. His thesis provided an exegetical challenge to Barth's doctrines of election and atonement in his Church Dogmatics and will be published with Wipf & Stock in the Princeton Theological Monograph Series. His doctoral studies also included time spent at the Karl Barth archives in Basel and an extended research trip to Princeton Theological Seminary.

Whilst working on his Ph.D., he also undertook ordination training in the Church of England, at Ridley Hall, Cambridge. On completing his doctorate, he moved to Lagos, Nigeria, to teach at a theological seminary for one year.

Dr. Grebe's research interests include the doctrine of atonement, twentieth-century German theology, theodicy and the question of evil, Biblical Theology, hermeneutics, and the overlap of Systematic Theology and Biblical Studies.

Heerak Christian Kim is an Adjunct Professor of Biblical Studies at Asia Evangelical College and Seminary and a member of Jesus College, Cambridge. Professor Kim has spent many years in Israel, researching Jewish history and Jewish identity, with Lady Davis Fellowship, Raoul Wallenberg Scholarship, and Goldsmith Foundation Fellowship. Prof. Kim was trained under some of the world's greatest scholars in Jewish studies in Israel, Europe, and the USA.

Prof. Kim is the author of many academic books relating to Jewish Studies, including *The Jerusalem Tradition in the Late Second Temple Period: Diachronic and Synchronic Developments Surrounding Psalms of Solomon 11* (2007), *Intricately Connected: Biblical Studies, Intertextuality, and Literary Genre* (2008), and *Zadokite Propaganda in the Late Second Temple Period: A Turning Point in Jewish History* (2013).

Prof. Kim is also well-known for having coined the literary device of "The Key Signifier" at the Society of Biblical Literature international conference in Singapore in 2005. An academic monograph, *Key Signifier as Literary Device: Its Definition and Function in Literature and Media* (2006), enumerates on the newly-coined literary device, which is particularly noteworthy for its functional aspects.

Paul David Landgraf is pastor of St. John Lutheran Church (Drake, Missouri) and Pilgrim Lutheran Church (Freedom, Missouri). He received his MDiv (1990) and two advanced degrees (STM 1998 and 2013) from Concordia Seminary (St. Louis, Missouri). He attended the St. Andrews conference on Hebrews and Christian Theology in 2006, and his paper on the literary structure of Hebrews was published in *A Cloud of Witnesses: The Theology of Hebrews in its Ancient Contexts* (London: T&T Clark, 2008).

Hyung S. Lee studied Bible, theology and music in California. Being a tech savvy, Lee has served as worship leader and youth pastor in Silicon Valley of California while working at numerous technological companies. And afterwards he served the churches in Vancouver, Canada as young adult pastor and pastoral intern while studying at Regent College, where he received a master's degree in New Testament.

Lee's research interests include intertextuality, the Gospel of John and Paul and his letters, as reflected in Lee's paper presentations at a number of academic venues such as the OT in NT Seminar (2011) and Galatians Conference (2012). He currently works for a tech company in California while researching Paul's use of OT in Galatians and working on ancient and modern language skills.

Lee is married and have two children with unique names in ancient Hebrew and Greek.

Sigve Tonstad completed a B.A. in theology at Middle East College, Beirut, Lebanon and Andrews University (1974), his MD from Loma Linda University (1979), an MA in Biblical Studies at Loma Linda University (1990), and a PhD in New Testament Studies at the University of St. Andrews (2005). He has also spent time at Duke University studying with E. P. Sanders and Richard B. Hays. He has written books and many articles in Norwegian. His books in English are *The Scandals of the Bible* (2000). *Saving God's Reputation: The Theological Function of Pistis Iesou in the Cosmic Narratives of Revelation* (T. & T. Clark, 2006), and *The Lost Meaning of the Seventh Day* (Andrews University Press, 2009). He is currently Associate Professor of Religion at Loma Linda University in California.

Inscribing Abraham:
Apocalyptic, the Akedah, and 'Abba! Father' in Galatians

Sigve K. Tonstad
Loma Linda University

When Paul in Galatians makes a sustained attempt to inscribe Abraham on the spiritual identity of his Gentile converts, he is up against opponents who are convinced that Abraham is the definitive placeholder for their circumcision message. In the following, I will argue that Paul's argument to the contrary depends on the apocalyptic and the Akedah, both elements finding expression in the exclamatory phrase, "Abba! Father!" (Gal 4:6). For Paul, this is a make-it-or-break-it argument for the crisis in Galatia.

The Quantitative Measure of Abraham
The quantitative measure of Abraham in Galatians is formidable, dominating the lion's share of two entire chapters (Gal 3:1-4:31). Gentile believers in Jesus will be "descendants of Abraham" (3:7); they will be "blessed with Abraham" (3:9); they are the recipients of "the blessing of

Abraham" (3:14); they will be, in a second iteration, "Abraham's offspring" and also his "heirs" (3:29); and they "are the children of the promise," meaning the promise to Abraham (4:28).

In the context of what we may call Paul's exegetical argument (3:1-4:7), Abraham is the reference point, not Moses (3:16-21); the promise takes priority, not the law (3:16-21); the founding figure has defining import, not the things that happened "four hundred and thirty years later" no matter how exceptional that event might seem (3:17). In the context of what we may call Paul's allegorical argument (4:21-31), the subversion of conventional referentiality is staggering, now framed with reference to the two women in Abraham's life. Hagar, the slave woman, "is Mount Sinai in Arabia and corresponds to the present Jerusalem" (4:25) while "the other woman," meaning Sarah, "corresponds to the Jerusalem above; she is free, and she is our mother" (4:26). Ratcheting up the theological rhetoric and the implied pastoral implication, Paul delivers a potential knock-out punch, "Drive out the slave and her child; for the child of the slave will not share the inheritance with the child of the free woman" (4:30). At this stage of the argument, Paul is not only remembering the Abraham story with his readers. They are also re-enacting it, complete with the not-so-subtle exhortation to "drive out the slave and her child" (4:30), whoever they may be in the present context.

If, at this point in the storied history of Pauline scholarship, we can agree that Paul's letter to the Galatians "is like coming in on a play as the curtain is rising on the third or fourth act," as J. Louis Martyn suggests,[1] we have admitted the need for reconstructing the first and the second act on the basis of the letter, our only available source. In the first act, Paul is preaching in person in the Galatian churches, a time nostalgically recalled (4:13-15).[2] In the second act, the Teachers arrive. With no other source at our disposal, their message and theological narrative must also be reconstructed from the letter (1:7, 9; 4:17; 5:10, 12; 6:12, 13).

Who, then, brought Abraham to the attention of the Galatians in the first place? Whose idea was it to introduce Gentiles in the remote

---

[1] J. Louis Martyn, *Galatians: A New Translation with Introduction and Commentary* (AB 33A; Toronto: Doubleday, 1997), 13.

[2] Richard B. Hays, *The Faith of Jesus Christ: An Investigation of the Narrative Substructure of Galatians 3:1–4:11* (SBLDS 56; Chico: Scholars Press, 1983; [repr. Grand Rapids: Eerdmans, 2002]), 33–117.

reaches of Asia Minor to the founding father of another religion and take them to Ground Zero of the ethnic lineage of another people? Why, five hundred miles from home, so to speak, and eighteen centuries removed, is Abraham a subject of intense interest and debate? At our point of entry to the drama in Galatians in the third act, we have more than one candidate for this honor. Did Paul bring up Abraham in Act One, or did the Galatians have to wait for the Teachers to hear the Abraham story in the second act?

Gordon D. Fee answers that "Abraham would have played no role at all had it not been for the 'agitators' who had tried to disrupt Paul's churches in Galatia by insisting on the circumcision of Gentile believers."[3] This view implies that Abraham is more serviceable to the cause of the Teachers than to Paul's message, a view I believe to be erroneous, with the combined force of apocalyptic and the Akedah pieces of evidence to the contrary.

Abraham as An Apocalyptic Figure

"For I want you to know, brothers and sisters, that the gospel that was proclaimed by me is not of human origin [οὐκ ἔστιν κατὰ ἄνθρωπον]," Paul writes in the autobiographical sketch in Galatians (1:11). In this section, Paul drives home lack of indebtedness to other sources of influence other than special revelation for his message (1:11-23). Moreover, as Martyn notes, the claim that his gospel *ouk estin kata anthrōpon* extends to content and not only to source: "The gospel I preach is *not* what human beings normally have in mind when they speak of 'good news.'"[4] By the measure of this claim, there is nothing by which to compare it, a message without precedent or antecedent.[5]

---

[3] Gordon D. Fee, "Who Are Abraham's True Children? The Role of Abraham in Pauline Argumentation," in *Perspectives on Our Father Abraham: Essays in Honor of Marvin R. Wilson*, ed. Steven A. Hunt (Grand Rapids: Eerdmans, 2010), 126. Martinus C. de Boer (*Galatians: A Commentary* [NTL; Louisville: Westminster John Knox, 2011], 186-187) does not say outright that the Teachers brought Abraham into the equation, but he seems to attribute the role of Abraham in the argument in Galatians to the influence of the Teachers.

[4] Martyn, *Galatians*, 178.

[5] Beverly Roberts Gaventa, "Galatians 1 and 2: Autobiography as Paradigm," *NovT* 28 (1986), 325.

But this is not the sole foundation for Paul's message. There is an Old Testament antecedent, another riveting singularity, in the story of the binding of Isaac on Moriah. For this reason we can easily imagine the Teachers piggy-backing on Paul's prior story of Abraham no less than they tap into Paul's prior story of Christ so as to turn it into "another gospel" (1:6). Indeed, if apocalyptic singularity without any need for Old Testament support had been Paul's persuasive strategy in Galatia, it is hard to see how the Teachers would have any opening for Abraham in any version. It will therefore be necessary to define *two* focal points of disagreement between Paul and the Teachers. They are contending on behalf of conflicting views of the good news in Christ, and they are also – and with equal intensity – battling over the legacy and meaning of Abraham.

Paul's deployment of the Abraham narrative is selective, with a determined tilt toward the Akedah. This possibility is suggested already at the beginning of his rapid-fire argument, my Exhibit One.

> And the scripture, foreseeing that God would set right the Gentiles by *pistis*, declared the gospel beforehand to Abraham, saying, "All the Gentiles shall be blessed in you" (3:8, translation mine).

In this text, Paul combines a phrase from the beginning of the story of Abraham in Genesis with a phrase taken from the ending and zenith of the story. As Scott W. Hahn has shown, the phrase 'shall be blessed in you' [ἐνευλογηθήσονται ἐν σοί] is taken from Genesis 12:3, but the object of the blessing, 'all the nations/Gentiles' [πάντα τὰ ἔθνη] is most compatible with Genesis 22:18.[6] Indeed, the latter phrase as direct speech by God to Abraham is found only in Genesis 22:18.[7] "Already in Gal 3:8," says Hahn, "Paul alludes to the covenant oath of the Akedah by forming a conflated quotation of Gen 12:3 and 22:18."[8]

---

[6] Scott W. Hahn, "Covenant, Oath, and the Aqedah: Διαθήκη in Galatians 3:15-18," *CBQ* 67 (2005), 92.

[7] Hahn ("Covenant, Oath, and the Aqedah," 92) discounts Gen 18:18 on the logic that in this verse God is not speaking to Abraham.

[8] Hahn, "Covenant, Oath, and the Aqedah," 92.

Paul's merger of the bookends of the Abraham narrative in Genesis is not contrived (3:8). When we turn to Genesis, similarities between the call at the beginning and the call to go to Mount Moriah are conspicuous. For instance, the call to Abraham to leave his country (Gen 12:1) and the call to give up Isaac (Gen 22:1, 2) follow the same pattern.[9]

> *Call at the beginning*: Go forth...to the land that I will show you (Gen 12:1).
>
> *Call at the end*: Go forth...to the land of Moriah...on one of the heights that I will point out to you (Gen 22:2).

The connection between these two points in the story is even more striking in Hebrew. Nahum Sarna emphasizes the link between the point of origin (Haran) and the destination (Moriah), observing that the Hebrew phrase *lekh lekha*, 'go forth' (Gen 12:1; 22:2) does not occur again in the Bible.[10] The calls to "go forth" mark the outer edges of the journey, *from* highlighting the point of origin and *to* marking the destination, the latter stated fully only in connection with the final call (Gen 22:2). In a construct conflating the two calls, God will be heard saying, 'Go forth *from* your country.... *to* the land of Moriah [*to*] one of the mountains that I will show you' (Gen 12:1; 22:1, 2). This linkage is further reinforced by the triple terms of endearment that run on parallel tracks in the two calls, the last one of which is especially poignant.[11]

> *Call at the beginning*: Go forth from your land, your homeland, and your father's house (Gen 12:1).
>
> *Call at the end*: Take your son, your only son, Isaac, whom you love and go forth (Gen 22:2).

The land at the beginning and the son at the end are more than

---

[9] Nahum Sarna, *Genesis* (JPSTC; Philadelphia: Jewish Publication Society, 1989), 150.

[10] Sarna, *Genesis*, 150.

[11] Ibid.

features of style. When these elements are given their due they suggest that in Genesis the call to Abraham at the end is not an afterthought. The phrase "I will show you" in connection with the first call (Gen 12:1) and the phrase "I will tell you" in the second (Gen 22:2) create the expectation of a 'show and tell' at the point of the destination. *The narrator is preparing the reader for the discovery that Abraham is not only a person who will believe in God, as at the beginning of the story* (Gen 15:6), *or a person who will obey God, as he is acknowledged to have done when we get to the ram with its horns caught in the thicket* (Gen 22:13, 18). The accent in Genesis is neither on belief or on obedience as the dominant images; *it is on revelation.*

More in the 'show and tell' category is evident in Genesis. Abraham is called to go to *Moriah* (Gen 22.2), best understood as a noun derived from the verb *rā'ā*, to 'see.' The place to which he will be going, therefore, is a "Place of Seeing."[12] Something beckons to be seen in Abraham's story. At the end of the journey there will be a revelation. When the cloud of gloom lifts from the Mount of Seeing, the naming of the place intensifies the revelatory thrust of Abraham's journey. Here, in the best translations of Genesis 22:14, Abraham sums up his experience in terms of a reality revealed by God and seen by Abraham.

> Ephraim Speiser:
> And Abraham named that site Yahweh-yireh, hence the present saying, "On Yahweh's mountain there is a vision."[13]
>
> Claus Westermann:
> And Abraham gave this place the name, "Yahweh sees," of which one says today: "On the mountain Yahweh makes himself seen."[14]
>
> Nahum Sarna:

---

[12] R. W. L. Moberly, *Genesis 12-50* (OTG; Sheffield: Sheffield Academic Press, 1992), 47.

[13] Ephraim A. Speiser, *Genesis* (AB 1; Garden City, NY: Doubleday, 1964), 162.

[14] Claus Westermann, *Genesis 12-36*, trans. John J. Scullion (Minneapolis: Augsburg Publishing House, 1985), 353.

And Abraham named that site Adonai-yireh, whence the present saying, "On the mount of the Lord there is a vision."[15]

If we make the LXX Paul's text, the emphasis on revelation is not diluted in the least although the combination of God who sees and God who is seen is demanding, "And Abraham called the name of that place 'the Lord sees' in order that [with the result that] they say today 'on the mountain the Lord is seen' (Gen 22:14 LXX, translation mine).[16]

Perhaps we can put it like this: The accent in the narrative that comes to a climax on the Mount of Seeing in Genesis 22 is neither on believing nor on obeying although both are in evidence in the Abraham narrative. The accent is on revelation – on God as the Revealer and on Abraham as the recipient and mediator of revelation. When we say with Ernst Käsemann or J. Christiaan Beker that Paul was an apocalyptic thinker,[17] as we should, we are telling a half-truth if we conclude that first century Jewish apocalyptic is the only source of Paul's 'apocalyptic' argument in Galatians. The other source of Paul's apocalyptic vision is Genesis. While Genesis is not an apocalyptic book in the scholarly and generic sense of the term, in the Akedah it becomes a book where the lid comes off to a degree that is fully in line with the root meaning of *apokálypsis*. Abraham is an apocalyptic figure, and the Akedah is the most spine-tingling apocalyptic occasion in the Old Testament.

In an essay subtitled, "What Kind of Exegete Was Paul?" C. John Collins concludes that Paul was a keen reader of the Old Testament, arguing that "we should give more room to the possibility that he saw things that are really there – things that we have not yet found."[18] The review of Genesis, above, will not be a case in point in a marginal sense

---

[15] Sarna, *Genesis*, 153-154.

[16] The *hina* construct can be either purposive or resultative.

[17] Ernst Käsemann, "Die Anfänge christlicher Theologie," *ZTK* 57 (1960); ET "The Beginnings of Christian Theology," in *New Testament Questions for Today*, trans. W. J. Montague (Philadelphia: Fortress Press, 1969), 102; J. Christiaan Beker, *Paul the Apostle: The Triumph of God in Life and Thought* (Philadelphia: Fortress Press, 1980), 15-16, 144.

[18] C. John Collins, "Galatians 3:16: What Kind of Exegete Was Paul?" *TynB* 54 (2003), 86.

only, as though it takes a microscope or a fine-tooth comb to discern what holds priority in the Abraham narrative.

This brings us to the second exhibit, Paul's argument about Abraham's singular seed in Gal 3:16 and the actual occasion for Collins' claim that Paul was an exegete who took the details in the text seriously.

> Now the promises were spoken to Abraham and to his seed. It does not say, 'And to his seeds [τοῖς σπέρμασιν], as to many but as to one, 'And to your seed [τῷ σπέρματί],' who is Christ (Gal 3:16, translation mine).

The negation at the center of this verse has a rationale, of course. "It does *not* say, 'And to his seeds,'" says Paul from a distance, virtually wagging his finger in the face of the Teachers, who are insisting on a collective meaning of *sperma*. At first sight, Paul's argument seems to arise from spectacularly unpromising raw material. How can he derive from the noun 'seed' an argument that points to a single referent only, to 'seed' and not to 'seeds,' when the word he uses just as well can have a collective referent?[19]

The answer, again, is found in the Akedah.[20] "No one can annul or add to a human covenant once it has been ratified," says Paul (Gal 3:15, translation mine). The promissory covenant in Genesis has several versions (Gen 15:17-21; 17:1-27), but when was it *ratified*? It was ratified on the Mount of Seeing when God confirmed it with a solemn oath (Gen 22:16-17). Adding it up, according to Hahn, the reasons for prioritizing Genesis 22:15-18 as Paul's primary background text is that (1) only there is the covenant "*ratified by God*;" (2) only there is the covenant "made with *Abraham and his 'seed'*" (22: 16, 18); (3) only there is there

---

[19] T. D. Alexander, "Genealogies, Seed, and the Compositional Unity of Genesis," *TynB* 44 (1993), 260.

[20] N. T Wright (*The Climax of the Covenant: Christ and the Law in Pauline Theology* [Minneapolis: Fortress Press, 1992], 162-168) assigns priority to Genesis 15 in Paul's 'argument from Abraham' in Galatians, arguing that Paul's concern is ecclesiocentric. Paul's *sperma* does not refer to a single individual but to the singularity of a family for which Christ is the corporate representative. My slight dissent from this view is not to deny the ecclesiological implication but that Paul's theocentric emphasis is enormous and explicit.

in the original story an emphasis on the single seed, 'take your son, your *only* son, Isaac' (22:2, 16); and (4), here too, the covenant "guarantees the divine *blessing to the Gentiles*" (22:14).[21] Moreover, Collins and T. Desmond Alexander have pointed to syntactical reasons for seeing a singular referent for the 'seed' in Genesis 3:15 as well as in Genesis 22:17-18, arguing that when the accompanying verb and pronouns are in singular, 'seed' is intended to have a single referent.[22] Even by exegetical criteria, the propulsive force at the 'apocalyptic' point of origin on the Mount of Seeing finds a perfect match in the magnetic pull of the apocalyptic point of destination in Abraham's singular seed (Gal 3:16).

Exhibit Three must necessarily be brief.[23]

> And because you are children, God has sent the Spirit of his Son into our hearts, crying, "Abba! Father!" (Gal 4:6)

This text is the climax of what we have called Paul's exegetical argument, an inclusio running from Galatians 3:1-4:7 in one recent and very competent reckoning.[24] The argument, we recall, began with Paul saying that the Galatians received the Spirit by hearing the message (3:2). How does it end, if "Abba! Father!" is the conclusion? From beginning to end Abraham has hovered over the subject. The Galatians received the Spirit when they heard the message (3:2), and the gift of the Spirit equals fulfillment of the blessing promised to Abraham (3:14).[25] And now,

---

[21] Hahn, "Covenant, Oath, and the Aqedah," 90-92.

[22] Alexander, "Genealogies, Seed, and the Compositional Unity of Genesis," 255-270; idem, "Further Observations on the Term 'Seed' in Genesis," *TynB* 48 (1997), 363-367; C. John Collins, "A Syntactical Note (Genesis 3:15): Is the Woman's Seed Singular or Plural?" *TynB* 48 (1997), 139-148; idem., "What Kind of Exegete Was Paul?" 75-86.

[23] See Sigve Tonstad, "The Revisionary Potential of "Abba, Father" in the Letters of Paul," *AUSS* 45 (2007), 5-18.

[24] de Boer, Galatians, 166-268.

[25] James D. G. Dunn (*The Epistle to the Galatians* [BNTC; London: A. & C. Black, 1993], 220, 221) rightly claims that the theological claim in Galatians 4:6 "is immeasurable."

toward the end of this recapitulation of Act One, the Spirit speaks, crying out, "Abba! Father!" (4:6)[26]

I suggest that three voices, not counting the Spirit, are blended into one in this exclamation. Voice number one is that of the Galatians, crying out at their baptism, "Abba! Father!"[27] Voice number two, and there has to be a second voice, for the wording is Aramaic, and Aramaic is not a language native to Galatia; voice number two is the voice of Jesus, possibly recalling his praying in Gethsemane (Mark 14:36; Rom 8:15).[28] We will be amiss if we do not hear a third voice, however, the 'Abba' that stands at the heart of the Akedah. This voice echoes from the apocalyptic point when Abraham is in conversation with his son, his only son, whom he loves, on their way to the Mount of Seeing (Gen 22:2, 16). '*Abi*,' says the son in that story. *Hinneni b^{e}ni*, the father answers, 'I am right here, my son' (Gen 22:7, translation mine). And this conversation, we recall, is accompanied by one of the most compelling visual images in all of literature, repeated twice, "So the two of them walked together" (Gen 22:6, 8).[29]

At this point in Galatians, Paul draws his strongest argument from the mouths of the people he seeks to persuade, invoking the prior, shared narrative. And the exclamation we hear is somewhat more than an "Aramaic sound bite," as Bruce W. Longenecker calls it.[30] It is a sharply focused and loudly proclaimed compression of the faith-identity of new

---

[26] "Affirmations about the Spirit which the Galatians received when they came to believe constitute the framework of Paul's discussion of the promise to Abraham (Gal. 3:1-5; 4:6-7)." Cf. Nils Alstrup Dahl, *Studies in Paul* (Minneapolis: Augsburg, 1977), 132.

[27] John A. T. Robinson, "The One Baptism," *SJT* 6 (1953), 262-263); T. M. Taylor, "'Abba, Father' and Baptism," *SJT* 11 (1958), 70; Hans Dieter Betz, *Galatians: A Commentary on Paul's Letter to the Churches in Galatia* (Hermeneia; Philadelphia: Fortress Press, 1979), 210; E. A. Obeng, "Abba, Father: The Prayer of the Sons of God," *ExpT* 99 (1988), 365; Martyn, *Galatians*, 391.

[28] Joseph A. Grassi, "*Abba*, Father" (Mark 14:36): Another Approach," *JAAR* 50 (1982), 455.

[29] See Erich Auerbach, *Mimesis: The Representation of Reality in Western Literature,* trans. Willard R. Trask (Princeton: Princeton University Press, 1953), 13-23.

[30] Bruce W. Longenecker, *The Triumph of Abraham's God: The Transformation of Identity in Galatians* (Edinburgh: T. & T. Clark, 1998), 62.

believers in Galatia, echoing an apocalyptic insight anchored in the Akedah.

The Faithfulness of God

I left *pistis* untranslated in Galatians 3:8, above, one reason being that *pistis* does not escape the combined influence of apocalyptic and the Akedah. Paul begins his 'argument from Abraham' by saying that "Abraham believed [*episteusen*] God" (3:6) before claiming that "it is those who are *ek pisteōs* who are the children of Abraham" (3:7). No one should be faulted for thinking that Paul's interest here is chiefly in Abraham as believer.

When we move into the thick of Abraham's story in Galatians, however, *pistis* is no longer centered on the faith of Abraham. It has acquired the texture of an apocalyptic event, aligning it with the mysterious "it" that God said would "surely come" in his answer to Habakkuk (Hab. 2:3).[31] "Now before *pistis* came [ρρὸ τοῦ δὲ ἐλθεῖν τὴν πίστιν], we were imprisoned and guarded under the law until *pistis* would be revealed [εἰς τὴν μέλλουσαν πίστιν ἀποκαλυφθῆναι]," says Paul (3:23), proceeding to press the point that *pistis* now "*has come*" [ἐλθούσης δὲ τῆς πίστεως] (3:25, italics mine). Here, the valence of *pistis* does not hail trust in God as the innovation that has burst upon the scene. *Pistis* has become shorthand for an event and not for the stance of the believer. Translations that convey Paul's intent might be "before the message came," "before Christ came," or even, grasping that *pistis* is shorthand for a larger story, "before [God's] faithfulness was demonstrated," especially when the last part of the verse says that *pistis* "would be revealed" (3:23). Hans Dieter Betz aptly notes that *pistis* "describes the occurrence of a historical phenomenon, not the act of believing of an individual,"[32] and Martyn takes the emphasis on an event even further.[33]

---

[31] "For there is still a vision for the appointed time; *it* speaks of the end, and does not lie. If *it* seems to tarry, *wait for it; it will surely come, it* will not delay" (Hab. 2:3).

[32] Hans Dieter Betz, *Galatians* (Hermeneia; Philadelphia: Fortress Press, 1979), 176, n. 120. Francis Watson, who vigorously defends the view that *pistis Christou* should be translated "faith *in* Christ," takes issue with the notion of revelation (and *pistis*) as an event; cf. "Is Revelation an 'Event'?" *Modern Theology* 10 (1994): 383–399; idem, *Paul and the Hermeneutics of Faith* (London and New York: T. & T. Clark, 2004), 127–163.

This bears on our subject because there is a forward movement in Paul's argument, a movement that is captured by *pistis* even in the 'argument from Abraham.' Under the influence of the Akedah, the focus shifts from Abraham as believer to Abraham as recipient of revelation and even to Abraham as a mediator of revelation. Believers in Galatia may be *ek pisteōs* in the sense that they, like Abraham, believe in God's promise (3:7), but this, too, will only be a half truth. "Now that *pistis* has come" (3:25) means that the burden placed on the shoulders of *pistis* as *faith* will be much less than it was for Abraham because much of that burden has been taken over by *pistis* as divine *faithfulness*. Abraham the believer has metamorphosed into Abraham the revealer.[34]

My reading aligns with Beker's claim that "Paul is an apocalyptic theologian with a theocentric outlook,"[35] but the apocalyptic thrust is refined by the role of the Akedah in the narrative.[36] Much as my reading has benefited from Martyn's emphasis on apocalyptic, it complements his idea of an "invasive movement from beyond" by placing *revelation* alongside, and ahead of, *invasion*.[37] Paul's argument certainly has a

---

The flaw in his argument is in my view that he does not allow sufficient playing room for the influence of Habakkuk in Paul's argument.

[33] J. Louis Martyn ("The Apocalyptic Gospel in Galatians," *Int* 54 [2000], 254) notes that to "explicate the verb *apokalyphthēnai*, Paul uses as a synonym the verb *erchomai*, 'to come on the scene.' And the result is startling, for it shows that Paul's apocalyptic theology—especially in Galatians—is focused on the motif of invasive movement from beyond."

[34] Echoing the Akedah in Romans, Paul asks, "He who did not withhold his own Son, but gave him up for all of us, will he not with him also give us everything else?" (Rom 8:32; cf. Gen 22:16). Here, the Akedah takes the measure of God's self-giving love; cf. Nils Alstrup Dahl, "The Atonement: An Adequate Reward for the Akedah?" in *Neotestamentica et Semitica: Studies in Honour of Matthew Black*, ed. E. Earle and Max Wilcox (Edinburgh: T. & T. Clark, 1969), 15–29.

[35] Beker, *Paul the Apostle*, 362.

[36] Beker (*Paul the Apostle*, x) suggested unnecessarily that Galatians was somewhat of an exception with respect to apocalyptic conceptions in Paul. J. Louis Martyn's corrective ("Apocalyptic Antinomies in Paul's Letter to the Galatians," *NTS* 31 [1985], 410-424) is well argued, but it is not sufficiently attentive to the distinctive scriptural features of Paul's 'apocalyptic' framework.

[37] Martyn, *Galatians*, 97-105.

strong participatory thrust.[38] When "Abba! Father!" is allowed to echo at full blast in his letter, it confirms that Paul's rhetoric in Galatians is "more revelatory and performative than hortatory and persuasive,"[39] but the theology of the expression is not a secondary matter. "Abba! Father!" is the view from the top of the mountain in Galatians,[40] where 'mountain' as metaphor is justified by the Akedah.

"I am astonished!" (1:6) "Are you so foolish?" (3:3) "How can you?" (4:9) Paul exclaims in the most concentrated piece of pathos and epideictic rhetoric in the New Testament. Such exclamations would be misplaced if Paul had not thought that the Teachers drew wildly misguided conclusions and not merely got the story wrong in a minor way. With the Twin Towers of the Akedah and the cross as reference points, Paul counts on self-evidence to carry his argument against circumcision even if he at some points adds specific reasons (5:2-3, 11-12; 6:12-13) and in two places (5:6; 6:15) relegates the subject to irrelevance. Among the many moving parts in Galatians, *God* is the stable, coherent center (4:6), and it is on the bedrock of Paul's God-centered vision that there will be a community in which there "is no longer Jew or Greek, there is no longer slave or free, there is no longer male and female; for all of you are one in Christ Jesus" (3:28). Paul is, as it were, along with Abraham, permanently encamped on the Mount of Seeing.

I will fortify this claim with a thought from Søren Kierkegaard, whose profound enchantment with the Akedah made him a better reader of the story than Paul's opponents in Galatia. Kierkegaard hails Abraham mostly for his exceptional faith, but he sometimes comes close to the apocalyptic, revelatory message of the story. "Venerable Father Abraham! When you went home from Mount Moriah, you did not need a eulogy to comfort you for what was lost; for you gained everything and kept Isaac– was it not so?" he asks.[41]

Given that persuasive strategy of Galatians is performative and participatory, it is now our turn. Was it so?

---

[38] Cf. E. P. Sanders, *Paul and Palestininan Judaism: A Comparison of Patterns of Religion* (Minneapolis: Fortress Press, 1977), 502, 552.

[39] Martyn, *Galatians*, 23.

[40] Tonstad, "The Revisionary Potential of 'Abba! Father,'" 12.

[41] Søren Kierkegaard, *Fear and Trembling*, ed. and trans. Howard V. Hong and Edna H. Hong (Princeton, NJ: Princeton University Press, 1983), 22.

Jesus Christ: Victim or Victor?
Revisiting Galatians 3:13 in conversation with Karl Barth and Scripture

Matthias Grebe*
Christ College, Cambridge

Introduction

Galatians 3:13 is arguably one of the most challenging Pauline verses, particularly with regard to the apostle's understanding of the salvation Christ attained for humanity on the cross.[42] How are we to

---

*Christ's College, Cambridge, CB2 3BU, UK. This article is a revised version of a paper that was presented in July 2012 at the '*Galatians and Christian Theology conference*' at St Mary's College, School of Divinity, University of St Andrews, UK.

[42] I must thank Professor David Ford for being such an excellent supervisor during my Ph.D., guiding me through Barth's theology with wisdom and patience and constantly encouraging me to bring Barth into conversation with Scripture. Thanks also to Professor Otfried Hofius, who first introduced me to Pauline theology when I was an undergraduate

understand the polemical concept of a 'cursed Messiah' hanging on the tree? Is Jesus cursed and condemned as a type of scapegoat, bearing the sins of humanity on the cross? Does Paul mean that Christ became the 'object' of the curse in humanity's place, as a means of propitiation? And if so, by whom – the Father, the Law, or both? This article seeks answers to these questions through an examination of the account of the doctrine of the atonement proposed by Karl Barth in his *Church Dogmatics* IV/1 (particularly his reading of Galatians 3:13),[43] and presents an exegetical challenge to Barth's reading by offering an alternative interpretation.

1. The fourfold *pro nobis*

In Volume IV of the *Church Dogmatics*, Barth discusses the doctrine of reconciliation. §59.1, *The Way of the Son of God into the Far Country*, focuses on the downward movement of Jesus Christ into human history – that is, the Lord who became a servant. In his incarnation the Son of God is seen as humbling himself as a servant, to be a "brother of man […] to take His place with the transgressors".[44] This humility is described in terms of the parable of the Prodigal Son (the journey of the Son of God, who went into the far country, emptying himself and taking the form of a human being upon whom the divine judgment was finally executed). For Barth the incarnation "means not only God's becoming a creature, [but also] His placing Himself under the judgment under which man has fallen in this contradiction, under the curse of death which rests upon Him."[45]

In the first exegetical small print section in §59, Barth uses passages like John 1:14 ("The word became flesh"), the Christ-Hymn of Philippians 2:6ff ("He emptied himself and became obedient…"), 2 Corinthians 8:9 ("He who was rich became poor"), Romans 8:3 ("God

---

at the University in Tübingen. His passion for Paul and his meticulous biblical exegesis sparked my own academic interest in New Testament Studies with particular regard to the atoning death of Christ. Final thanks must go to Mike Bigg, Ashley Cocksworth and Robert Leigh, whom I have had the privilege to have as dialogue partners on St Paul and Karl Barth – many of the issues raised in this article have arisen out of our conversations.
[43] Karl Barth, *Church Dogmatics*, ed. G.W. Bromiley and T.F. Torrance (Edinburgh: T.&T. Clark, 1956–75). Hereafter *CD*.
[44] *CD* IV/1, p. 157.
[45] *CD* IV/1, p. 185.

sent his Son in the likeness of sinful flesh"), Hebrews 5:8 ("He who is the Son learned obedience in what He had to suffer"), as well as Galatians 3:13 ("He was made a curse for us") as his exegetical bolsters.

In the next section of the *CD*, the famous *The Judge Judged in Our Place* of §59.2, Barth explores the doctrine of the atonement and expounds the fourfold *pro nobis* (what Jesus Christ has done 'for us') in juridical terms. The notion of Christ being simultaneously the Judge and the judged corresponds to Barth's doctrine of election in *CD* II/2 where he states that Christ is both "electing God and elected man in one",[46] who is elected as well as rejected. Barth argues that Jesus Christ has taken our place in four specific ways: (I) as Judge; (II) as the judged; (III) as the judged in our place; and (IV) as the one who acted justly in our place.[47] What Barth stresses, therefore, is that Jesus Christ is the sole actor with respect to humanity's salvation.

2. Barth on Galatians 3:13

This article focuses on (II) and (III): Barth's understanding of Jesus Christ as the judged (II), who is judged in our place (III). It is here that Barth reveals his interpretation of Galatians 3:13 and the way he views the 'mechanics' of Jesus' dealing with sin and becoming a curse. But before any examination of this, we first need to clarify two things: (1) What does Barth mean by 'judged'? Does he regard Jesus as being judged by God and does this mean that the Father judges the Son? And (2) what does Barth mean by 'in our place'?

Barth sees Jesus as being 'for us' in that "he took the place of us sinners."[48] He understands the passion of Jesus as the "judgment of God in which the Judge himself was the judged."[49] For Barth, God has "caused Him [Jesus] to be regarded and treated as a sinner [...] He was made a curse for us."[50] Barth writes that in Galatians 3:13, Jesus

---

[46] *CD* II/2, p. 116.
[47] See *CD* IV/1, p. 273.
[48] *CD* IV/1, p. 235.
[49] *CD* IV/1, p. 254.
[50] *CD* IV/1, p. 165.

pursues our interest in our place. [...] There is no suggestion of our participating in this action. He is made a curse for us (Gal. 3:13) to free us from the curse: for us, but without us – everything depends on this – without our having any longer to bear or partially to bear the curse. We are simply those who have been redeemed from the curse by Him.[51]

De Boer points out that the "substitutionary meaning ('in our place' or 'in our stead') would imply that Christ took upon himself a penalty that ought to be imposed on human beings."[52] And this is exactly how Barth reads Galatians 3:13 when he writes that

> when in fulfilment of the divine judgment it took place that He willed to make our sin His own, and did in fact make it His own, it was decided that in no other way could it cease to be our sin which as such would inevitably bring us to eternal perdition.[53]

Barth explains that "our sin is no longer our own. It is His sin, the sin of Jesus Christ."[54] Thus for Barth, in the "death of Jesus Christ it has come to pass that in His own person He has made an end of us as sinners and therefore of sin itself by going to death as the One who took our place as sinners."[55] According to Barth, the cross is the sign of an enactment of God's judgment, his *No* to sinful humanity. The *Deus pro nobis* means that "God in Jesus Christ has taken our place when we become sinners, when we become His enemies, when we stand as such under His accusation and curse, and bring upon ourselves our own destruction."[56]

3. An exegetical challenge to Barth

(a) Galatians 3:13

---

[51] *CD* IV/1, p. 231.
[52] Martinus C. de Boer, *Galatians* (New Testament Library; Louisville, Kentucky: Westminister John Knox Press, 2011), p. 211.
[53] *CD* IV/1, p. 238.
[54] *CD* IV/1, p 238.
[55] *CD* IV/1, p. 253.
[56] *CD* IV/1, p. 216.

But how far can we agree with Barth in his contention that the cross is God's *No*, executed over the Son? Is Jesus really the 'Judged Judge', the one who bears the curse on the cross on humanity's behalf? Paul does not say that Christ was 'cursed' for us – in fact, nowhere does he suggest that the Father cursed the Son, or laid a curse upon him. All Paul writes is that Jesus 'became' a curse *pro nobis*. We therefore need to examine Galatians 3:13 in the context of Galatians 3 and Paul's overall intention for the letter.

After an autobiographical sketch in Chapter 1 and a section on the conference in Jerusalem and the conflict in Antioch, Paul comes to the conclusion in Chapter 2 that both Jews and Gentiles are justified through faith. He then begins Chapter 3 with what Betz calls his *probatio*,[57] highlighting Paul's view of the primacy of faith over Law. He presents a chain of arguments, reaching the most challenging in verse 13. Paul's argument goes as follows: that "the 'curse of the law' is the curse pronounced on the law-breaker."[58] And that it is this curse from which Christ has redeemed humanity. Yet what remains to be seen is just *how* he did this.

We see that Paul's argument is based on the fact that observance of the Torah does not lead to salvation – instead, those who follow the Torah are under a curse, because no one is able to fulfill the Torah and thus no one is justified before God through the works of the Law. As Sanders puts it: "It is by definition impossible."[59] In this context, those Galatians who seek justification before God 'by works of the Law' place themselves under a curse, because for them the Law becomes a curse the Law brings, by not fulfilling it, and by "doing so they deprive themselves from the blessing of Abraham given to 'men of faith'."[60] In verse 13 Paul goes on

---

[57] See Hans Dieter Betz, *Galatians: A Commentary on Paul's Letter to the Churches in Galatia* (Hermeneia; Philadelphia: Fortress, 1979), p. 128.
[58] See F.F. Bruce, *The Epistle of Paul to the Galatians: A Commentary on the Greek Text* (The New International Greek Testament Commentary; Exeter: Paternoster Press, 1982), p. 164.
[59] E.P. Sanders, "*On the Question of Fulfilling the Law in Paul and Rabbinic Judaism*," in *Donum Gentilicium: New Testament Studies in Honor of David Daube*, eds. E. Bammel, C.K. Barrett, and W.D. Davies (Oxford: Calrendon, 1978), p. 106.
[60] Betz, *Galatians*, p. 149.

to state that Jesus has redeemed humanity from the 'curse of the Law' by dying on the cross. To understand what the apostle means by 'redemption', we need to remember that Paul presupposes that humanity is enslaved by the curse of the Law. The verb 'redeemed' (*exagorazo*) has biblical associations of liberation from slavery (e.g. the Exodus from Egypt). So what Paul is referring to is the 'new' slavery and bondage brought by the curse of the Torah. As de Boer argues then, according to Paul, "human beings apart from Christ are already under a curse", and thus the issue at stake is "redemption from this already-existing situation."[61] In his love, God has sent his Son into the world to liberate humanity from this terrible fate.[62] The Son frees humanity by becoming a human being himself. He is born by a woman under the Law (4:4), and so is able to redeem humanity, enabling their adoption as 'sons of God' (4:5). The way Christ accomplishes this redemption is therefore by 'becoming a curse for us' (3:13).

But a full interpretation of Galatians 3:13 and Paul's assertion that Jesus becomes 'a curse for us' requires yet more excavation of the text. Does Paul mean that Christ became the 'object' of the curse in humanity's place, as a means of propitiation? Martyn talks about the crucifixion as "a head-on collision between the Law and Christ."[63] And yet according to Scripture the curse is pronounced only on the law-breaker, and Paul is very clear that Christ did not break the law but was obedient unto death (Philippians 2:8). In fact, according to Paul, Jesus "by his lifelong obedience (cf. Romans 5:19) [...] remained immune from the curse of the law."[64]

Rather than seeing the cross as a collision with the Law, then, we have to understand Paul's view Jesus' death as a sacrifice within the cultic setting of the atonement. Paul sees Christ as free from all sin (2 Corinthians 5:21), as the sinless lamb (1 Corinthians 5:7), and as such he is not a criminal who hangs cursed on the tree, but instead he dies as a cultic atoning sacrifice for cursed humanity. As Dunn highlights, "the curse is not rebuked but remedied. 'Having become a curse for us' is a

---

[61] de Boer, *Galatians*, p. 211.
[62] See Betz, *Galatians*, p. 149.
[63] J. Louis Martyn, *Galatians: A New Translation with Introduction and Commentary* (Anchor Bible 33A; New York: Doubleday, 1997), p. 320.
[64] Bruce, *Galatians*, p. 164.

combination of martyr theology (itself using the imagery of the sacrificial cult) and Adam christology."[65] By Jesus' acting as a representative of humanity "his death and its consequences were an enactment of human destiny with effects on humanity."[66] The "idea is not that Christ became the curse from which 'we' are then granted an exemption, but that Christ shared 'our' predicament in order to liberate 'us' from that predicament."[67] As Paul writes in Galatians 2:20, "I have been crucified with Christ". In fact, it is not that Christ 'saves' or 'protects' humanity from the Law but that 'in Christ' the Law is fulfilled and executed on humanity too, as Paul stipulates in the previous verse ("For through the law I died to the law" – Galatians 2:19). In being executed over Jesus, the Law is also executed over humanity. But whereas if a law-breaker were to die, his or her own death as the accursed would lead to eternal separation from God, in Christ's death (understood from the perspective of cultic sacrifice), a person is united with him, and is therefore brought into contact with God through this cultic sacrificial death.

> Within this understanding, the act of atonement is not so much about paying a debt to a God who is offended by humanity's sins. Instead, humanity is understood as a victim of her own sins. Humanity in and of herself – her entire being – is the cause of the broken relationship with God. It is humanity that bars fellowship with God, standing in her own way, 'blocking' communion with God.[68]

Again, Christ is not a 'scapegoat', bearing away the sin that had otherwise stood between humanity and God; it is not that sin is a 'blockage' that needs to be removed for humanity to have access to God. Instead, through baptism the individual (whose entire nature is sinful) participates in Christ's death (Romans 6:4) and is freed from sin (Romans 6:6). But moreover, because the individual participates in Christ's death she will

---

[65] James D. G. Dunn, *The Epistle to the Galatians* (Black's New Testament Commentary; Peabody, MA: Hendrickson, 1993), p. 177.
[66] Dunn, *Galatians*, p. 177.
[67] Ibid. p. 212.
[68] Matthias Grebe, "*Election and Atonement in Karl Barth's Church Dogmatics: A Systematic and Exegetical Study*" (Doctoral thesis of the University of Cambridge 2012), p. 167.

also partake in his resurrection (Romans 6:5), and is thus brought into contact with God in and through Christ. It is through death *under* the Law – through Christ's sinless death on the cross – that humanity is freed from sin and brought into contact with a holy God. Thus the means of dealing with sin should therefore be examined from a cultic point of view:

> Christ took the individual's sinful existence with him into death, establishing a covenant between himself and humanity through the act of spiritual circumcision in baptism. Through Christ's sacrifice, the sinful nature and thus sin itself was cut off, freeing the sinner from the body of death and making him alive in Christ (Col 2:11ff.).[69]

Consequently, death to the Law is the presupposition for the 'life for God' found at the end of verse 19.[70] This death to the Law through the Law is achieved in union with Christ on the cross, as Dunn explains: "Union with Christ is nothing if it is not union with Christ in his death."[71] It is this that constitutes the core of Paul's Gospel therefore – the idea that "believers are counted acceptable to God because they are 'in Christ'";[72] it is the "transition of believing in Christ as a dying which results in a different kind of living."[73]

(b) Deuteronomy 21:23 and the Law

The analysis of Galatians leads us to question how we are to understand Paul's citation of Deuteronomy 21:23 "Cursed it everybody who hangs on a tree". Galatians looks at how Jesus frees humanity (which otherwise stands cursed and convicted by the Law) by coming under the Law himself and becoming a subject to the Law in the incarnation, redeeming humanity by and through the Law's requirements in his own death on the cross. According to the Law, in being hanged on the cross,

---

[69] Grebe, *Election and Atonement*, p. 175.
[70] See Betz, *Galatians*, p. 122.
[71] James D. G. Dunn, *Unity and Diversity in the New Testament* (London: SCM, 1977), p. 195.
[72] Dunn, *Galatians*, p. 141.
[73] Ibid. p. 143.

Christ was seen as accursed. However, as de Boer emphasizes, Deuteronomy 21:23 has "nothing to do with execution by crucifixion, but with the display of an already-executed criminal on a tree."[74] It is not that a person was accursed because he died on a tree – one's death on the cross does not automatically identify the individual as accursed. Instead, according to Deuteronomy 21:23, it is the other way around – that is, if somebody was regarded as accursed, the Law required him to be hanged on a tree. Thus, being hanged on a tree did not constitute the curse itself, but was rather the public proof that this person was accursed by God.

So it was with Jesus' death: because the High Priest and elders saw him as accursed, as a blasphemer, they consequently demanded he be hanged on the cross as a sign of him being accursed by God. We see this notion reflected in Paul's letter. "Since the Messiah, almost by definition, enjoyed the unique blessing of God, whereas a crucified person, according to the law, died under the curse of God, the identification of the crucified Jesus with the Messiah was a blasphemous contradiction in terms."[75] Paul tells the Judaizers that according to their understanding of the Law's requirements, which they so fervently seek to uphold and force upon those in the Galatian Church, Jesus had died. But Paul does not stop there – he goes on to say that through his death, Jesus redeemed those who put their faith 'in Christ' from the Law, leaving the Law void.

Furthermore, Bruce points out that Paul omits *hypo theou* in verse 13 "to avoid the implication that Christ in his death was cursed by God."[76] "This implication," Bruce continues, "would conflict with Paul's conviction that Christ's enduring the cross was his supreme act of obedience to God (see Romans 5:19) and that 'in Christ God was reconciling the world to himself' (2 Corinthians 5:19)."[77] Therefore the question 'Who made Christ a curse?' is left unanswered by Paul. What Paul *does* make plain (Bruce argues) is that "the curse which Christ

---

[74] de Boer, *Galatians*, p. 212. See also Bruce, *Galatians*, who writes that in the "NT period, however, Deuteronomy 21:22-23 was applied both to the exposure of a dead corpse on a tree or pole and the impalement or crucifixion of a living person", p. 122.
[75] Bruce, *Galatians*, p. 166.
[76] Ibid. p. 165.
[77] Ibid. p. 165.

'became' was his people's curse, as the death which he died was their death."[78]

Therefore we can conclude that Christ was not the object of God's reprobation – instead, Christ redeemed humanity from the curse of the Law. With this polemical statement Paul highlights the "cost at which he achieved the deliverance of men from the curse of the law, *genomenos ... katara*, referring to the reprobation of Christ by men."[79] The Old Testament passage is then rightly understood as a rhetorical device in Paul's argument, which explains "why the death on the cross led men to look on him with reprobation as one accursed."[80]

As a result, Paul's statement in Galatians 3:13 should be read not simply as a soteriological statement of Christ's bearing a curse, but rather as part of Paul's wider argument in Chapter 3, as a polemical remark about the Law. It should be seen not merely as an explanation of Christ's death itself, but rather as a statement of what he achieved through his death – redemption from the Law. As Burton argues,

> If *katara* refers to the curse of the law, then the quotation maybe be understood to define precisely how and in what sense he became a curse of the law. Inasmuch as the law affirms that whoever is hanged on a tree is accursed, and Jesus died on the cross, he falls under this verdict and the curse of the law. But inasmuch as this verdict is manifestly false and monstrous, in it the law does not so much condemn Christ as itself.[81]

Thus Galatians 3:13 indicates that for those 'in Christ', the Law should be regarded as void and meaningless (with regard to salvation!) in the light of Christ's death. If read from this perspective, then the passage expresses what Christ has achieved with his atoning and purifying death and must be seen as part of Paul's argument against the Judaizers. Paul tells them that *even if* their interpretation of the Law were right, it would have no

---

[78] Ibid. p.166.
[79] Ernest De Witt Burton, *A Critical and Exegetical Commentary on the Epistle to the Galatians*, ICC, ed. S.R. Driver, A. Plummer, and C.A. Briggs (Edinburgh: T.&T. Clark, 1921; reprint, Edinburgh: T.&T. Clark, 1980), p. 175.
[80] Ibid. p. 175.
[81] Burton, *Galatians*, p. 173.

sustained implications for the Galatian Church since the Law's 'rule' as a custodian (Galatians 3:25) is abrogated after Christ's death (Jesus made an end to the Law (Romans 10)).

Conclusion

According to the Law, therefore, hanging on a tree was viewed as a public display of a person's being cursed, a sign that he or she had broken the Law. We saw that even though the sinless Jesus did not break the Law (and was "obedient unto death") he died the death of a law-breaker for humanity's sake. Galatians 3:13 is Paul's most radical depiction of the death of Christ and I argue that his statement that "Jesus became a curse" is provocative one made to silence his opponents who emphasize the necessity of following the Torah to achieve salvation. Paul refers to Jesus' death as that of a law-breaker in order to take the Judaizers' argument about the Law directly onto their 'turf', using their own terminology and argument about the Law and in this way debunking their own insistence to the Galatian Church that they must adhere strictly to the Law. In doing this, therefore, Paul undermines the Judaizers' very own argument, which from Paul's perspective leads only to a curse that Christ has already dealt with on the cross. This liberation from the curse of the Law by faith in Christ is Paul's primary point in his epistle to the Galatians. Paul uses the death of Christ to refute the legalists, arguing that "legalism makes that death needless, here that it proves Christ accursed."[82] He overcomes the Judaizers' charge that he is ignoring some parts of the Law by arguing that their argument is defunct since Christ has made an end to the Law altogether.

Returning now to Barth's forensic *pro nobis*: Barth is partly right when he asserts that Jesus became the 'Judge Judged' and was 'judged in our place'. However it was not the Father but rather humanity as whole who judged Jesus. As we saw, for Paul, Christ became the "object of human execration – he was cursed by men"[83] and the cross therefore demonstrates the cost for which Jesus redeemed humanity from the curse of the Law (see Hebrews 12:2; Philippians 2:8).

---

[82] Ibid. p. 174.
[83] Burton, *Galatians*, p. 172.

Galatians as Examined by Diverse Academics

Pannenberg comments that the Son's offering himself up on the cross is not "identical with his rejection by the Father."[84] In fact, Jesus was rejected by others and "precisely herein he was not rejected by his Father. Instead he was obedient to the mission he had received from the Father."[85] It is this obedience to the will of the Father that is confirmed in the resurrection. Just as God redeems Israel from slavery in Egypt and goes on to make a covenant with her at Mount Sinai, so too does God in Christ redeem humanity from the curse of the Law and establish the covenant with her in Christ's body. Thus,

> Jesus' death is not about the Father punishing the Son, and therefore the Father and the Son are not separated in the cross event, but rather the cross is about humanity coming back to God through death. Since Jesus did not bear sin [as a scapegoat], he is not a covenant-breaker. The death on the cross not only highlights humanity's sinfulness, but also reveals and bears witness to the fact that not even death can separate and destroy the covenant with God that has been established in Jesus Christ.[86]

We can therefore conclude with Barth that in the flesh "victory is won".[87] Jesus is the victor over sin and death on the cross, freeing humanity – the victim – from the curse of the Law through his sacrificial death. Galatians 3:13 – Christ's becoming a curse *pro nobis* – must be seen in the same light as Galatians 4:4, where Christ's being under the law redeems humanity from its curse. What Paul seeks to do in verse 13 is to "call attention to the depth of Christ's love (2:20)" for humanity,[88] to demonstrate his willingness to give up his glory (Philippians 2:6ff.) and to show how Christ finally went to the cross to die for the redemption of his creation.

---

[84] Wolfhart Pannenberg, *Systematic Theology, Vol. 3*, Geoffrey Bromiley (trans.) (Grand Rapids: Eerdmans, 1991), p. 452.
[85] Ibid. p. 452.
[86] Grebe, *Election and Atonement*, p. 172.
[87] *CD* III/2, p. 336.
[88] de Boer, *Galatians*, p. 211.

Galatians as Examined by Diverse Academics

Bibliography

Barth, Karl. *Church Dogmatics*, ed. G.W. Bromiley and T.F. Torrance (Edinburgh: T. &T. Clark, 1936–77).

Betz, Hans Dieter. *Galatians: A Commentary on Paul's Letter to the Churches in Galatia* (Hermeneia; Philadelphia: Fortress, 1979).

Bruce, F.F. *The Epistle of Paul to the Galatians: A Commentary on the Greek Text* (The New International Greek Testament Commentary; Exeter: Paternoster Press, 1982),

Burton, Ernest De Witt. *A Critical and Exegetical Commentary on the Epistle to the Galatians*, ICC, ed. S.R. Driver, A. Plummer, and C.A. Briggs (Edinburgh: T.&T. Clark, 1921; reprint, Edinburgh: T.&T. Clark, 1980).

De Boer, Martinus C. *Galatians* (New Testament Library; Louisville, Kentucky: Westminister John Knox Press, 2011).

Dunn, James D. G. *The Epistle to the Galatians* (Black's New Testament Commentary; Peabody, MA: Hendrickson, 1993).

Dunn, James D. G. *Unity and Diversity in the New Testament* (London: SCM, 1977).

Grebe, Matthias. "*Election and Atonement in Karl Barth's Church Dogmatics: A Systematic and Exegetical Study*" (Doctoral thesis of the University of Cambridge 2012).

Martyn, J. Louis. *Galatians: A New Translation with Introduction and Commentary* (Anchor Bible 33A; New York: Doubleday, 1997).

Pannenberg, Wolfhart. *Systematic Theology*, Vol. 3, Geoffrey Bromiley (trans.) (Grand Rapids: Eerdmans, 1991).

Galatians as Examined by Diverse Academics

Sanders, E.P. "*On the Question of Fulfilling the Law in Paul and Rabbinic Judaism*," in *Donum Gentilicium: New Testament Studies in Honor of David Daube*, eds. E. Bammel, C.K. Barrett, and W.D. Davies (Oxford: Calrendon, 1978), 103-26.

Apocalyptic Allegory:
Paul's Use of Genesis and Isaiah in Galatians 4:19–5:1

Joseph Hyung S. Lee
Regent College

Paul's use of the verb, ἀλληγορέω, which does not appear anywhere else in the scriptures, neither from the OT in LXX nor the NT in Greek, except in Gal 4:22 and other ancient Graeco-Roman and Jewish literature, and the apostle's use of the Genesis narrative and the prophetic text have perplexed many readers and opened a wormhole of speculations with such claims as that Paul was a Hellenic interpreter (or Homeric allegoriser; cf., Philo). On the other hand, other readers of the apostle ground his interpretation to be, in a great extent, derivative of Jewish worldview in the first century. And because of such suspicion for Paul to be a Hellenic allegoriser, not only a few Pauline scholars have described the apostle's allegory to be not much different from that of Philo's and later Origen's, but also some argued that the allegoriser of Gal 4:21– 5:1 cannot be the apostle Paul but must be another allegoriser, who was heavily influenced by Graeco-Roman rhetoric in a same degree as that of Philo of Alexandria. However, in Gal 4:21–5:1, as the climax of this letter, Paul is allegorically/correspondingly identifying the condition, the fate and the identity of the people of God in their history from Abraham, the Exodus, the prophets to Paul's and Galatians' contemporary in the light of the history and the oracles of exile and restoration from Isaiah 40–66 and in accordance with a reoriented Jewish apocalyptic perspective on three different levels – 1) intertextuality; 2) historical narrative; and 3) apocalyptic perspective. The apostle is writing in such a way in Gal 4 in order to claim that in a new age/new exodus, which has dawned with Christ and the Spirit, the freedom that the Messiah has set us free (i.e., the content of the Isaianic εὐαγγελίον from Isa 61:1) belongs both to the Jews and the Gentiles, hence the Galatians, who are part of the children no longer in slavery (i.e., exile) but the heirs with inheritance, Abrahamic children, according to the covenantal promise of God.

INTERTEXTUALITY IN GAL 4:19–5:1

Isaianic Echoes in Gal 4:19–20

As Prof. J. Louis Martyn observed in his commentary, Gal 4:19 possibly might echo a travail metaphor from Isa 45:7–11, especially Isa 45:10 where Yahweh declares, "Woe to him who says to a father, 'What are you begetting?' or to a woman, 'With what are you in travail (ὠδινήσεις; תְּחִילִין)?'" to the exiled people who were complaining about Yahweh's choice of Cyrus as their messiah (Isa 45:1). However, in Gal 4:19–20, Paul more likely has Isa 51:1–3 in his mind on two grounds. Firstly, the text of Isa 51:1–3 is not only another section where ὠδίνω (הוּל)

appears in Isaiah (51:2), but it is also one of the sections where "the idea of 'comfort' for Jerusalem is key to the opening proclamation" as in Isa 40:1; 52:9; and 54:11. And, this theme of comfort for Jerusalem climaxes in Isaiah's anticipated new exodus throughout Isa 40–66, especially in 57:18; 61:2 and 66:13 where Yahweh comforts his people in the restored Jerusalem.

As Paul changes his tone with τέκνα μου in Gal 4:19 and his wish to be present with the Galatians in v. 20, the apostle seems to have Yahweh's comfort for Jerusalem-Zion in Isa 51:1–3 in mind. Secondly, with the second time of the use of the word, ὠδίνω in Paul's quotation of Isa 54:1 in Gal 4:27, the apostle penned 4:19–20 as a bridge text between the content of Gal 4:21–5:1 and the one prior to 4:19–20. Hence, the apostle's intertextual echo from Isa 51:1–3, where Yahweh demands a heed from Jerusalem-Zion to remember the moment of Abraham and Sarah, who bore/travail (ὠδίνω), giving birth to God's people, prepares the auditors of the Galatians to hear the allegorical text of 4:21–5:1.

Isaiah 54:1 in Its Context

Moving onto Paul's use of the OT in Gal 4:20–5:1, we will deal with his explicit quotation from Isa 54:1 first. For Paul the Septuagint is his scripture as evidenced in his quotation in Gal 4:27. After allegorical correspondences (συστοιχέω) with two sons (δύο υἱούς), two covenants (δύο διαθῆκαι), two women (δουλεὰν καὶ ἐλευθέρα) and two Jerusalems (ἡ νῦν Ἰερουσαλὴμ καὶ ἡ ἄνω Ἰερουσαλήμ), Paul quotes in verbatim the Septuagint version of Isa 54:1 with an introductory formula, γέγραπται γάρ. For us, the question is why Isa 54:1 is used along with the tale of two sons from Gen 15–21 by the apostle. With the quotation from Gen 21:10 in Gal 4:30, would it not fit better to use an explicit quotation from Gen 15 or 16 in order to mark inclusio of his argument in Gal 4:21–5:1? In fact, if this passage is the final argument of Paul's rhetorical probatio where the apostle incorporates an allegory as a rhetorical device, Isa 54:1 weighs less significantly as the allegory appears to function between the two women and two sons from Genesis to the two Jerusalems. Then, why is the text of the prophet is being appropriated by the apostle?

Isa 54:1 is a climactic moment in Deutero-Isaiah (Isa 40–55) where a new exodus was announced with "the return of Yahweh's actual presence" (40:3) to "a restored Jerusalem-Zion" at its centrality. However, in spite of a hopeful proclamation of a new exodus, Deutero-Isaiah contains the prophet's (or Yahweh's) polemical language towards Jacob-Israel (40:27; 46:9, 12; 48:1) because of her rebellion, rejecting Yahweh's agent, Cyrus as messiah and shepherd (44:28; 45:1, 13; 46:13) and being blind and deaf (42:18ff), unable to understand/perceive God's wisdom for the restoration of Jerusalem. Hence, with the appearance of an enigmatic, unidentified עֶבֶד as a newly appointed agent to heal Jacob-Israel's wounds (53:4–6) in the future, the promise of Jerusalem-Zion's restoration is once again being anticipated to be an unknown future for the exilic people; the new exodus is not yet fulfilled and has been postponed as indicated in Isa 56–66. Within this context of Deutero-Isaiah, an unthinkable demand has been proclaimed by Yahweh to a barren woman, that is to burst out with shout for joy (רָנִּי עֲקָרָה לֹא יָלָדָה) in Isa 54:1. Then, who is this barren woman in Isa 54:1 in the prophetic utterance and in the apostle's letter?

In Deutero-Isaiah, there are three instances where a barren woman motif appears in Isa 49:19–21; 51:1–3 and 54:1–3. In Isa 49:19–21, connecting the experience of Zion's barrenness to exile, Yahweh declares that Zion herself would ask this question about the children in exile, "Who has borne me these? I was bereaved and barren, exiled and put away, but who has brought up these? Behold, I was left alone; whence then have these come?" (v. 21). The implication from Zion's barrenness is that these exilic children in Babylon were not born by Jerusalem-Zion but were born for her by someone else, just as Hagar gave birth to a child instead and in spite of Sarah's barrenness (Gen 16:15); nevertheless, the apostle does not site this text from Isaiah 49. However, in Isa 51:1–3 the barren woman motif is embedded within the name of THE mother, Sarah, which only appears once here in the Hebrew scriptures outside of the Pentateuch. As observed before, this section of Deutero-Isaiah (51:1ff) is where the prophet comforts Jerusalem-Zion reminding those who seek Yahweh and his deliverance in their exile (v. 1) to behold Abraham and Sarah (v. 2) as recapitulated Adam and Eve in the Garden of Eden (v. 3), hence a new creation will dawn, and this is the promise and the destiny for soon-to-be restored Jerusalem-Zion in the future.

In Isa 54:1 the barren woman is unnamed and enigmatic just as the עֶבֶד in the servant song in 52:13–53:12. The words, Jerusalem and Zion appear five and seven times in Isa 51:1–52:12, so the readers like ourselves may conclude that this barren matriarch to be Jerusalem-Zion in the line of the barren matriarch motif with Sarah as pioneer, however, the disappearance of the names, not only Sarah, but Jerusalem and Zion altogether until Isa 59 would make the prophetic auditors to wonder the identity of this woman in Isa 54. This enigmatic characteristic seems to be one of the points from the barren matriarch in Isa 54 as well as the servant song, that the auditors of the prophet in exile would wonder who the barren woman and her children are as well as the identity of עֶבֶד in the fourth servant poem. That is one of the reasons why the apostle Paul seems to be appropriating Isa 54:1 in Gal 4:27 because one of points for this quotation, and also the allegory, is the identity of true Abraham's children in a new exodus as we shall see an Isaianic new exodus motif later, in Gal 5:1.

So, who is this barren woman in both Isa 54:1 and Gal 4:27? For Isaiah it is the exiled Jerusalem-Zion to-be restored in a future new exodus; and for Paul, it is also Jerusalem-Zion who was barren as Sarah was but is now restored also as Sarah gave birth to Isaac. However, for all the barren matriarchs in the OT, with Sarah as pioneer (i.e., Rebekah, Rachel, Manoah's wife and Hannah), they had travailed the birth pangs (חוּל), giving birth to one child. But from the unnamed barren woman in Isa 54:1, her birth narrative, and even her birth pangs (i.e., the curse of Eve in Eden in Gen 3:16), is reversed in that the barren matriarch in 54:1 would be a mother to many children (i.e., the people) without having been in travail (ἡ οὐκ ὠδίνουσα; לֹא חָלָה). Not only that, for this barren woman, Yahweh himself will wed her as the prophet proclaimed in v. 5. Hence, the woman who has a husband (ἡ τῆς ἐχούσης τὸν ἄνδρα) in Isa 54:1 is not a particular woman (e.g., Hagar in Gal 4) but all the matriarchs who bore children. And the point is that when the widowed barren women who will be newly wedded, in other words, when exiled Jacob-Israel is restored to be a newly wedded Jerusalem-Zion (Isa 66:7–14), she will be, even without birth-pangs, more fruitful and fertile than any matriarch on earth, which necessitates for the woman to enlarge her tent as expansive as possible (Isa 54:2). Hence, if the barren woman in Isa 54:1 is Jerusalem-Zion in a future restoration, new exodus, how was this passage understood in Jewish literature, and how does Paul incorporate it along with the Genesis narrative?

A Matriarch Motif in Jewish Literature

Not too far distant from Isa 54:1, in Trito-Isaiah, in Isa 66:7–14 to be more specific, Yahweh's song for Zion from a new temple (66:5) picks up a barren matriarch motif from Deutero-Isaiah again by giving birth to a people without birth-pangs, but this time the name of the one who gives birth is explicitly announced as 'Zion' (v. 8) and 'Jerusalem' (v. 10). Also, Jacob-Israel's blindness and deafness will be cured as prophesied in the servant song (Isa 52:12–53:4) when all see and hear something they have never seen or heard before (66:8). Hence, as what was promised to the exiled Jerusalem-Zion in Isa 54:1 was postponed to a future, the oracle for Jerusalem-Zion in 66:7–14 for the post-exilic people is looking towards the ultimate eschatological future in the new exodus.

This Jerusalem-Zion matriarch motif is also seen in Apocrypha. In Bar 4:8–11, the image of Jerusalem as a birthing and nurturing mother is embedded into the comfort and the restoration section for Israel (4:5–5:9). The mother Jerusalem is widowed and left desolate because of the sins of her children, Israel (4:7, 11, 12, 16, 19). And, the comfort for Jerusalem comes as she anticipates to "take off the garment" of her sorrow (5:1) and affliction and to "stand upon the height," looking to the east and the west and witnessing the gathering of her children (5:5).

In a first century apocalyptic work, the Fourth Book of Ezra, Zion is also depicted as a barren woman who has had and lost a son and now wishes to die in the field of Ardat in Ezra's vision (9:43–10:4). Then Ezra rebukes this woman, without knowing her identity, that Zion their mother is in a sorrowful state (4 Ezra 10:7, 23) and then to find that the woman he was speaking to was an established city, Zion (10:25–28, 45–46).

Targumic and Rabbinic literature also inhabit a Jerusalem-Zion matriarch and barren motif. Targum Isaiah interprets a barren woman in Isa 54:1 to be Jerusalem along with 49:18–20 and 66:7, but the woman with a husband in 54:1 is interpreted to be "inhabited Rome." In Midrash Rabbah for the Song of Songs 4:9, Isa 54:1 is employed as a fulfilment that, in spite of Jerusalem's desert condition (i.e., exile), she has produced more righteous men for Yahweh such as "Daniel and his associates, Mordecai and his associates, Ezra and his associates," so "more are the children of the desolate than the children of the married wife" (Isa 54:1).

Implications from these Jewish texts for us with the Galatians text, are that, on the one hand, a barren matriarch motif has been part of Jewish understanding and communication for their exilic condition and eschatological anticipation, but on the other hand, two female figurines representing two Jerusalems from these texts are rare or none. However, as we have seen in Isa 40–66 and also from Jewish literature, there is one Jerusalem-Zion but with two conditions, one barren and desolate, representing an exile, and the other who would bear many children and marry Yahweh, a restored Jerusalem-Zion. With this in view, we move onto how Paul uses two female matriarchs and two Jerusalems in Galatians 4.

Hagar, Exile and 'Jerusalem Now'

The peculiarity of Paul's allegory for Hagar in Gal 4:21–5:1 boils down especially to two correspondences the apostle makes - Sinai mountain or Sinaitic covenant in Arabia and a present/now Jerusalem in vv. 24–26. Even if Hagar in v. 25 should be omitted from a text-critical point of view (hence, τὸ δὲ Σινᾶ ὄρος ἐστὶν ἐν τῇ Ἀραβίᾳ), there is no doubt that Paul connects Hagar with Sinai in Arabia and 'Jerusalem now.' But, shouldn't Mt. Sinai be reminiscent of a great exodus moment for Israel's history? How do Hagar and Sinai mountain/Sinatic covenant in Arabia corresponds to (στοίχεω) 'now Jerusalem' in slavery or exile for the apostle and his auditors, specifically, Galatians?

If the quotation of Isa 54:1 is being employed in connection with the Jerusalem-Zion matriarch who gives birth to the children of freedom according to promise as Paul lays out in Gal 4:27, the quotation of Gen 21:10 in Gal 4:30 corresponds with 'Jerusalem now' as this text originally applies to Hagar, the slave Egyptian in Genesis. Paul's quotation of Gen 21:10 for some has been regarded to be an imperatival call for the Galatians to expel the apostle's opponents or Jews/Jewish Christians, but a second person singular imperatival form, ἔκβαλε is being retained from the Septuagint translation of Gen 21:10 and other imperatival verbs in its proximity being addressed in the second person plural form speak against such notion (e.g., γίνωεσθε in 4:12, λέγετέ in 4:21 and στήκετε in 5:1).

I propose that along with Paul's use of Gen 21:10 in Gal 4:30, the apostle is pointing to exile with phrases, 'now Jerusalem,' Hagar, Sinai moutain/Sinaitic covenant and Arabia. So in Gal 4:21–5:1, Paul connects 'Hagar' as the slave woman and her son, Ishmael as the slave son being exiled (ἐκβαλε), losing prerogative to be an Abrahamic inheritor to Sinai and Sinaitic covenant by which the first generation of the old Exodus had become wilderness wanderers because of their rebellion against Yahweh (Num 13:33; 14:34; Ps 107:4), being cut off from the inheritance of the Land promised to Abraham. Also, the later generation of Israel from a prophetic era, still under the effect of the Sinaitic covenant, Jacob-Israel was exiled because of her harlotry/idolatry against her husband Yahweh. And perhaps, a geographical remark, 'Arabia' might also function as to reiterate this Hagar/Sinai connection to exile, because 'Arabia' was geographically in a great extend 'desert/wilderness.' 'Now Jerusalem' in Gal 4, therefore, is not a geographical reference but the state of Jerusalem-Zion in exile as in Isa 64:8–10, "Thy holy cities have become a wilderness, Zion has become a wilderness, Jerusalem a desolation" (Isa 64:8; cf. Isa

1:21). But for Paul, it is no longer under the Babylonian or the Roman superpower that the people of God are exiled but in the apostle's apocalyptic view, under the evil age (Gal 1:4) by which people are enslaved, an exilic condition was still in effect. And if Paul, prior to encountering Jesus, and his contemporary Jews were perceiving the state of their people still in a continuous exile, the allegory of Hagar, Sinai in Arabia and νῦν Ἰερουσαλήμ with slavery could bring exile to the minds of the apostle's auditors who were well acquainted in the narrative and the history of God and his people by the apostle's teaching.

Barren Matriarch, a New Exodus and 'Jerusalem Above'

On the other hand, the barren matriarch from Isa 54:1 in Gal 4:27 brings forth Jerusalem-Zion in restoration, hence a new exodus in view, however, for Paul, instead of calling this Jerusalem, 'future' or 'new' Jerusalem, which seems to be more fitting since her antitype is 'present/now' Jerusalem, nor even 'heavenly' Jerusalem, but the apostls calls this Jerusalem-Zion matriarch 'above Jerusalem' (ἄνω Ἰερουσαλήμ). For Paul, with a hopeful fate and the eschatological destiny of Jerusalem in Isa 40–66 in view, 'above Jerusalem' is a reference to 'Jerusalem-Zion,' which has been arisen to the glory by Yahweh's intervention for an Isaianic new exodus/restoration (Isa 2:2; 52:2; 60:1; 66:20). In Isaiah as well as other apocalyptic literature, there are rarely two Jerusalems but one Jerusalem with two states or two ages - one in the age of an exile, characterised as desolate, barren and enslaved; and the other in the age of a new exodus, restored, glorified and married to Yahweh. Paul's reorientation of this apocalyptic two ages is that the eschatological age of a new exodus/restoration by Yahweh's own intervention was supposed to follow consequently at the end of the evil age of exile (Gal 1:4), but because of the death and the resurrection of Jesus and the advent of the Spirit, Paul's Jewish apocalyptic eschatology has been reoriented in that an eschatological triumphal age has been realised with the death and the resurrection of Jesus the Messiah.

Hence, two stages/states of Jerusalem, exile and restoration of which in the mind of the prophet Isaiah were consequent event, present and future, are now concurrently present as there are two groups of children on the earth, of the slavery and of the freedom. And also, I concur with Professors Dunn and Nanos that there is one covenant, namely Abrahamic covenant of which Paul concerns deeply in Galatians, instead of two.

Therefore, Paul's allegory in Gal 4:21–5:1 is inhabited with a reoriented Jewish apocalyptic perspective in its undercurrent as the apostle is intertextually working with Gen 15–21 and Isa 40–66. Should we, then, categorise the apostle's allegory, instead of typology for he would be able to inform his readers explicitly what he thinks of typological category as his typological interpretation shown in 1 Cor 10:6, 11 and Rom 5:14, simply 'allegory,' not necessarily a Philonic allegory, but allegory of which one corresponds or calls to mind (συστοιχέω) from/to another? We should perhaps acknowledge that the text of Gal 4:21–5:1 is allegory that corresponds multiple traditions of Israel's text and history - Genesis, Exodus and Isaiah - intertextually, historically and apocalyptically.

Apocalyptic Allegory and Isaianic New Exodus

I do not think that we need to create another allegorical category called 'apocalyptic allegory,' however, for the sake of auditors' intrigue, I have chosen the title of this paper as such, implying that Paul's allegory in Gal 4 demonstrates that the influence of Jewish apocalyptic is weightier than some of us would credit him for. As Professor Ernest Käsemann has pointed out, saying, "Apocalyptic – since the preaching of Jesus cannot really be described as theology – was the mother of all Christian theology," we may not invalidate the important role of Jewish apocalyptic thoughts in the shaping of NT text and theology during the first century even if one takes this teacher's claim to be exaggeration. Nevertheless, an apocalyptic Paul does not necessarily mean that the apostle is divorced from salvation history and Jewish/prophetic eschatology, but rather in Paul, if not pioneered by him after the Damascus experience, the marriage of salvation history, prophetic eschatology and Jewish apocalyptic thoughts has reoriented how the apostle views what it truly means to partake in the Abrahamic covenantal inheritance, namely the covenantal people of Yahweh. Then, how is this redefined apocalyptic view of two concurrent ages in two Jerusalems has been incorporated with an Isaianic new exodus in Israel's salvation history in Gal 4:19–5:1?

Just as Paul's choice of unique phrase ἐξαιρέω in Gal 1:4 signals exodus tradition with (Exod 18:8–10; Isa 57:13), the apostle's use of ἐλευθεια in Gal 5:1 echoes Isa 61:1 where it says:

> 1 The Spirit of the Lord GOD is upon me, because the LORD has anointed me to bring good tidings (εὐαγγελίσασθαι) to the afflicted; he has sent me to bind up the brokenhearted, to proclaim liberty to the captives, (κηρύξαι αἰχμαλώτοις ἄφεσιν; לִקְרֹא לִשְׁבוּיִם דְּרוֹר) and the opening of the prison to those who are bound; 2 to proclaim the year of the LORD's favour, and the day of vengeance of our God; to comfort all who mourn; 3 to grant to those who mourn in Zion – to give them a garland instead of ashes, the oil of gladness instead of mourning, the mantle of praise instead of a faint spirit; that they may be called oaks of righteousness, the planting of the LORD, that he may be glorified (Isa 61:1–3, RSV).

Here our focus is on the phrase "to proclaim liberty to the captives (κηρύξαι αἰχμαλώτοις ἄφεσιν; לִקְרֹא לִשְׁבוּיִם דְּרוֹר)" from the verse 1. This language of ἄφεσις is used for the phrase, "forgiveness of sins" (ἄφεσιν ἁμαρτιῶν), which signifies "return from exile" in the NT (Matt 26:28; Mark 1:4; Luke 1:77; 3:3; 24:47; Eph 1:7; Col 1:14). But in Gal 5:1, the apostle proclaims, "For freedom (τῇ ἐλευθερίᾳ) Christ has set us free" (RSV). In Jewish literature, the word, ἐλευθερία also signifies return from exile (1 Esd 4:53; 1 Macc 14:26–27; Praem. 164); and the apostle deliberately has chosen this word ἐλευθερία for the Hebrew word דְּרוֹר

from Isa 61:1 in order to maintain this apocalyptic allegorical category between slavery/exile and freedom/new exodus. For the apostle, the text of Isa 40–66 is in view for using Gen 15–21 in Gal 4:19–5:1. As Paul declares, "For freedom Christ has set us free," echoing Isa 61:1 along with an explicit citation from Isa 54:1, an Isaianic new exodus/restoration is in view for his letter to the Galatians. Hence, for the Galatians Christians to relapse to the exilic/enslaved condition of 'Jerusalem now' with circumcision is abhorrent to the apostle's mind.

Conclusion

In summary, I have examined Gal 4:19–5:1 with Isa 40–66 and Gen 15–21 in view, in order to see how Paul uses the OT in this part of the letter's argument. I have argued that in Gal 4:21–5:1, with also vv. 19–20 in mind, Paul, in his apocalyptic allegory, that is one corresponds to another with a reoriented Jewish apocalyptic view, is identifying the condition, the fate, and most importantly, the 'identity' of the people of God within the framework of exile and restoration/new exodus on three different levels – 1) intertextual; 2) historical/narrative; and 3) apocalyptic. On an intertextual level, Paul, not only incorporates two citations (Isa 54:1 in v. 27; and Gen 21:10 in v. 30) in the Galatians text, but also has inhabited in the texts of Gen 15–21 and of Isa 40–66 intertextually. On a historical/narrative level, Hagar, Ishmael, Sinai in Arabia and 'Jerusalem now' correspond to an exilic condition of Jacob-Israel/Jerusalem-Zion with the word 'slavery' (δουλεία); but on the contrary, free woman, Isaac, 'Jerusalem above' to the restoration of Jerusalem-Zion in a new exodus. Lastly, on an apocalyptic level, the Jewish apocalyptic framework of two ages – an evil age and the eschatological age – has been redefined in that there are now dual-Jerusalemite ages concurrently continuing to give a birth to the children of slavery/exile on one hand and of the promise/inheritance/new creation on the other, because the new exodus has already broken into this world with Jesus and the Spirit. Henceforth, for the Galatians to live as the Torah-binding proselytes for Paul is absolutely abhorring for such means that the Galatians are acting as if they are the children of and in an exile, desolate and enslaved without Yahweh.

For Paul, at the new exodus, Jews and Gentiles in Christ together are Abraham's children, the heirs with inheritance, and the one covenantal people of Yahweh, and so shall our ecclesiology be. "Peace and mercy be upon all who walk by this rule – for in Christ Jesus neither circumcision nor uncircumcision, but a new creation – ἐπὶ τὸν Ἰσραὴλ τοῦ θεοῦ (Gal 6:15–16).

Galatians as Examined by Diverse Academics

Bibliography

Becker, J. Christiaan. *The Triumph of God: The Essence of Paul's Thought*. Translated By Loren T. Stuckenbruck. Minneapolis: Fortress Press, 1990.

Betz, Hans Dieter. *Galatians: A Commentary on Paul's Letter to the Church* in Galatia Hermeneia. Philadelphia: Fortress Press, 1979.

Callaway, Mary. *Sing O Barren One: A Study in Comparative Midrash* (Society of Biblical Literature Dissertation Series 91. Atlanta, Ga.: Scholars PRess, 1986.

Child, Brevard S. *Isaiah*. The Old Testament Library. Louisville, Ky.: Westminster John Knox Press, 2001.

Duncan, George S. *The Epistle of Paul to the Galatians*. The Moffatt New Testament Commentary. London: Hodder and Stoughton, 1934.

Eastman, Susan G. "'Cast Out the Slave Woman and Her Son.'" *Journal for the Study of the New Testament* 28.3 (2006): 309-336.

Evans, Craig A. "Jesus & the Continuing Exile of Israel." Pages 77-100 in Jesus & the Restoration of Israel: A Critical Assessment of N. T. Wright's Jesus and the Victory of God. Edited by Carey C. Newman. Downers Grove: InterVarsity Press, 1999.

Freedman, H., and Maurice Simon., eds. *Midrash Rabbah: Song of Songs*. Translated by Maurice Simon. London: The Soncino Press, 1939.

Goldingay, John. *The Message of Isaiah 40–55: A Literary-Theological Commentary*. London: T&T Clark, 2005.

Hansen, G. Walter. *Abraham in Galatians: Epistolary and Rhetorical Contexts*. Journal for the Study of the New Testament Supplement Series 29. Sheffield: JSOT Press, 1989.

Harmon, Matthew S. *She Must and Shall Go Free: Paul's Isaianic Gospel in Galatians*. Beihefte zur Zeitschrift für die neutestamentliche Wissenschaft 168. Berlin: De Gruyter, 2010.

Hays, Richard B. *Echoes of Scripture in the Letters of Paul*. New Haven: Yale University Press, 1989.

Kamesar, Adam., ed. *The Cambridge Companion to Philo*. Cambridge: Cambridge University Press, 2009.

Longenecker, Richard N. *Galatians*. Word Biblical Commentary 41. Dallas, Tex.: Word, 1990.

Longenecker, Bruce W. *The Triumph of Abraham's God: The Transformation of Identity in Galatians*. Nashville, Tenn.: Abingdon Press, 1998.

Martyn, J. Louis. *Galatians: A New Translation with Introduction and Commentary*. The Anchor Bible 33A. New York: Doubleday, 1997.

Metzger, Bruce M., ed. *The Apocrypha of the Old Testament: The Oxford Annotated Apocrypha*, Revised Standard Version. New York: Oxford University Press, 1965.

Morris, Leon. *Apocalyptic*. Grand Rapids: Eerdmans, 1972.

Nanos, Mark D. "What Does "Present Jerusalem" (Gal 4:25 in Paul's Allegory Have to Do with the Jerusalem of Paul's Time, or the Concerns of Galatians. Paper presented at the annual meeting of the Central Region of the SBL., St. Louis, Miss., March 28-29, 2004.

O'Neill, J. C. "'For This Hagar is Mount Sinai in Arabia' (Galatians 4.25)." Pages 210-219 in *The Old Testament in the New Testament: Essays in Honour of J. L. North*. Journal for the Study of the New Testament: Supplement Series 189. Edited by Steve Moyise. Sheffield: Sheffield Academic Press, 2000.

Oswalt, John N. *The Book of Isaiah: Chapters 40–66*. The New International Commentary on the Old Testament. Grand Rapids: Eerdmans, 1998.

Schweitzer, Albert. *Paul and His Interpreter: A Critical History*. Translated By W. Montgomery. London: Adam and Charles Black, 1912.

Thompson, J. A. "Arabia." Pages 179-181 in vol. 1 of *The Interpreter's Dictionary of the Bible*. Edited by G. A. Buttrick. 4 vols. Nashville: Abingdon, 1962.

Watts, Rikki E. *Isaiah's New Exodus in Mark*. Biblical Studies Library. Revised and updated ed. Grand Rapids: Baker Academic, 2000.

Westermann, Claus. *Isaiah 40–66: A Commentary*. The Old Testament Library. Translated By David M. G. Stalker. Philadelphia: The Westminster Press, 1969.

Wright, N. T. *The New Testament and the People of God*. Christian Origins and the Question of God 1. Minneapolis: Fortress Press, 1992.

_____. *Jesus and the Victory of God*. Christian Origins and the Question of God 2. Minneapolis: Fortress Press, 1996.

Promise, Law, Faith:
Covenant-Historical Reasoning in Galatians

T. David Gordon
Grove City College

Introduction

Many years ago, my doctoral advisor (Paul J. Achtemeier) suggested that someone study the relation of law and covenant in Paul's thought. While I did not pursue that avenue during my doctoral studies (pursuing instead the closely-related matter of Paul's Understanding of the Law), the thought was well-planted, and I have been intrigued with the question for almost three decades. In addition to Professor Achtemeier's influence, I must mention my former colleague at Gordon-Conwell Theological Seminary, the late Meredith G. Kline. Professor Kline's study of Ancient Near Eastern covenant treaties, and the bearing of such on biblical studies, has stimulated the thinking of all who have known his work. He also has stimulated my interest in the relation of law and covenant, whether in the Bible generally, or in Paul's letters specifically. Whether Professors Achtemeier or Kline would be satisfied or instructed with the results of my pursuing this line of question I may never know, but I do know that I am grateful to them both for stimulating the pursuit.

I should also herein acknowledge my appreciation to those students at Gordon-Conwell Theological Seminary, Westminster Theological Seminary, and Covenant Theological Seminary, who have studied Galatians and/or Paul with me since 1984. They have dutifully fulfilled their assigned task in the scheme of things, by playing "stump the teacher" with untiring, if not always equally cogent, zeal (One student objected to my views, on the ground that he couldn't find them represented in the current commentaries. I asked him if he would believe them if I wrote a commentary, and he looked even more puzzled than before, if that were possible in his case). In the process, they have caused me to modify and more-carefully express a number of my thoughts about Galatians. Just as importantly, not one has come even close to shaking my confidence in my fundamental perspective (regarding the problem at Galatia or the nature of Paul's reasoning therein). Considering how motivated they ordinarily are to rebut the cockamamie hypotheses of their professors, their inability to shake my confidence in my position has, in fact, enhanced that confidence.

E. P. Sanders has served the field of Pauline scholarship well in recent decades. Aspects of his theses have not enjoyed universal popularity, yet he has stimulated the field to re-evaluate Paul in a profoundly fresh way. Whether Palestinian Judaism was precisely as Sanders described it, or perhaps more "variegated," is now somewhat irrelevant to Pauline studies. The important contribution is this: we no longer assume, prima facie, that Paul's "problem" with the law was exclusively or primarily due to an alleged meritorious abuse thereof. While Professor Dunn, referring primarily to Sanders, may have been optimistic in referring to a single "New Perspective on Paul," I think it is fair to say that there are many new perspectives on Paul that have arisen from Sanders's raising the question of whether there may not be more to Paul's polemic with the law than merely meritorious legalism. Indeed, it is easy to agree with Professor I. Howard Marshall's assessment that many of the newer interpretations need not be perceived as mutually exclusive.

Galatians as Examined by Diverse Academics

At least in two areas, if I read the literature optimistically, consensus may be developing in the study of Galatians that undergird much of what I am attempting to accomplish. First is the lexical observation that ὁ νόμος in Paul's vocabulary ordinarily refers to the Mosaic law, or even more precisely to the Mosaic covenant itself (by synecdoche, since the covenant is so characterized by law-giving). So Frank J. Matera suggests regarding Galatians 3:17: "The Law (nomos) is the Mosaic Law given to the Israelites on Mount Sinai." Second is the now-common historical observation that Paul's difficulty with the Law is motivated largely, primarily, or even exclusively by the reality that the Law separated Jews from Gentiles.

Exegetical progress sometimes results from new discoveries in archaeology, history, lexicography, text-criticism, grammar, or semantics. Just as often, exegetical progress results from a different paradigm; a different way of construing the available data (as argued in Thomas Kuhn's The Structure of Scientific Revolutions). If exegetical progress is made from this labor, it will not be due to my discovering much new about grammar, lexicography, the transmission of the NT text, or any other technical matter. Rather, it will be due to my raising slightly different questions than have been raised in the past. The paradigm from which Paul (indeed, the Bible) was interpreted for many years was largely dominated by systematic theological considerations of an ordo salutis nature; in the twentieth century, Paul's students have profited greatly by complementing such studies with biblical-theological or redemptive-historical considerations of an historia salutis nature (Geerhardus Vos, Herman N. Ridderbos, Werner Georg Kümmel, Ernst Käsemann, et al.). Closely related to the latter, though different from it in precise detail, is what I will endeavor to encourage here: a consideration of those matters that might be called historia testamentorum, the history of God's various covenanting acts. This work attempts to understand Galatians as Geerhardus Vos recommended for understanding the entire Bible:

The Bible is, as it were, conscious of its own organism; it feels, what we cannot always say of ourselves, its own anatomy. The principle of successive Berith-makings (Covenant-makings), as marking the introduction of new periods, plays a large role in this, and should be carefully heeded.

The difference between salvation-historical/redemptive-historical categories and covenant-historical categories is this: the former (salvation/historical) narrates those particular events or deeds that are judged to be significant in the overall work of redemption, overcoming what is lost in the first Adam and restored in the last. But the latter (covenant-historical) narrates the successive covenant-administrations by which God binds himself to his people (and vice versa). Thus, the exodus is a significant salvation-historical event, but it introduces, by itself, no covenantal change. Not until the event at Mt. Sinai is a covenant instituted that relates Yahweh to those he delivered from Egypt in a particular way. Similarly, the Incarnation is a monumental act in salvation history--so much so, that Eastern and Western Christendom sometimes debate whether it is equal in prominence with the Passion. But the Incarnation, significant enough as it is in redemptive-historical terms, does not, by itself, inaugurate any change in covenant-administration. The Incarnate Christ was born "under the Law," under the Sinai covenant-administration, and lived out his earthly existence submissive to its stipulations, teaching his followers to do the same (Matt. 5:17-21). But later, a "new covenant" was inaugurated in his sacrificial death "This cup is the new covenant in my blood" (1 Cor. 11:25, cf. Luke 22:20). Each successive covenant-administration institutes some new practices (some sacramental) and stipulations. Abraham's descendants were not required to offer animal sacrifices until the Sinai covenant was administered; after that, they were. Similarly (and importantly, in Galatians), his descendants were not required to be ritually or dietarily separate from the Gentiles until the Sinai covenant was administered; after that, they were.

It is common—and helpful—for students of Galatians to be cognizant of redemptive-historical categories. Don Garlington, for instance, refers to the difficult statement that ὁ δὲ νόμος οὐκ ἔστιν ἐκ πίστεως in Gal. 3:12, and rightly says that "the law and faith belong to distinctly different historical realms: the former does not occupy the same turf in the salvation-historical continuum as the latter." Similarly, Moisés Silva, also commenting on Gal. 3:12, says, "In other words, to say that 'the law' is not of faith is to claim that the Sinaitic Covenant belongs to a different redemptive-historical epoch than the gospel." Such comments take us significantly beyond the more-static systematic theological understanding that has characterized so much of Galatians interpretation in the past. But they do not go quite far enough in being expressly covenant-historical; Paul's reasoning is not merely that the Abrahamic (or New) covenant is located at a different season of salvation history than the Sinai covenant; his point is that these covenants themselves have different characteristics. The Abrahamic covenant is characterized by believing that God will fulfill several remarkable pledges; the Sinai covenant is characterized by doing the things the same God commanded on the tablets of the covenant. In this sense, the law is not of faith (ὁ δὲ νόμος οὐκ ἔστιν ἐκ πίστεως). The Sinai covenant is not essentially characterized in the same manner as the Abrahamic covenant; whatever its proposed benefits are, they will not arrive (as the benefits proposed to Abraham did) by believing, but by doing the things commanded.

Paul, in Galatians, traces how three of these covenant-administrations differed in their stipulations, and especially in those stipulations that related Jew to Gentile. My approach greatly appreciates that of Ben Witherington III, and goes further. Witherington says, "As this commentary develops it should become clearer all the time that Paul does indeed operate with a two—or perhaps even three-covenant theology (depending on whether one sees the new covenant as the fulfillment of the Abrahamic one or and therefore part of it, or as fulfillment without being part of it)." My approach (disclosed in the title) is self-consciously tri-covenantal throughout (and there is no "perhaps" in my poly-covenantalism). In Galatians, Paul does not provide a complete history of God's covenanting. He says nothing expressly about any covenant with Adam, nothing about any covenants with Noah (whether ante-diluvian or post-diluvian), nothing about any covenant with Phineas to be a priesthood, and nothing about a covenant with David to build God a house. Paul's exclusive covenantal interest in this letter is with three covenants, and how they are like and unlike each other (especially in terms of the relation of Jew and Gentile). Obviously, as a minister of the New Covenant, he is interested in the New Covenant. Additionally, because of the insistence of the Judaizers at Galatia on the observance of the stipulations of the Mosaic covenant, Paul wishes to discuss the relation of these two. However, he finds it expedient to do so in terms of a third covenant (though temporally prior to the other two), the Abrahamic. Indeed, Paul argues that the New Covenant and the Abrahamic covenant are profoundly similar in kind; while the Sinai covenant is different from these two in some important ways. There are also some similarities between Abraham/New on the one hand and Sinai on the other; but Paul does not mention them in this letter because his concern is local, practical and polemical. Therefore, one could derive a somewhat distorted picture of Paul's thought by reading Galatians alone; the Roman letter, being less polemical, provides an occasion in which Paul's statements about the Sinai administration are somewhat more favorable (because more comprehensive and less polemical) than they are in Galatians.

It is no part of my thesis to attempt to determine when Paul first arrived at his covenant-historical reasoning. I leave it to Hans Hübner, Seyoon Kim, Francis Watson, et al. to trace the development (if any) of Paul's thinking. Whether Paul's understanding of the Abrahamic and Sinai covenant changed after Damascus or not is also no part of my thesis (though surely his understanding of the New covenant did). My thesis is concerned to demonstrate that the reasoning in the letter itself, regardless of when or where it was originally derived, was/is covenant-historical: Paul addressed issues in the New Covenant community in light of the realities associated with two previous covenants—one with Abraham and one with the Israelites at Sinai.

In the following, building upon what others have argued recently, I will attempt to persuade the reader that Paul's argument in Galatians is not in the first place (if at all) designed to correct systematic theological errors of an ordo salutis nature (i.e. faith as the instrument of justification); rather, his argument in Galatians is designed to correct implicit errors of an historia testamentorum nature (whether Israel's Messiah has brought blessings only to the members of the Sinai covenant community or also to individuals from all nations; and what this means for observing the stipulations, especially the segregating/marking stipulations, of the Sinai covenant). Paul's argument in Galatians is covenant-historical; he corrects misbehaviors (requiring observance of the Mosaic Law) associated with the New Covenant by describing the relation of that New Covenant to two covenants that were instituted before it, the Abrahamic and the Sinaitic. The error of the Galatian community resides in its (practical, if not theoretical) insistence that the Sinai covenant is everlasting, with the logical corollary that the stipulations of that covenant, including those that distinguish one ethnic group from another, are also everlasting. Effectively, Paul argues that the New Covenant is not merely a new reality associated with the Sinai covenant; rather, it is a covenant in its own right that displaces the temporary, Christ-anticipating, Jew-threatening and Gentile-excluding Sinai covenant.

Throughout this work I will argue that Paul conceived the Sinai covenant as "temporary," which could be misunderstood by some. In employing the term "temporary," I mean that the covenant itself, made at Sinai with the Israelites, governed the children of Abraham from that time until Christ came. I do not mean that its instructive benefits were merely temporary; to the contrary, both Jews and Christians continue to find themselves instructed by the realities of that covenant. John the Baptist, for instance, could not have referred intelligibly to Jesus as "the lamb of God, who takes away the world's sins" (John 1:29) had there never been a Passover lamb or other Jewish sacrifices. The epistle to the Hebrews largely consists of explaining the work of Christ in terms of those theological types that antedated him and created a theological matrix by which his person and work were comprehensible. We continue to benefit from the things we learned from the Sinai covenant. But that covenant itself, made with the Israelites, came after the Abrahamic covenant and before the new covenant (and ended therewith). The covenant itself was, therefore, temporary, even though its typological instructions continue to benefit us today. Some years from now, I will pay the last payment on my house, and my mortgage contract will then end, because it is a temporary contract. I will still benefit from the contract, because I will still live in the home. But I will no longer have any obligation to that covenant or its requirements; neither I nor anyone else will be obligated to it.

Why Not Covenant-Theological? Why Covenant-Historical?

Some may wonder why I do not describe Paul's reasoning in the Galatian letter as covenant-theological. I could do so, and if one did so, the explanation could work reasonably well. But "covenant-historical" is better suited to Galatians, because so many of Paul's statements are of a temporal nature (see more below), where he reminds that the Abrahamic covenant antedated the Sinai covenant by 430 years, and thus temporalized/relativized the Sinai administration (Gal. 3:17). In this letter, Paul conceived the Sinai covenant as a temporary, provisional covenant-administration that governed between the other two covenants; it governed after the Abrahamic covenant and before the New Covenant. The temporal analogies Paul employed to describe the tutelage of the Sinai covenant ("guardians," "managers," "trustees") all point to this temporary/provisional nature of the Sinai covenant, and to understand Paul we must adjust our thinking to his thoroughly historical reasoning.

It may be helpful to entertain the possibility that the problem at Galatia may have been entirely practical, and not theoretical at all. That is, in practice, the Galatian Judaizers required the participants in the New Covenant to observe the rites and ordinances of the Mosaic covenant. We do not know what their theoretical rationale for this practice was, and perhaps it is unnecessary to speculate further. Paul considered the practice to be inconsistent with the theoretical realities of the New Covenant, but it was the practice itself, not necessarily the theory (theories?) behind it that was the problem. That is, contrary to nearly all previous interpretations of Galatians, we might consider the possibility that, for Paul, some practices are wrong in themselves, regardless of the theoretical foundations behind them.

Theoretical foundations are sometimes implicit rather than explicit; and it is true that the implicit foundation to the Galatian error was that, in some sense or senses, the Sinai covenant (and its stipulations) was eternal. This tendency, at an implicit level, to regard the Mosaic covenant and/or its stipulations as eternal, is still with us, and is enshrined in the confession of my own tradition, the Westminster Confession of Faith. In chapter 19:1, the divines at Westminster affirmed that God "gave to Adam a law…" In the next section, 19:2, they said: "This law, after his fall, continued to be a perfect rule of righteousness; and, as such, was delivered by God upon Mount Sinai, in ten commandments…" While not explicitly saying that the Mosaic law was eternal, Westminster appears to have implied that the Mosaic law had, in some senses, been published first in the garden, and that it was "perfect." So, if after sixteen centuries of the common era, Christian confessional literature tends to regard the Mosaic covenant as eternal, we can be patient with the fact that perhaps some first century Jewish Christians had a similar misunderstanding.

For whatever theoretical reasons, then, the practical reality was that Gentiles were being required to observe those very Mosaic practices that had been designed to exclude them, and to protect the Israelites from inter-marriage and corruption by them. Those very stipulations of the Mosaic covenant that had been designed to preserve Israel as a "peculiar people," distinct from and indeed separate from the nations of the world, were being required of members of those nations. But for Paul (though unlike for the Galatians or the Westminster Assembly), the stipulations of a covenant cannot simply be lifted from their covenantal context; they are part and parcel of that covenant. If we still observe the Gentile-excluding stipulations of the Mosaic covenant, if we still regard the nations as unclean, then the promises to Abraham that his "Seed" would bless all the nations appears not to have been fulfilled. On the other hand, if the promise to bless the nations through Abraham's Seed has been fulfilled, then there is no longer any purpose for the covenant administration that excluded those nations; far from leading us away from faith in Abraham's God, such Gentiles believe in Abraham's God also.

Paul's thinking in Galatians is also deeply *historia salutis*; as well as pervasively eschatological. The reader will quickly discover my dependence upon those twentieth-century interpretations of Paul that have (rightly) disclosed the pervasively eschatological nature of his theological conceptions (including, but not limited to, his eschatological understanding of the Spirit, his eschatological conception of justification, and his eschatological understanding of Abraham's promised blessings to the nations). Thus, in introducing somewhat more overtly the category of *historia testamentorum*, it is not in any way my intention to diminish the importance of *historia salutis* categories in the deeper substructure of Paul's thought. Rather, it is designed to facilitate understanding how it is that Paul reasons about the New Covenant realities in light of two previous covenants, the Abrahamic and the Mosaic covenants.

In a variety of ways, the New Covenant is profoundly and pervasively eschatological, and it would require an additional monograph to demonstrate how eschatological the "new covenant" was conceived by Jeremiah even before Paul. I cannot do justice to the relationship between "new covenant" and eschatology in this monograph, but I mention it here because any emphasis on eschatology will eventually lead to an appreciation of covenant-historical reasoning, and vice versa. Consider just the expression "the days are coming" from Jeremiah, an expression that does not merely appear in verse 31 "when I will make a new covenant with the house of Israel and the house of Judah." Consider these also:

Jer. 23:5 "Behold, the days are coming, declares the LORD, when I will raise up for David a righteous Branch, and he shall reign as king and deal wisely, and shall execute justice and righteousness in the land.

Jer. 30:3 For behold, days are coming, declares the LORD, when I will restore the fortunes of my people, Israel and Judah, says the LORD, and I will bring them back to the land that I gave to their fathers, and they shall take possession of it."

Galatians as Examined by Diverse Academics

Jer. 31:38 "Behold, the days are coming, declares the LORD, when the city shall be rebuilt for the LORD from the tower of Hananel to the Corner Gate.

Jer. 33:14 "Behold, the days are coming, declares the LORD, when I will fulfill the promise I made to the house of Israel and the house of Judah.

Jer. 49:2 Therefore, behold, the days are coming, declares the LORD, when I will cause the battle cry to be heard against Rabbah of the Ammonites; it shall become a desolate mound, and its villages shall be burned with fire; then Israel shall dispossess those who dispossessed him, says the LORD.

Jer. 51:47 "Therefore, behold, the days are coming when I will punish the images of Babylon; her whole land shall be put to shame, and all her slain shall fall in the midst of her.

Jer. 51:52 "Therefore, behold, the days are coming, declares the LORD, when I will execute judgment upon her images, and through all her land the wounded shall groan.

We observe then, that "new covenant," long before Paul, was itself deeply eschatological—an aspect of the coming days--and I therefore appreciate those various approaches to his letters that are sensitive to such. My only point here is that my covenant-historical approach does not exclude the validity of the various eschatological interpretations; it augments them.

If we permit Paul to reason covenant-historically, and if we permit ourselves to reason, with Paul, using the categories of historia testamentorum, we will find his argumentation in Galatians to be more accessible than if we approach Galatians by other categories. Indeed, even in the very helpful discussions of Paul by James D. G. Dunn, the categories are not quite right, though they are very close. Dunn's approach is essentially sociological: Jews and Gentiles are united in Christ, and are not, therefore, to be separated by those "works of the law" that have that tendency. This is very close to the heart of the matter, but is unsatisfactory apart from historia testamentorum categories. The Jews and Gentiles were not separated merely because they were ethnic or geo-political competitors or strangers. Xenophobia was not the entire problem, and plausibly was no part of the problem at all. They were separated by the terms of the Mosaic administration itself; not by ethnic or geo-political suspicions or hatreds. To the contrary, the entire history of the Israelites from the time of the Conquest on was one of being too "Gentile-friendly," as it were. It was Yahweh who insisted on the Israelites being separate, and the Israelites who did not desire to be so. It was Yahweh who insisted on destroying utterly the Am ha-Aretz during the Conquest, and the Israelites who did not do so. It was Yahweh who proscribed intermarriage with the Am ha-Aretz, and the Israelites who insisted on doing so. So it was not ordinary sociological differences that separated Israel from the nations; it was the Mosaic covenant and its stipulations that did so.

Paul's historia testamentorum categories are not always overt, and he only employs διαθήκη three times explicitly in Galatians. Sometimes the terminology he employs for describing these realities can be misleading to us, unless we consider that he may be using terms in a particular manner. Note, for instance, the use of νόμος and ἐπαγγελία in Galatians 3:17:

This is what I mean: the law, which came 430 years afterward, does not annul (ἀκυροῖ) a covenant previously ratified (προκεκυρωμένην) by God, so as to make the promise void.

Note here that whatever Paul means by law/νόμος on the one hand, and promise/ἐπαγγελία on the other, they are separated by 430 years. To what, then, does he refer? He refers to two covenant-administrations ("does not annul a covenant"), one with Abraham, and one with Moses, separated by 430 years (which Stephen, in his speech, "rounded off" to 400 years). So Paul's actual reasoning in this verse is, if I may paraphrase:

This is what I mean: the Sinai covenant, which came 430 years afterward, does not annul a covenant previously ratified by God, so as to make the Abrahamic promissory covenant void.

That is, for Paul in Galatians, "law" is ordinarily a synecdoche for the Sinai covenant-administration, an administration characterized by law-giving. And "promise" in the same letter is ordinarily a synecdoche for the Abrahamic covenant-administration, a covenant characterized by promise-giving.

In Galatians 3:17, this way of reading the matter is not difficult, and most people find it fairly straightforward, because of the temporal language of 430 years. But in other Galatian passages, Paul's reasoning is the same, yet to some minds it is less obviously so. "Law" still sounds to some like God's moral will (or, to some, legalism), and "promise" sounds to some like a vague theological category. As I will argue in the appropriate places, the matter is even more complex, because Paul often uses a third synecdoche, "faith," to refer to the New Covenant. He does so because it is a covenant characterized by faith in the dying-and-rising Christ. But this synecdoche evades us also, because to our minds "faith" is a reference to the human/existential act of trust (and indeed, Paul sometimes uses πίστις to refer to such in Galatians). So then, ordinarily when Paul speaks in Galatians of promise, law, and faith, he means the Abrahamic covenant (characterized by promise-giving), the Sinai covenant (characterized by law-giving), and the New Covenant (characterized by faith in the dying-and-rising Christ); but we (mistakenly) hear him speaking of general theological categories/realities of God's pledges, God's moral demands, and our faith in such a God.

That is, for Paul in Galatians, "law" is ordinarily, if not regularly, a synecdoche for the Sinai covenant-administration, an administration characterized by law-giving. And "promise" in the same letter is ordinarily a synecdoche for the Abrahamic covenant-administration, a covenant characterized by promise-giving. If this is so, then Paul's reasoning is much more covenantal than we may think at first blush, because the three uses of διαθήκη are not the only instances of his reasoning covenantally. The 32 uses of νόμος and the ten uses of ἐπαγγελία (ordinarily) are also covenantal in substance. And, if this is so, when discussing who "inherits" the promises of the Abrahamic covenant (employing κληρονομέω, κληρονομία, or κληρονόμος), we find six more occasions of covenantal reasoning, which is also the case when "ratify/annul" (κυρόω, ἀκυρόω, or προκυρόω) language is employed. Similarly, a statement such as Ὅσοι γὰρ ἐξ ἔργων νόμου εἰσίν, ὑπὸ κατάραν εἰσίν• ("all who are of works of the law are under a curse," Gal. 3:10) does not employ the lexical stock of διαθήκη, but the reasoning is covenantal: all who are parties to the Sinai covenant fall under its threatened curse-sanctions (as the following quote from Deut. 27:26 demonstrates, γέγραπται γὰρ ὅτι ἐπικατάρατος πᾶς ὃς οὐκ ἐμμένει πᾶσιν τοῖς γεγραμμένοις ἐν τῷ βιβλίῳ τοῦ νόμου τοῦ ποιῆσαι αὐτά).

A good example of this use of synecdoche for covenant-administrations is found in Gal. 3:23-25:

Now before faith came (Πρὸ τοῦ δὲ ἐλθεῖν τὴν πίστιν),
we were held captive under the law (ὑπὸ νόμον),

imprisoned until the coming faith would be revealed.
So then, the law was our guardian until Christ came (εἰς Χριστόν),
in order that we might be justified by faith.
But now that faith has come (ἐλθούσης δὲ τῆς πίστεως),
we are no longer under a guardian.

Note here the contrast between the two temporal clauses, "before faith came" and "now that faith has come." On first blush, it may appear that Paul was employing ἡ πίστις to refer to the human, existential capacity to exercise trust. However, in 3:6-9, Paul had made it abundantly clear not only that Abraham had faith, but that he was, therefore, the father of all who also had faith: just as Abraham "believed (ἐπίστευσεν) God, and it was counted to him as righteousness..." Know then that it is those of faith (οἱ ἐκ πίστεως) who are the sons of Abraham. ...So then, those who are of faith (οἱ ἐκ πίστεως) are blessed along with Abraham, the man of faith (τῷ πιστῷ Ἀβραάμ).

For Paul, faith, as an existential human capacity, even faith as the instrument of justification, had been here since Abraham. Therefore, when Paul in the same chapter says "before faith came, we were...under the law," he must be using "faith" as a reference to the New Covenant, so that "before faith came" and "before Christ came" mean virtually the same thing. Indeed, many commentators have routinely recognized that "before faith came" in this passage refers to the New Covenant realities, and that "faith" here is a synecdoche for the New Covenant, or realities associated with it. What they less frequently recognize, at least explicitly, is that ὁ νόμος here is a synecdochal reference to the Sinai covenant-administration, a point that I will attempt to argue throughout.

Static systematic-theological categories are incapable of processing the deeply historical/temporal (and covenantal) reasoning in Galatians. Paul understands God to have unfolded his redemptive purposes in a series of covenants over time, and Paul's reasoning is therefore profoundly temporal. Notice, even in the stretch from 3:17-4:4, the frequency of temporal language, indicating in the following by italics:

This is what I mean: the law, which came *430 years afterward*, does not annul a covenant *previously* ratified by God, so as to make the promise void. ...Why then the law? It was added because of transgressions, *until* the offspring should come to whom the promise had been made... Now *before faith came*, we were held captive under the law, imprisoned until the coming faith would be revealed. So then, the law was our guardian until Christ came, in order that we might be justified by faith. But now that faith has come, we are no longer under a guardian... I mean that the heir, as long as he is a child, is no different from a slave, though he is the owner of everything, but he is under guardians and managers until the date set by his father. In the same way we also, when we were children, were enslaved to the elementary principles of the world. But when the fullness of time had come, God sent forth his Son...

Paul reasons here that things change with the introduction of each distinctive covenant, and that, especially, the Sinai covenant was temporary; it had a beginning, 430 years after the Abrahamic, and an end, with the arrival of what was pledged to Abraham in the coming Christ/seed and his new covenant. The problem, therefore, was neither with the Sinai covenant nor some alleged abuse thereof; the problem resided in regarding a temporary covenant (and/or its Gentile-excluding stipulations) as permanent.

I therefore understand why Paul's interpreters have not yet, in my judgment, correctly understood the Galatian letter. The purpose of this work is to promote the category of *historia testamentorum* to Paul's interpreters (I don't recall Vos using that exact expression), and to suggest that reading Paul's letter by means of such a category provides a more-satisfactory reading. But sociological categories won't work, and the traditional systematic-theological categories won't work. They are not Paul's categories in Galatians, and his thought can no more fit into such categories than can square pegs fit into round holes.

If we return to a confessional standard that informed what Sanders called the "dominant Protestant" approach, consider again our earlier citation of portions of chapter 19 of the Westminster Confession of Faith. In chapter 19:1, the Westminster Confession affirmed that God "gave to Adam a law, as a covenant of works, by which he bound him and all his posterity to personal, entire, exact, and perpetual obedience." In the next section, 19:2, it said: "This law, after his fall, continued to be a perfect rule of righteousness; and, as such, was delivered by God upon Mount Sinai, in ten commandments..." Note, then, that Westminster 19 tended (and intended) to do with "law" the precise opposite of what Paul tended (and intended) to do with ὁ νόμος in the Galatian letter: Westminster 19 eternalized "law"; Paul temporalized ὁ νόμος. Westminster 19 thereby absolutized "law"; Paul relativized ὁ νόμος. Westminster 19 universalized "law"; Paul localized ὁ νόμος (as a covenant that excluded all nations but Israel). Paul not only did not drive ὁ νόμος back into Eden; he expressly argued that sin (Genesis 3) was in the world before ὁ νόμος (Rom. 5:13). And in Galatians, he argued that ὁ νόμος was relativized even by the Abrahamic administration, which antedated it by at least 430 years. Westminster 19 made "law" a universal reality, "by which he bound him (Adam) and all his posterity to personal, entire, exact, and perpetual obedience" (WCF 19:1); whereas Paul understood ὁ νόμος to be a covenant that excluded all but the Israelites.

Alongside this tendency in Westminster chapter 19, however, there was another use of "law" in the Westminster standards that comports very closely with Paul's usage, as at WCF 25:2: "The visible church, which is also catholic or universal under the gospel (not confined to one nation, as before under the law), consists of all those throughout the world that profess the true religion; and of their children: and is the kingdom of the Lord Jesus Christ, the house and family of God, out of which there is no ordinary possibility of salvation" (parenthesis theirs, emphases mine). This appears to be the same usage at WCF 7:5: "This covenant was differently administered in the time of the law, and in the time of the gospel: under the law, it was administered by promises, prophecies, sacrifices, circumcision, the paschal lamb, and other types and ordinances delivered to the people of the Jews, all foresignifying Christ to come..." In passages that say "under the law," "law" is a synecdoche, by which that covenant-administration so characterized by law-giving is referred to by its central feature. However, apart from the almost-technical phrase, "under the law," elsewhere in the Westminster Confession (and many Protestant confessions) "law," unless qualified in some other way, means God's moral will.

It is not surprising, then, that the "dominant Protestant" approach has had difficulty making good sense of Galatians. It has been forced, as I say, to "read between the lines" of Galatians rather than read the lines themselves. It has been forced to invent a problem never expressly mentioned in the letter, and contrary to much/most of what the reliably-dated and pertinent sources actually say. Not only has that approach misunderstood late Second Temple Judaism, it has sometimes projected its own use and understanding of "law" onto Paul's use of ὁ νόμος, which makes of the Galatian letter an utterly inexplicable puzzle. Until and unless interpreters grasp that in Galatians ὁ νόμος is ordinarily employed as a synecdoche for the particular and temporary treaty Yahweh made with the Israelites at Sinai 430 years after making unconditional pledges to Abraham, the Galatian letter will remain to us what the Soviet Union remained to Prime Minister Churchill: "a riddle, wrapped in a mystery, inside an enigma."

I expect to encounter some objections to the thesis. I also anticipate, however, that they will not be due to my making idiosyncratic or risky conclusions of a grammatical, lexical, or historical nature. Rather, they will be due, largely, to other considerations, arising from three entirely different directions. On the one hand, the post-holocaust study of Paul's relation to the Jews and their covenant(s) is profoundly intent on discovering that Paul does not perceive Judaism and Christianity as being, in any significant way, different from each another. In such an environment, it would be preferable for Paul to conclude that God has made in history only one covenant, one that embraces Jew and Gentile alike. Regrettably, such a conclusion is not possible (though the Abrahamic covenant pledged blessings to all the tribes of the earth). It will not arise from the available literature, and it will not fit well if imposed upon it. The Jews themselves had several covenants, not one, as Paul himself observed: "They are Israelites, and to them belong the adoption, the glory, the covenants" (αἱ διαθῆκαι, Rom. 9:4).

On another hand, some North American covenant theologians of the twentieth century (with a little help from the seventeenth-century's nomenclature of a single "covenant of grace"), in their debates with dispensational theologians, have adopted a biblical theology that is also (implicitly if not explicitly) mono-covenantal, in their desire to avoid what they perceive to be the errors of American Dispensationalism. Such, I would argue elsewhere, is contrary to the majority report of historic covenant theology, and it is surely contrary to Paul. "These are two covenants (αὗται γάρ εἰσιν δύο διαθῆκαι, 4:24)" cannot responsibly be construed to mean "These are one covenant." If Paul's reasoning in Galatians addresses three specific covenants in terms of their distinctive features, we will not be able to assess well his reasoning if we refer to all three, or even two of the three, as "the covenant."

Third, in the ongoing "faith-works" discussion (a discussion that has, in dogmatic history, both a Lutheran and an Evangelical host), there are those for whom the categories of "faith" and "works" have never been covenantal, but theological and/or existential. It will quickly be evident that I think they use Pauline terms in a way that Paul himself did not. They tend to use "faith" and "works" abstractly, whereas Paul contrasts specifically "faith in Christ" and "works of the Law." Whether the conclusions they reach theologically, with their re-defined terms, are true or Pauline is not a matter I have much publication interest in; but I expect to encounter some resistance from them for my arguing for what I perceive to be a different definition of those terms.

To the reader, then, I offer a "covenant-historical" model for reading Galatians. I do not offer it on the ground that such a model solves all of the interpretive difficulties in the letter. I merely offer it on the two-fold ground that it solves difficulties that other models do not solve, and that it provides a method for reading the entire book without major difficulty or inconsistency. I assume that the test of any model is its comparative adequacy: Does it account for more of the available evidence and data than alternative models? If it does, it is to be preferred, at least until another model comes along, more adequate to the task.

It should be evident that this volume is not a commentary on Galatians, at least in any ordinary sense. It is designed to explain the forest more than the trees, and the trees only insofar as they explicate the forest. It is an endeavor to explain the argument or thought of the letter, and is unlike a commentary in this way (though it might be beneficial if such commentaries were occasionally written, and Charles Cousar's is to be commended on this ground). My ongoing decisions regarding which details to include or exclude are consistently guided by this one consideration: that I wish to offer an alternative reading to both the dominant Protestant understanding and the New Perspectives understanding. I therefore include those details that I regard as significant in demonstrating either the inadequacy of the other positions or the comparative adequacy of mine. Some readers will think I have included unnecessary detail; others will judge that I have excluded necessary detail, and I do not flatter myself that I will please all. But I do owe to all a candid discussion of what considerations informed my decisions, even if the judgment I exercise in the process is quite imperfect. Similarly, this volume is not intended as a survey of recent scholarship on the questions of Paul and the Law; others have covered this material ably. Rather, I attempt to interact (primarily in the notes) with recent scholarship sufficiently to indicate awareness of the discussion and/or where my perspective differs from other known perspectives. I attempt to avoid/evade cluttering the manuscript with such references, but again: some will understandably claim that there are too many such references while others will equally understandably claim that there are too few; I had hoped Goldilocks would edit the manuscript, but she was busy furniture-shopping.

After several introductory matters are dealt with, and the historical narrative in Galatians 1 and 2 is briefly surveyed, I will present a pericope-by pericope discussion of the central argument of the letter in Galatians 3 and 4, followed by an abbreviated discussion of chapters 5 and 6. For the student of Galatians, this work needs to be supplemented by the standard commentaries, which continue to appear faster than either my mind or wallet can accommodate them. If this work contributes at all to understanding Galatians, it will not do so because it comments exhaustively on each of the letter's respective details. To the contrary, I deliberately intend to omit mentioning those details (and the arguments about them in the secondary literature) except insofar as they are necessary to establish what I judge to be an over-all way of reading Galatians that is more adequate than the known alternatives.

While I will endeavor to state my case positively, offering the reasoning for why I believe this covenant-historical approach illuminates Galatians well, implicit throughout is my dis-satisfaction with two other approaches: the dominant Protestant approach prior to E. P. Sanders, and the so-called New Perspective(s) approach. The first always tended to misunderstand Galatians in two ways: First, it tended to read "between the lines," rather than the lines themselves, assuming that Palestinian Judaism taught a meritorious theory of justification, and that Paul was correcting such an error at Galatia. Paul's negative comments about ὁ νόμος were assumed to be negative comments about alleged first-century legalism, rather than negative comments about the law itself. While I do not believe the dust has finally settled on the nature of Palestinian Judaism of the first century, Sanders has demonstrated, at a minimum, that this older Protestant view was a caricature. The dominant Protestant therefore never appreciated properly how significant the Gentile-excluding nature of Sinai was to the apostle to the Gentiles. F. C. Bauer's criticism of the dominant Protestant perspective on this point was just:

"Thus, not only was he the first to lay down expressly and distinctly the principle of Christian universalism as a thing essentially opposed to Jewish particularism...In his Christian consciousness his own call to the apostolic office and the destination of Christianity to be the general principle of salvation for all people were two facts which were bound up inseparably in each other, and could not be disjoined."

Second, and related, the dominant Protestant approach never really heard Paul's reasoning in Galatians correctly; it viewed the passages regarding justification as though Paul were arguing *for* the doctrine, whereas I read those passages as though Paul is arguing *from* the doctrine. As we will see at the appropriate points, my judgment is that Paul in Galatians does not argue for justification as though it were disputed, but from justification (as undisputed) in order to argue for the full inclusion of the Gentiles in the church, without their observing Mosaic ceremonies (wherein the dispute truly resided). In Galatians, "we who are Jews by nature" are those who know "that a man is not justified by observing the law" (Gal. 2:15-16). Since we Jews know this, Paul reasons, we see no barrier to the justification of the non-law-observing Gentiles. What distinguished us (the law) did not justify anyway, so there is no reason that the Gentiles need to observe a law that never justified us Jews anyway.

Regarding the New Perspectives on Paul, three matters (that appear with differing emphases among different representatives) that characterize that approach strike me as unsatisfactory. First, Prof. Dunn's "sociological" discussion of Galatians is largely right and helpful, but is not the right term, and is a tad off in substance. While it is true that Jews and Gentiles were members of different societies, and while it is true that the unity of believing Jews and Gentiles is a very important Pauline concern in the letter (indeed, in all of Paul's letters), what separated Jew and Gentile (in Paul's mind) was not their ethnic or cultural differences, but the Sinai covenant itself, a covenant God made with the Israelites that deliberately excluded the Gentiles, proscribed inter-marriage with them, and even proscribed much of the Gentile diet.

A second feature that often appears in the New Perspectives on Paul is an express or implicit monocovenantalism; a tendency to perceive only one covenant in the Hebrew Bible, or at least to define "covenant" as some single, over-arching plan to redeem. Many authors within the New Perspectives approach are aware of the importance of "covenant" in understanding the Scriptures. Regarding Galatians 3, for instance, note how N.T. Wright, in one of his earlier writings, called attention to this:

"The basis thesis I wish to argue here hinges on Paul's use of the covenantal theme…First, the chapter as a whole should be seen as an extended discussion of Genesis 15. This is one of the great covenantal chapters in the Jewish scriptures...Second, Paul's use of the 'curse' terminology here belongs exactly within this overall covenantal exposition, since it comes from one of the other great covenantal sections, Deuteronomy 27-8."

Wright correctly observed the "covenantal" theology of Galatians 3, and was right to refer to Genesis 15 and Deuteronomy 27-28 as among the "great covenantal chapters" or "great covenantal sections" of the Scriptures. But Wright's over-all approach makes it difficult for him to see that these are not only different "sections" or "chapters," but different covenants in their own respective rights; one (Genesis 15) made with Abraham and another, of a different kind, later instituted through Moses that segregated Israel from the nations (Deut. 27-28). In his volume on justification, note how Wright defines "covenant:"

"Here we have it: God's single plan, through Abraham and his family, to bless the whole world. This is what I have meant by the word covenant when I have used it as shorthand in writing about Paul....The 'covenant,' in my shorthand, is not something other than God's determination to deal with evil once and for all and so put the whole creation (and humankind with it) right at last."

Wright understands "covenant" to be God's eternal redemptive plan, a mis-definition not entirely unlike the mis-definition found in the Reformed confessional literature (which, ironically, Wright routinely chastises). Wright's definition of "covenant" is very like the Reformed confessional "covenant of grace," and each is misleading, because biblically, "covenant" is never some eternal plan, but always some ratified-in-space-and-time treaty. Since the nature of Paul's argumentation in Galatians is to compare and contrast the New covenant with the Abrahamic and Sinai covenants, any monocovenantalism, or any tendency to confuse "covenant" with a timeless or eternal plan, is fated beforehand to misunderstand Paul significantly. Note again Wright's comments on Galatians 3:10-14:

"He is expounding covenant theology, from Abraham, through Deuteronomy and Leviticus, through Habakkuk, to Jesus the Messiah...For Paul, then, the covenant is not detached from the realities of space and time, of the this-worldly orientation which was characteristic of Israel's covenant. Rather, the covenant was precisely working its way out through exile and restoration."

Galatians as Examined by Diverse Academics

Wright refers to several covenants (inaugurated with Abraham, Moses, and Christ) as "the covenant" or "Israel's covenant." But Abraham's covenant (which was also Israel's) threatened no one with exile; the threat of exile was exclusively associated with the Sinai covenant. Wright's view differs from that of interpreters such as Charles Talbert:

"When employed theologically, covenant can describe very different types of relationships. On the one hand, there are covenants in which God binds himself. When talking about such promissory types, covenant and oath are often synonymous (Testament of Moses 1:9; 3:9; 11:17; 12:13), as are covenant and promise (1 Kgs. 8:25). Such covenants are not conditional. On the other hand, there are covenants in which Israel is bound. When talking about such obligatory types, covenant and law are often synonymous...Such covenants are conditional on the people's obedience."

Beginning with E. P. Sanders, the expression "covenantal nomism" has come to be one of the most common errors in contemporary Pauline studies; because the expression ends up homogenizing the several covenants found in Tanakh. The promissory covenant with Abraham, the works-demanding, curse-threatening, Israel-segregating covenant instituted with Moses, the covenant with Phinehas that his descendants would offer sacrifices, the pledge to David to put a descendant on an everlasting throne, are all tossed into a theological Waring blender, out of which emerges a single slurry that, ironically, bears almost no resemblance to any of the particular covenants found in Tanakh. Indeed, from my perspective, much of the discussion of what we call "the Quest for Second Temple Judaism" is crippled by the fact that so many participants in the quest—on either side of the conversation—are mono-covenantal. Are there some Second Temple texts that demand rigorous obedience to the Laws of Moses? Of course; the covenant instituted via Moses demanded such. Are there some Second Temple texts that regard the pledges Yahweh made to Abraham as entirely gracious? Of course; that covenant was a promissory covenant. Are there Second Temple texts that require the strictest observance of the holiness code? Of course; both the Mosaic covenant and the one with Phinehas demanded such. Whatever one calls the monocovenantal slurry that emerges from a blended Tanakh—whether it is called "covenantal nomism" by Sanders et al. or "the covenant" by Wright et al.—it will never make adequate sense of Paul's reasoning in Galatians, which was rigorously poly-covenantal. Paul perceived more difference between the Abrahamic covenant and the Sinai covenant than, perhaps, Friar Martin did between the Sinai covenant and the New Covenant.

A third area where I find the New Perspectives approach unsatisfactory in Galatians resides in its teaching about justification and the covenant community. Here are two representative samples, from James D. G. Dunn and N. T. Wright:

> "God's justification is rather God's acknowledgement that someone is in the covenant." "Justification in this setting, then, is not a matter of how someone enters the community of the true people of God, but of how you tell who belongs to that community."... "Within this context, 'justification,' as seen in 3:24-26, means that those who believe in Jesus Christ are declared to be members of the true covenant family."

The problem with this view is that throughout most of her history, Israel plainly was in a covenant relationship with Yahweh that condemned her rather than justified her. To be in the Sinai covenant community placed the nation under conditional cursings as well as conditional blessings. So there is not only a lexical problem here (it is not at all clear that the δικ-language means anything about covenanting or covenant communities; as we will see it was and is routinely ethical or forensic language, as I discuss in the lengthiest excursus in this volume), but also an historical problem of great significance: Israel was united covenantally to God by the Sinai covenant, but she was routinely condemned (and almost never justified) by the prophets who were the executors of that covenant. Indeed, both the Hebrew Bible and the New Testament Scriptures record the relationship of the Israelites to their prophets as murderous:

1Kings 19:10 He said, "I have been very jealous for the LORD, the God of hosts. For the people of Israel have forsaken your covenant, thrown down your altars, and killed your prophets with the sword, and I, even I only, am left, and they seek my life, to take it away."

Neh. 9:26 "Nevertheless, they were disobedient and rebelled against you and cast your law behind their back and killed your prophets, who had warned them in order to turn them back to you, and they committed great blasphemies."

Matt. 23:31 Thus you witness against yourselves that you are sons of those who murdered the prophets.

Luke 11:47 Woe to you! For you build the tombs of the prophets whom your fathers killed.

Acts 7:51-53 "You stiff-necked people, uncircumcised in heart and ears, you always resist the Holy Spirit. As your fathers did, so do you. Which of the prophets did not your fathers persecute? And they killed those who announced beforehand the coming of the Righteous One, whom you have now betrayed and murdered, you who received the law as delivered by angels and did not keep it."

1Th. 2:14 For you, brothers, became imitators of the churches of God in Christ Jesus that are in Judea. For you suffered the same things from your own countrymen as they did from the Jews, 15 who killed both the Lord Jesus and the prophets, and drove us out.

Why would the Israelites have murdered the prophets if the prophets exonerated them, acquitted them or justified them? Would they not rather have welcomed them with open arms? But the pervasive witness of the Hebrew Bible is consistently the same: The Sinai covenant (and its "servants the prophets") ordinarily condemned the covenant people; it did not acquit/justify them. By the standards of that covenant itself, the covenant people were judged to be unrighteous, not righteous, as even a small representation of prophetic testimony against that covenant people (not against the nations) demonstrates:

Hos. 5:3-5 I know Ephraim, and Israel is not hidden from me; for now, O Ephraim, you have played the whore; Israel is defiled. Their deeds do not permit them to return to their God. For the spirit of whoredom is within them, and they know not the LORD. The pride of Israel testifies to his face; Israel and Ephraim shall stumble in his guilt (ταῖς ἀδικίαις); Judah also shall stumble with them.

Hos. 7:1 When I would heal Israel, the iniquity (ταῖς ἀδικίαις) of Ephraim is revealed…

Hos. 8:13-14 As for my sacrificial offerings, they sacrifice meat and eat it, but the LORD does not accept them. Now he will remember their iniquity (τὰς ἀδικίας) and punish their sins; they shall return to Egypt. For Israel has forgotten his Maker and built palaces, and Judah has multiplied fortified cities; so I will send a fire upon his cities, and it shall devour her strongholds.

Is. 59:1-4 Behold, the LORD's hand is not shortened, that it cannot save, or his ear dull, that it cannot hear; but your iniquities have made a separation between you and your God, and your sins have hidden his face from you so that he does not hear. For your hands are defiled with blood and your fingers with iniquity; your lips have spoken lies; your tongue mutters wickedness (ἀδικίαν). No one enters suit justly (οὐδεὶς λαλεῖ δίκαια); no one goes to law honestly; they rely on empty pleas, they speak lies, they conceive mischief and give birth to iniquity.

Jer. 2:22 Though you wash yourself with lye and use much soap, the stain of your guilt (ταῖς ἀδικίαις σου) is still before me, declares the Lord GOD.

Jer. 3:13 Only acknowledge your guilt (γνῶθι τὴν ἀδικίαν σου), that you rebelled against the LORD your God...

Jer. 11:10 They have turned back to the iniquities of their forefathers (τὰς ἀδικίας τῶν πατέρων αὐτῶν), who refused to hear my words.

To be sure, the Sinai covenant also provided the covenant community with a means of atonement. But if such atonement was necessary, then the covenant community otherwise stood condemned as "unrighteous" (ἀδικία). Atonement is not needed for the righteous but for the unrighteous:

Lev. 16:21-22 And Aaron shall lay both his hands on the head of the live goat, and confess over it all the iniquities (πάσας τὰς ἀνομίας) of the people of Israel, and all their transgressions (πάσας τὰς ἀδικίας), all their sins (πάσας τὰς ἁμαρτίας). And he shall put them on the head of the goat and send it away into the wilderness by the hand of a man who is in readiness. The goat shall bear all their iniquities (τὰς ἀδικίας) on itself to a remote area, and he shall let the goat go free in the wilderness.

Thus, before offering the required atoning sacrifice, the covenant people were unrighteous; and after offering such sacrifice, they were (for the moment) acquitted. But both before the atonement/acquittal and after the atonement/acquittal they were still the covenant people. They were the covenant people before atonement; they were the covenant people after. They were the covenant people when they were declared unrighteous; they were the covenant people when they were declared righteous, both when they were condemned and when they were acquitted. Therefore, any suggestion that there is some lexical or theological relation between justification/δικαιοσύνη and being in a covenant with God has profoundly misunderstood the covenant God made with Israel through Moses and enforced through the prophets. Israel would have avidly welcomed such a new "perspective" in her day; she would have been more than delighted to know that merely by being in the Sinai covenant she was regarded as righteous or justified. And surely the prophets she murdered would have been much happier to have been able to declare "peace, peace," when there was none (Jer. 6:14, 8:11).

Ironically perhaps, there is a tendency shared by both the dominant Protestant approach and by the New Perspectives where I believe they are both mistaken: Each, at times, suggests that Palestinian Judaism of the era misunderstood the Mosaic Law; one suggests she misunderstood it by attempting to keep its commands (ostensibly in order to be justified) and the other suggests she misunderstood its "badges" as segregating her from the nations. But while I do not deny that Palestinian Judaism believed both things, neither is erroneous. The Mosaic covenant required comprehensive obedience: "Cursed is everyone who does not abide by all the things written in the book of the Law, to do them (τοῦ ποιῆσαι αὐτά)" (Deut. 27:26 cited in Gal. 3:10), and "The one who does them (ὁ ποιήσας αὐτὰ) shall live by them" (Lev. 18:5 cited in Gal. 3:12). And the Mosaic covenant required Israel to remain separate from the nations:

> "When the LORD your God brings you into the land that you are entering to take possession of it…You shall make no covenant with them and show no mercy to them. You shall not intermarry with them, giving your daughters to their sons or taking their daughters for your sons…Then the anger of the LORD would be kindled against you, and he would destroy you quickly…For you are a people holy to the LORD your God. The LORD your God has chosen (προείλατο) you to be a people for his treasured possession, out of all the peoples (παρὰ πάντα τὰ ἔθνη) who are on the face of the earth." (Deut. 7:1-6)

The stipulations of Israel's covenant required her to be distinct from the other peoples of the earth: "You shall not eat anything that has died naturally. You may give it to the sojourner (τῷ παροίκῳ) who is within your towns, that he may eat it, or you may sell it to a foreigner (τῷ ἀλλοτρίῳ). For you are a people holy to the LORD your God." (Deut. 14:21). Regarding the various laws (e.g. diet, Sabbath, circumcision), James D. G. Dunn in his original "New Perspective" address said, "Covenant works had become too closely identified as Jewish observances, covenant righteousness as national righteousness. But to maintain such identifications was to ignore both the way the covenant began and the purpose it had been intended to fulfill in the end." But the Jews did not "ignore" the teachings of Moses nor how the Sinai covenant began: It began when the Israelites were separate, wandering in an uninhabited region between Egypt and Canaan; and the covenant required the Israelites to remain separate from the peoples of the land she would inherit. Dunn's confusion is due to his conflating the Abrahamic covenant with the Sinai covenant (the paragraph previous to the quote above referred to the pledge to Abraham to be a blessing to the nations). But the Sinai covenant itself required the Israelites to be separate from the nations about her (for reasons I will discuss later). So, ironically, both approaches believe that Paul needed to correct Jewish misunderstandings of the Sinai covenant; whereas I think the Jews understood that covenant correctly, and it is Paul's interpreters who misunderstand it (and therefore him). It did require works (it was not "of faith," Gal. 3:12); and it did require that the Israelites segregate themselves from the nations around them. Eagerly pursuing the righteousness it demanded and rigorously separating themselves from the Am ha-Aretz were precisely what the Mosaic covenant required; they were not misunderstandings of what it required.

 My voice, then, differs both from the dominant Protestant approach to Galatians and from the New Perspectives on Paul approach; I suppose mine could be regarded as a "third perspective on Paul." I regard each of those approaches as containing many interesting and valuable insights and truths, but I also regard them each as being incapable of making sense of Paul's theological reasoning in Galatians. I offer this alternative reading as merely that: an alternative that I have found satisfactory since I began teaching the Greek text of Galatians in 1984. If others find this approach more satisfactory than other approaches, I invite them to join me in this way of reading Galatians.

 I should make a final introductory comment about my perspective and its relation to the two other prevailing perspectives. My understanding of Galatians antedated most of the New Perspective discussion; it grew out of my sense of the inadequacy of the dominant Protestant approach, but without any reference to the (then-emerging) New Perspective. As time has passed, I have recognized that my view is as far from the one as it is from the other; it is largely independent of the other approaches, and was developed largely independently of them. As I look at the matter now, however, I recognize that my viewpoint may have the unintended benefit of bridging the gap that now separates those two points of view, because I think there is something in my perspective that each may find harmonious with its own views. The New Perspective will probably appreciate my understanding of the importance of the Jew-Gentile issues in Paul's writings (and specifically in his negative comments about ὁ νόμος), and will probably appreciate my unwillingness to believe that one must "scold a first-century Jew to be a Christian"; one can embrace the teachings of the New Covenant without accusing anyone else of having misunderstood the Sinai covenant. Further, they will probably appreciate the corporate approach I take to a number of interpretive matters; I ordinarily regard ἡμεῖς and ὑμεῖς throughout Gal. 3 and 4 as referring, respectively, to Jews and Gentiles, as they irrefragably do in Ephesians 2. The dominant Protestant approach may appreciate the fact that I regard Paul's soteriology as being essentially that of the Protestant confessions, and that I regard δικαιοσύνη to denote ethical uprightness (and, by extension, to denote declarative/forensic statements or judgments about such), and not "covenant faithfulness" or "apocalyptic power." If the two find it possible to regard ὁ νόμος as a synecdoche for the Sinai covenant, all three of us will be able to find a congenial meeting place.

On the Greek and English of Galatians

I must explain to the reader two things about this work: First, I routinely refer to the Greek text. Almost always, the English will also appear, at least parenthetically (or vice versa), so even those whose Greek is rusty or non-existent will ordinarily be able to follow my reasoning. But I have all but given up on attempting to make sense of Paul (or any other New Testament author) from English translations, for two reasons. First, their name is legion, for they are many. There are so many different English translations, each with its own respective strengths and weaknesses, that it is no longer realistic to expect that there will be a single, common translation to which all public discourse refers. The Greek text may simply have to serve as the common text for academic discussion of the New Testament. Second, the sheer number of English translations that has appeared since the Second World War is rather significant; and the market niche of each depends, obviously, on its being different from existing translations. Therefore, each newer translation (with some occasional exceptions) has tended to be remarkably adventurous, to justify commercially its raison d'être.

For the sake of illustration, consider several translations of the fairly straightforward comment in Galatians 3:10: Ὅσοι γὰρ ἐξ ἔργων νόμου εἰσίν, ὑπὸ κατάραν εἰσίν. The Authorized/King James Version translated this in a fairly straightforward and literal manner: "For as many as are of the works of the law are under the curse." The KJV translators followed the similar substantive use of the preposition ἐκ from the previous verses: οἱ ἐκ πίστεως εὐλογοῦνται σὺν τῷ πιστῷ Ἀβραάμ (3:7 and 9), which the KJV similarly translated: "So then they which be of faith are blessed with faithful Abraham." But note what other translations have done with this:

> For all who rely on works of the law are under a curse (Revised Standard Version, New Revised Standard Version, English Standard Version. Mild variation: "All who rely on observing the law are under a curse," New International Version).
> But those who depend on the law to make them right with God are under his curse (New Living Translation).
> Anyone who tries to please God by obeying the Law is under a curse. (Contemporary English Version).
> A curse is on all people who are trying to become good by obeying the law. (Worldwide English New Testament)
> But those who depend on following the law to make them right are under a curse (New Century Version)

Note that, beginning with RSV, the simple "ἐκ /of" became "rely on," suggesting, I suppose, some inappropriate (legalistic?) self-reliance. But this unsubstantiated and gratuitous mis-translation is mild compared to what followed, when the simple substantive use of the preposition ἐκ became such things as "depend on...to make them right," "tries to please God by," "trying to become good by," and "depend on following...to make them right." And none of these translations felt any obligation to translate the preposition in the previous verses in a consistent manner, so Paul's parallel, by employing ἐκ characteristically ("of faith" and "of works of the law," or "characterized by faith," and "characterized by works of the law"), is almost entirely camouflaged. I join Alice here: "'Curiouser and curiouser,' cried Alice."

It is often easier, therefore, simply to refer to the original text as our common text, with enough surrounding information (such as a verse reference) so that the reader can check the English if unsure about the Greek. For the sake of consistency, however, some English translation must be selected as the default translation to which I ordinarily refer unless I indicate otherwise. To serve this purpose, I have selected the English Standard Version. It has its flaws (which I point out whenever pertinent to interpreting Galatians), as do the other English translations, but since its editors claim that it is "literal where possible," (gratuitously, I might add, in light of what they did with Gal. 3:10), it is a tad less adventurous (less "curious") than many other contemporary translations. The NRSV is also a fairly restrained translation; overall, it is probably as good as ESV, and more widely used in academic circles, so I had intended to employ it in this book. Its commitment to gender-inclusive language, however, is a liability in Galatians, where so often Paul refers to Abraham's progeny, yet does so by employing different terms for different purposes. He employs "seed/offspring" (σπέρμα, 3:16 [thrice], 3:19, 3:29), "children" (τέκνα, 4:25, 27, 28, 31), or "sons" (υἱοί, 3:7, 26; 4:6, 7, 22, 30), the latter of which NRSV cannot employ by its own strictures, even though it is interpretively significant in a letter where inheritance is an important consideration, and the relationship between the κληρονομ-language and the υἱο-language is almost certainly intentional for Paul yet verboten for NRSV (which translates both υἱοί and τέκνα as "children"). My choice of ESV, therefore, is merely due to my judgment that it obscures Paul's reasoning in Galatians less frequently than do other contemporary English translations, which, admittedly, is damning with faint praise. On those occasions where I judge it to be necessary, I simply provide my own English translation, and notify the reader of doing so.

Some lament the absence of a common vernacular translation as the basis of public discourse, and I suppose I find the absence somewhat lamentable myself. But there was always some price to be paid for vernacular translations, even when they were fairly restrained; and now they tend to be so imaginative and unrestrained as to be unreliable on their good days and misleading on others. So there may be some advantage in making the original text our common text anyway; I will often do so here.

Introductory Issues

In the next chapter, we will consider several historical issues that are pertinent to understanding Paul's reasoning in Galatians 3 and 4. Here, however, I wish to introduce three matters that inform my understanding of those chapters: First, I regard ὁ νόμος throughout the Galatian letter to be a synecdoche for the Sinai covenant. Second, I regard Paul's reasoning in Galatians 3 and 4 to be covenant-historical in its nature. Third, I believe Paul argues from justification by faith (as a settled doctrine), not for justification by faith (as though it were a disputed doctrine). It will help the later discussion to introduce these three briefly here, since these three govern my approach throughout.

1. ὁ νόμος as Synecdoche for the Sinai Covenant

On several occasions in the last thirty years or so, some hapless individual has felt constrained by the bounds of courtesy to ask me what my dissertation topic was. When I have responded, "Paul's understanding of the Law," the eyes glaze over, disclosing only regret for having asked the question. Reading through the glaze and regret, I believe I can surmise what is going through the mind: "Oh no, another arcane dissertation on some Pauline minutia. I wish I hadn't asked." Not entirely immune to the demands of courtesy myself, I ordinarily change the topic, and enjoy watching the glaze disappear from the eyes with a satisfaction perhaps matched only by that of Ananias, when he saw the scales disappear from Paul's. At the risk of sounding defensive, however, I would suggest that my topic was not as arcane as most think it is. If one evaluates the vocabulary of Romans and Galatians, and dismisses words that have no particular religious or theological meaning (e.g. prepositions, conjunctions, the verb εἰμί, etc.), one finds that only one term appears with greater frequency than νόμος in Romans, and that is θεός. If one does the same search for frequency in Galatians, one finds that, again, only one term appears with more frequency than νόμος, though in this case it is Χριστός. Only terms for the Godhead appear with greater frequency in these two letters. Here are the data:

Romans
θεός = 153
νόμος = 74
Χριστός = 65
ἁμαρτία = 48
κύριος = 43

Galatians
Χριστός = 38
νόμος = 32
θεός = 31
πίστις = 22
πνεῦμα = 18

In each case, νόμος appears more frequently than some terms for the Godhead itself (more frequently than Χριστός or κύριος in Romans; more frequently than θεός in Galatians). At least in these two letters, then, νόμος is a significant concern for Paul, and a significant part of his thought. To grasp his thought, we must understand what he means by νόμος. That is, we study νόμος in Paul not merely because it is a "problem" or conundrum to be solved--Paul says both positive and negative things about it--we study νόμος because it figures so prominently in these two important letters. We might state the matter negatively, and say: Insofar as one misunderstands Paul's use of νόμος, one misunderstands Romans and Galatians.[89]

One of the controlling factors in my reading of Galatians is my belief that the prevailing usage of ὁ νόμος throughout the letter is as a synecdoche for the Sinai covenant in its entirety. In this sense, Gal. 3:17 has profound interpretive consequences, because in this verse, ὁ νόμος not only appears to be used as such a synecdoche, but almost no other understanding of the term would make any sense at all: "This is what I mean: the law, which came 430 years afterward, does not annul a covenant previously ratified by God, so as to make the promise void." Suppose the word "law" here were replaced with the word "giraffe." Then the sentence would read: "This is what I mean: the giraffe, which came 430 years afterward, does not annul a covenant previously ratified by God..." But what able-minded person would suppose that the arrival of a giraffe could have the consequence of annulling a covenant? Suppose, then, a less-fanciful example, and replace the word "law" with "moral directions." Then we get this: "This is what I mean: moral directions, which came 430 years afterward, do not annul a covenant previously ratified by God..." Well, zoologically this is less problematic, but logically it is just as difficult. Who would imagine that the arrival of moral information would annul a previous treaty? What kind of moral information would require one to renege on one's commitments? The only thing that might reasonably be expected to nullify a *previous* treaty is a *new* treaty. For all I know, the Treaty of Westphalia is routinely broken today, as is the Treaty of Versailles. Why? Because the relevant parties entered

---

[89] Indeed, one could make a case that this term is important to understanding Paul per se. νόμος appears 121 times in his letters; whereas ἀγάπη/ἀγαπάω appear 109 times and δικαιοσύνη/δικαιόω/δίκαιος appear 102 times. As a mere matter of lexical statistics, the term concerns Paul more than love and more than justification.

subsequent treaties by which they related to each other on different terms. So what understanding of *nomos* makes sense of Galatians 3:17? I suggest that it only makes sense to take it as referring to the *covenant* God made with the Israelites at Mount Sinai, a covenant characterized by law-giving, and characterized by the threats of severe sanctions upon those who violate those laws/commands.[90]

Paul appears here to be alluding to Ex. 12:40-41, which also enumerates the time between the patriarchal/Abrahamic covenant and the Sinai covenant the same way: "The time that the people of Israel lived in Egypt was 430 years. At the end of 430 years, on that very day, all the hosts of the LORD went out from the land of Egypt."[91] Further, Paul in this text refers to a *"covenant* previously ratified by God," a matter also implied by the two verbs προκεκυρωμένην and ἀκυροῖ.[92] And Paul characterizes that previously-ratified covenant as one of "promise." Implicit in Gal. 3:17 is that ὁ νόμος is itself a covenant, but a different *kind* of covenant than the one characterized by "promise." And, as we all know from Exodus and Deuteronomy, it was not just a single "law" that came 430 years later, nor even a *body* of such laws, but a covenant: "The LORD our God made a covenant with us in Horeb (Deut. 5:2; cf. also Deut. 29:1; 1 Kings 8:9; 2 Chr. 5:10). Whatever else was true about this covenant made at Horeb, it did not annul the previous promissory covenant made with the patriarchs.

Note also that in Galatians 3:17, Paul employs the synecdoche "promise" (ἐπαγγελία) for the Abrahamic covenant. He could have spoken otherwise; he could have spoken of "the covenant made with your fathers" (Deut. 4:31; 5:3; 7:12; 8:18, et al.), for instance, but he did not. He called it "the promise." Was only a single promise made to Abraham? No; several promises were made: to make his descendants numerous, to

---

[90] As we shall see when we get to the text, other covenantal language is present also, including the verbs ἀκυρόω and προκυρόω, as well as the obvious διαθήκη.

[91] Actually, Moses's record, adequate by the standards of his day, is not quite precise. The Abrahamic covenant was ratified in Abraham's generation, some time before Joseph (and/or other descendants of Abraham) was enslaved in Egypt. The time of the original covenant with Abraham (Gen. 15:18) until the covenant at Sinai was closer to five hundred years. Paul probably cites the "430 years" figure by attraction to Ex. 12:40-41.

[92] English has difficulty preserving the Greek word play, because our word "annul" differs from our word "ratify." We could only preserve the Greek by employing a neologism, saying "The law, that comes 430 years after, cannot de-ratify a covenant previously ratified by God…"

give him a land, and through one of his descendants to bless all the nations of the earth (Gen. 12:1-3, 7; Gen. 15:4-7; Gen. 17:1-8; Gen. 28:14). Nevertheless, promise-giving so characterized the Abrahamic covenant that the word "promise" could justly be employed as a synecdoche for the covenant itself.

By its very nature, synecdoche is a figure of speech employed to designate a reality by a dominant or characteristic feature.[93] Twice in Galatians 3 (verses 23 and 25), Paul refers to the new covenant by the word "faith," because faith in Christ is such a dominant or important feature. Luke employs such a synecdoche when he describes the early meetings of the apostolic church: "On the first day of the week, when we were gathered together *to break bread*, Paul talked with them" (Acts 20:7, emphasis mine). We know from other records of the early assemblies of the apostolic church that they were characterized not exclusively by the breaking of bread, but also by apostolic instruction, prayers, and collections (Acts 2:42). But, because the Supper was such a dominant, perhaps even climactic, feature of those assemblies, they could be spoken of, by synecdoche, by such an expression as "to break bread."

The Sinai covenant is therefore justly spoken of as ὁ νόμος.[94] The dominant feature of the covenant made at Sinai was law-giving. Of the

---

[93] Actually, synecdoche can be employed also to refer to less-dominant features; but insofar as synecdoche and metonomy differ from one another, it may be that metonomy can employ almost anything associated with a reality for the reality itself, even if that associated thing is not very central to the reality; whereas synecdoche tends to refer to an aspect of a reality that is essential to it. Examples of such metonomy might be "the White House" for the executive branch of government, since the branch could exist elsewhere, and often does (e.g. in Air Force One). Similarly, the "arm of the law" as a metonomy for the police department has almost nothing to do with arms, and everything to do with radar guns, cameras at intersections, and snide State Police officers (who appear to take out their unresolved marital frustrations on their hapless fellow-citizens, but I digress).

[94] In saying this, I am not suggesting that there is any difference between the anarthrous νόμος and the articulated one. With most contemporary students of Paul, I believe the presence or absence of the definite article is irrelevant. In Gal. 3:11-12, for instance, the term can be used either with or without the definite article, as it can in the LXX. Cf. the discussion by Douglas J. Moo, "'Law,' 'Works of the Law,' and Legalism in Paul," *Westminster Theological Journal* 45 (1983), pp. 75-76, and Thomas R. Schreiner, *The Law and Its Fulfillment: A Pauline Theology of Law* (Grand Rapids: Baker, 1993), pp. 33-34. Note also J. Louis Martyn's recognition that only 8 of the 32 uses of *nomos* in the

ten covenantal words Moses brought down from Horeb, nine were commands.[95] And later these nine were expanded into a body of legislation consisting of over 600 commandments. Because a dominant feature of this covenant was law-giving,[96] Paul refers to the covenant itself as ὁ νόμος.

Paul did not invent this covenantal understanding of ὁ νόμος out of whole-cloth. Twice in the LXX, διαθήκη is used to translate the Hebrew *torah*:

> As it is written in the Law of Moses (בתורת משה, LXX: ἐν διαθήκῃ Μωσῆ), all this calamity has come upon us; yet we have not entreated the favor of the LORD our God, turning from our iniquities and gaining insight by your truth (Dan. 9:13).

The Masoretic text plainly says "in the Torah of Moses," but the LXX translators say "in the *covenant* of Moses." A similar thing occurs at 2 Chron. 25:4:

---

letter are articulated, yet, "as the contexts show, all are definite references to the Law, except for 3:21a, a condition contrary to fact." *Galatians*, n. 40, p. 555.

[95] It is not necessary to our purposes here for me to indicate why I agree with the Jewish enumeration of the Decalogue, rather than with the three different Christian enumerations. But I do agree that the Jewish enumeration, whereby the first word is the word of preamble and historical prologue ("I am the Lord your God who brought you out of the land of Egypt...") is the correct enumeration, and that all three of the Christian enumerations (the Roman Catholic, Lutheran, and Reformed) have serious difficulties. These difficulties are self-inflicted; in the effort to universalize the Decalogue, the various Christian traditions have attempted to find "ten" words that omit the opening words (since these opening words so evidently describe the peculiar relationship between Yahweh and Israel). Once these words are omitted, however, it is difficult to find "ten" words; only nine are left. So the Reformed tradition divides into two different words the prohibiting of having any gods before Yahweh and the making of images, despite the fact that the explanatory clause ("for I the Lord your God am a jealous God") appears to govern the first at least as much as the second. The Roman Catholic and Lutheran enumerations face their own difficulty; each attempts to make two separate words out of the anti-coveting prohibitions.

[96] And, perhaps because of the highly conditional nature of the Sinai covenant, in which Yahweh pledged either to bless or to curse Israel on the condition of Israel's obedience or disobedience.

But he did not put their children to death, according to what is written in the Law, in the Book of Moses (ספרב שהמן בתורה, LXX: κατὰ τὴν διαθήκην τοῦ νόμου κυρίου καθὼς γέγραπται).

Note here that there are two parallel prepositional phrases in the original Hebrew:

"in the Torah" (בתורה) and
"in the Book of Moses" (בספר משה).

But the LXX renders the first one: "according to the *covenant* (κατὰ τὴν διαθήκην) of (not "in") the law of the Lord." It is even possible that the genitive in the expression τὴν διαθήκην τοῦ νόμου κυρίου is appositive, "the covenant that *is* the Law of the Lord." These LXX realities may have influenced Paul, for whom Torah was not merely moral wisdom of a timeless character, but a *covenant*-administration that had a good deal of moral wisdom in it. Or, perhaps Paul never noticed these two unusual translations of תורה with διαθήκη. But, whether he noticed or not, and whether he was lexically influenced or not, he joined the LXX translators in *regarding* Torah covenantally. For both the LXX and for Paul, Torah was not mere wisdom (though it was wise) and Torah was not mere law (though it contained many laws), Torah was a covenant, filled with wise stipulations, made with the Israelites alone at Mount Sinai, segregating them from the Gentiles and threatening them with curses if they disobeyed.

These LXX translations are doubly striking. First, they are remarkable for the fact that they diverge from the literalism so common in the LXX translation.[97] While there is indeed a range of translation within the LXX, its overall tendency is fairly literal, creating a number of somewhat awkward renderings in Greek that have often been called, for lack of a better designation, "Semitisms" or "Hebraisms." To diverge from this pattern is somewhat bold, especially on so well known and religiously important a term as *Torah*. One would have thought that here

---

[97] I am not suggesting that all portions of the LXX are translated in the same manner, nor equally literally. I merely suggest that, taken as a whole, the LXX is ordinarily fairly literal, and in many cases, surprisingly so.

especially the literal/conservative tendency of the LXX would have been preserved by translating with the ordinary νόμος.[98] Second, they are striking because, in each case, the divergence is identical; תורה is translated by διαθήκη. That is, if each diverged in a different way (e.g., if one had substituted ἡ σοφία, "the book of the *wisdom* of Moses"), it might merely indicate the kind of idiosyncrasy associated with scribal transmission--too little light, too little sleep, too much wine, etc. Translating late at night, wearied by the process, perhaps a translator simply got careless, made a mistake, and no one else noticed and corrected the idiosyncrasy. But the divergent, less-literal translations are less-literally translated in the identical manner, suggesting that the translators always had the overtones of the Sinai תורה at this point recognized that *covenant* about it, but that the Greek νόμος did *not* necessarily have the same lexical overtones. Thus, to preserve the covenantal associations , they felt compelled to substitute διαθήκη for the ordinary (and תורה with expected) νόμος.

Consider also the Greek title for the fifth book of Moses: "Deuteronomy." What is contained in that book? Merely a second law? No, the book contains the account of the renewal of the Sinai covenant itself, after the Israelites had broken it. It contains, as it were, a second covenant (and indeed διαθηκη appears therein 28 times, whereas νόμος appears there 24 times), even though the LXX refers to it as τὸ δευτερονόμιον, and Odes refers to Deuteronomy 32 as ᾠδὴ Μωυσέως ἐν τῷ Δευτερονομίῳ. As Deut. 29:1 itself says, "These are the words of the covenant (οἱ λόγοι τῆς διαθήκης) that the LORD commanded Moses to make with the people of Israel in the land of Moab, besides the covenant that he had made with them at Horeb (πλὴν τῆς διαθήκης ἧς διέθετο αὐτοῖς ἐν Χωρηβ)." Of course the Law was republished therein, but only because the original Law-covenant had been violated. Therefore, even the nomenclature of τὸ δευτερονόμιον associated a "second law" and a "second covenant."

---

[98] An example of this conservative tendency in the LXX resides in the "righteousness" language. According to David Hill, of the 476 uses of the –group in the Hebrew צדק Bible, the LXX employs the δικ–root to translate them 462 (97%) times. Cf. Hill, *Greek Words and Hebrew Meanings: Studies in the Semantics of Soteriological Terms*. SNTSMS 5 (Cambridge: Cambridge University Press, 1967), p. 104.

Galatians as Examined by Diverse Academics

Much confusion has occurred in Galatians studies (and Pauline studies more generally) when people assume that Paul uses ὁ νόμος in many ways, differing ways, even within the same context. While it is possible for this to be done with words, there is a simpler explanation.[99] Ordinarily, Paul uses the term as he does at Galatians 3:17, where it manifestly refers to the covenant made at Sinai. This prevailing usage, however, can also lead to slightly extended uses as well. An expression such as "the law says" can refer either to the covenant/treaty itself, which requires certain things, or it can refer, by extension, to the treaty *document*, wherein such words can be found. Referring to Clement's use of *diatheke*, for instance, A. H. J. Gunneweg says "The term means both the covenant, the establishment of divine salvation, and also the *documents* which belong to it and bear witness to it."[100] It would have been unusual (if not impossible) in the Ancient Near East to have a treaty without a treaty document, and therefore the one can often be spoken of as the other.[101] Paul followed Moses in associating closely the covenant itself and its written record.

> Then Moses wrote this law (LXX, "Moses wrote this law *in a book*," ἔγραψεν Μωυσῆς τὰ ῥήματα τοῦ νόμου τούτου εἰς βιβλίον) and gave it to the priests, the sons of Levi, who carried the ark of the covenant of the LORD (τοῖς αἴρουσιν τὴν κιβωτὸν τῆς διαθήκης κυρίου), and to all the elders of Israel.... Take this Book of the Law (τὸ βιβλίον τοῦ νόμου τούτου) and put it by the side of the ark of the covenant of the LORD your God (τῆς κιβωτοῦ τῆς διαθήκης κυρίου τοῦ

---

[99] Whether we join philosophers in approving "Ockham's razor," or join empiricists in treasuring "parsimony," join them we do. If a simpler explanation makes sense of the data, whether philosophically, empirically, or exegetically, there is no good reason to prefer a more complicated explanation.

[100] *Understanding the Old Testament*, trans. John Bowden (Philadelphia: Westminster, 1978), p. 36, italics mine.

[101] Note how easily Paul can say, "For to this day, when they *read the old covenant* (τῇ ἀναγνώσει τῆς παλαιᾶς διαθήκης), that same veil remains unlifted" (2 Cor. 3:14), because when they read "the old covenant" they are reading what was written on "tablets of stone" (2 Cor. 3:3), "carved in letters on stone" (2 Cor. 3:7). The Sinai covenant itself was so associated with the stone tablets, that when one "reads" what is inscribed there one "reads the old covenant." At least at 2 Cor. 3, what Paul regards as being contained on the "tablets of stone" is "the old *covenant*," not God's moral will, and surely not legalism.

θεοῦ ὑμῶν), that it may be there for a witness against you (Deut. 31:9, 12).

Thus, with verbs of communication (speaking, reading, writing), ὁ νόμος can refer either to what the *treaty* "says," or to what the treaty *document* "says," since there is little practical difference.[102] We do a similar thing in English when a banker reminds someone who is late paying the mortgage, "Don't forget; we have a *contract* here." The word "contract" in such a sentence can refer to the business relationship itself or to the written document in which the contract has been formally recorded. While it is true, therefore, in such circumstances, that ὁ νόμος has more than one usage, the latter use is but an extension of the more basic usage. Some would suggest that an expression such as ὁ νόμος λέγει could/should be translated "the Scripture says," and the suggestion is not farfetched. I am suggesting, however, that even in such an expression, it is the covenant document that is being referred to, and it just happens, in this case, that the covenant document is part of the Jewish/Christian Scriptures. To say that ὁ νόμος *means* "the Scriptures" in such an expression, while not entirely objectionable, is an extension of an extension ("covenant" extends to "covenant document" extends to "Scripture") that simply is not necessary, and that may obscure the deeply covenantal nature of Paul's thought.[103]

I am especially resistant to the once-common habit of "solving" the problem of Paul and the law by arguing that ὁ νόμος is an arbitrarily polyvalent term in Paul that can mean different things in different settings. The dominant Protestant approach, for instance, "solved" the tension between Paul's positive and negative statements about the Law by defining the term differently; when Paul viewed the Law positively, he was referring to the rich moral wisdom found in Torah, whereas when he viewed it negatively, he was referring to a meritorious/legalistic abuse

---

[102] Cf., e.g., Rom. 3:19; 7:7; 1 Cor. 9:8; 14:21; Gal. 3:10; 4:21.

[103] Additionally, though somewhat irrelevant to my purposes, to translate ὁ νόμος with "Scripture" might contribute to misunderstanding the public nature of writing in early manuscript cultures. In such cultures, due to the expense of writing material and scribal activity, things that were written were ordinarily matters of significant public importance (such as treaties) or of significant cultural heritage (e.g., *The Iliad*). For this reason, we ought to treat ἡ γραφὴ with special care, and ordinarily translate it as "Scripture" or "what is written," and *not* confuse it with a particular treaty that happens to have a large amount of commanding in it.

thereof. Douglas J. Moo observed that students of Paul have suggested that Paul uses the term to mean as many as seven different things.[104] I do not object to polyvalency *per se*, nor do I insist that Paul employs ὁ νόμος without any variation. However, I am very nervous about solving the tension between Paul's negative and positive statements about the Law in this manner; and my nervousness is due to three considerations.

First, polyvalent terms are not capriciously so. When a term (or expression) has more than one usage, almost always this is due to its having a different use within different semantic settings (or, as some call them, within different "language games" or semantic fields/domains). As Mark A. Seifrid has observed regarding another lexical stock, "All too frequently, scholars investigating –terminology continue to overlook צדק the semantic insight that any proper definition of a word or word-group must describe the *contexts* which call forth the various meanings of the terms."[105] That is, one could say that the English word "run" is polyvalent; but this could be misleading. When one is returning an item to a hosiery store, it only has one meaning; when one looks at a baseball scoreboard it only has one meaning; and when one is discussing a cold-ridden nose, again it has but a single meaning. The term may be employed in many different ways, but it is ordinarily employed only one way in a given semantic setting. So the real question is whether Paul, when in mid-argument about the Law somewhere, can simply change his meaning "on the fly," with any hope that his audience could possibly know that he is doing so. In most of Paul's uses of ὁ νόμος, the expression appears several times within a sustained argument, and I regard it as highly unlikely that Paul could continue to discuss the same thing while switching the definition of one of the more important vocabulary terms he employs.

A second consideration grows out of the ordinarily conservative nature of the LXX translators, and the particular caution they would have accorded to appears 208 times in the Hebrew תורה. By my count, תורה

---

[104] "'Law,' 'Works of the Law,' and Legalism in Paul, *Westminster Theological Journal* 45 (1983), pp. 73-100.

[105] Mark A. Seifrid, "Righteousness Language in the Hebrew Scriptures and Early Judaism," in D. A. Carson, Peter T. O'Brien, and Mark A. Seifrid, eds., *Justification and Varied Nomism*, vol. 1, *The Complexities of Second Temple Judaism* (Grand Rapids: Baker, 2001), p. 422.

Galatians as Examined by Diverse Academics

Bible in the singular. Of those, I could only find 19 that were not translated by ὁ νόμος in the LXX. Three of those, by their own contextual qualifications, are manifestly not "the Law of Moses":

> Prov. 1:8 Hear, my son, your father's instruction, and forsake not your mother's *teaching*, (, θεσμοὺς תורת אמך μητρός σου)
>
> Prov. 7:2 keep my commandments and live; keep *my teaching* (, τοὺς δὲ ἐμοὺς λόγους) as the apple of ותורתי your eye;
>
> Prov. 31:26 ... and the *teaching of kindness* (, ותורת חסד τάξιν) of kindness is on her tongue.

And four others are translated with a derivative of ὁ νόμος:

> Deut. 17:18 "And when he sits on the throne of his kingdom, he shall write for himself in a book a copy of this law (התורה משנה הזאת, δευτερονόμιον), approved את by the Levitical priests.
>
> Jer. 26:4 You shall say to them, 'Thus says the LORD: If you will not listen to me, to walk in my law (, ἐν בתורתי τοῖς νομίμοις μου) that I have set before you,
>
> Hos. 8:12 Were I to write for him my laws (, νόμιμα) תורתי by the ten thousands, they would be regarded as a strange thing.
>
> Prov. 3:1 My son, do not forget my teaching (, ἐμῶν תורתי νομίμων), but let your heart keep my commandments.

If we remove these seven, we find only 12 (5.7%) that are translated with anything other than ὁ νόμος; the other 94.3% are translated with ὁ νόμος. I regard it as unlikely, therefore, that Paul, trained under Gamaliel, would have monkeyed around a good deal with ὁ νόμος. It was, in Paul's circles, simply the Greek equivalent of תורה, and the likelihood of Paul introducing substantively new denotations to such a theologically important term are slender. For Paul, תורה was the distinctive deliverance of God to the Israelites, the covenant he made with them at Sinai recorded on the "tablets of the covenant" and stored in the "ark of the covenant." Note several texts where תורה is employed by texts that refer to the covenant itself:

> Deut. 29:21 And the LORD will single him out from all the tribes of Israel for calamity, in accordance with all the curses of the covenant (τὰς ἀρὰς τῆς διαθήκης) written in this Book of the Law (τῷ βιβλίῳ τοῦ νόμου τούτου).
> Deut. 31:9 Then Moses wrote this law (τὰ ῥήματα τοῦ νόμου τούτου) and gave it to the priests, the sons of Levi, who carried the ark of the covenant (τὴν κιβωτὸν τῆς διαθήκης) of the LORD, and to all the elders of Israel.
> Deut. 31:26 "Take this Book of the Law (τὸ βιβλίον τοῦ νόμου τούτου) and put it by the side of the ark of the covenant (τῆς κιβωτοῦ τῆς διαθήκης) of the LORD your God, that it may be there for a witness against you.
> Hos. 8:1 Set the trumpet to your lips! One like a vulture is over the house of the LORD, because they have transgressed my covenant (τὴν διαθήκην μου) and rebelled against my law (τοῦ νόμου μου).
> Psa. 78:10 They did not keep God's covenant (τὴν διαθήκην τοῦ θεοῦ), but refused to walk according to his law (ἐν τῷ νόμῳ αὐτοῦ).

A third concern relates to those who have argued that Paul employs ὁ νόμος sometimes to refer to legalism, to a meritorious/legalistic abuse of the law.[106] This I regard as extremely unlikely; bordering on

---

[106] Ernest de Witt Burton, *A Critical and Exegetical Commentary on the Epistle to the Galatians* ICC (Edinburgh: T. & T. Clark, 1921), p. 458; Daniel P. Fuller, *Gospel and Law: Contrast or Continuum?* (Pasadena, CA: Fuller Theological Seminary, 1990), pp. 97-99; et al. Perhaps ironically, James D. G. Dunn does a very similar thing regarding "works of the law" when he claims that it can mean, generally, "what the law requires (355)," but also "Israel's misunderstanding of what her covenant law required (366)." Dunn, *The Theology of Paul the Apostle.* (Grand Rapids; Edinburgh: Eerdmans; T & T Clark, 1998). This is R. Barry Matlock's criticism of Dunn: "How exactly can Dunn have 'works of the law' signify *both* 'what(ever) the law requires' *and* a particular perversion of the law, the 'misunderstanding' and its characteristic emphases and effects?"

semantically impossible. Why would Paul employ ὁ νόμος to mean both the good Law that God gave to the Israelites, and to mean an *abuse* of the same good thing? Could ὁ νόμος mean both "God's Law, *rightly* understood and used," and "God's Law, *wrongly* understood and used"? I doubt any language could do such a thing with a single word. Could the term "antibiotic" refer to that which kills microorganisms and to the microorganisms themselves? Far more likely for a first-century Palestinian Jew such as Paul, ὁ νόμος meant what it did when he defended himself in Jerusalem: "I am a Jew, born in Tarsus in Cilicia, but brought up in this city, educated at the feet of Gamaliel according to the strict manner of the law of our fathers (τοῦ πατρῴου νόμου), being zealous for God as all of you are this day" (Acts 22:3). It would hardly have served Paul's defense to have accused himself here of misunderstanding or mis-using the Law; to the contrary, his Law-observance was evidence of his zeal for God. Paul would have employed ὁ νόμος as did the LXX before him, as the Greek term for the Hebrew *torah*, which God gave the Israelites at Sinai. The only thing I suggest beyond this is that I view ὁ νόμος (in Paul's usage) not primarily as a compendium of moral wisdom, but as a covenant; the "tablets of the covenant" (Deut. 9:9, 11, 15) were placed in the "ark of the covenant," because what was inscribed on those tablets was the covenant God instituted at Sinai. And even here, I argue that this is what it sometimes meant *before* Paul also.

Further, as I will suggest at appropriate places, not only does ὁ νόμος, by synecdoche, suggest "the Sinai covenant," it also suggests "the Sinai covenant that excludes Gentiles." That is, Paul is deeply aware of the segregationist nature of the Sinai covenant.[107] The previous

---

Cf. Matlock, "Sins of the Flesh and Suspicious Minds : Dunn's New Theology of Paul," *Journal for the Study of the New Testament*, (72, 1998), p. 78 (emphasis his).

[107] This segregationist nature of Sinai is even disclosed in the circumstances under which it was inaugurated. Yahweh did not make covenant with the Israelites while they were slaves to the large civilization of Egypt; nor did he make covenant with them while they were in the well-populated and highly civilized land of Canaan; rather, he made covenant with them in a deserted wilderness. If it had been Yahweh's intention for this covenant to have comprehended other nations, or for its ten words to have been ten timeless words of moral counsel given to the human race *per se*; then his publicist ought to have been fired. If the Egyptians were to have been benefactors of these ten words, Yahweh should have given them while the Israelites were still there; and were the Canaanites to have been its benefactors, it should have been delivered after the crossing of the Jordan. But

(Abrahamic) covenant would one day bring blessings to "all the families/nations of the world" (Gen. 12:3; 22:18). But the Sinai covenant segregated the descendants of Abraham from such families and nations. When Paul asks the rhetorical question Τί οὖν ὁ νόμος in Gal. 3:19, he could be paraphrased as asking this: "Why was there an Israel-segregating covenant for so many years, since the earlier covenant comprehended all the nations in its pledged blessings?"[108] His question was not merely "Why have *another* covenant?" His question was: "Why have a *different* covenant, that segregated the descendants of Abraham from the nations? What was the purpose of this segregation? What good could possibly come from such a segregationist covenant, when the earlier covenant had pledged one day to employ the 'seed of Abraham' to bless all of those other nations?"[109]

That is, Paul asked precisely the opposite question that Luther and Calvin asked when they formulated three uses of the Law. Luther and

---

they manifestly were not; because the Sinai covenant was made with God's "chosen people," *with* them alone *when* they were alone.

[108] James D. G. Dunn has rightly called attention to this segregating aspect of the Sinai covenant itself: "In sociological terms the Law functioned as an identity marker and boundary, reinforcing Israel's sense of distinctiveness and distinguishing Israel from the surrounding nations." Dunn, "The New Perspective on Paul," in Karl P. Donfried, ed., *The Romans Debate* (Peabody, Mass.: Hendrickson, 1991), p. 303. Heikki Räisänen also rightly notices that "In summary, *nomos* in Paul refers to the authoritative tradition of Israel, anchored in the revelation on Sinai, which separates the Jews from the rest of the mankind." *Paul and the Law* (Philadelphia: Fortress, 1983), p. 16.

[109] I have been surprised recently to encounter occasional individuals who deny that the Sinai covenant segregated Israel from the nations. I had anticipated many objections, but not this one. Were the Israelites not prohibited from intermarrying with the people of the land before they entered it (Deut. 7:3ff.)? Was not the entire program of return from exile threatened because they had done this very thing (Ezra 9:14), to the point that the Israelites were required to put away the wives and children? Does not Ephesians 2 regard the law as creating a wall between Israel and the nations, saying that Christ "has broken down in his flesh the dividing wall of hostility (τὸ μεσότοιχον τοῦ φραγμοῦ) by abolishing the law (τὸν νόμον) of commandments and ordinances (2:13-14)? Segregation was so necessary that Yahweh demanded that the Am-haAretz be put to death: "But in the cities of these peoples that the LORD your God is giving you for an inheritance, you shall save alive nothing that breathes, but you shall devote them to complete destruction, the Hittites and the Amorites, the Canaanites and the Perizzites, the Hivites and the Jebusites, as the LORD your God has commanded, that they may not teach you to do according to all their abominable practices that they have done for their gods, and so you sin against the LORD your God." (Deut. 20:16-18).

Calvin effectively asked this question: "What are three good uses of the Law, that it universally and always has *today*?" But Paul asked just the opposite question: "What was the *temporary* purpose of a covenant that appeared, in some ways, to be a disruption of the Gentile-including covenant that antedated it?" Luther and Calvin asked: "What are the uses of the law that it *still* has?" Paul asked: "What was the purpose of the Sinai covenant that it *no longer* has (οὐκέτι, Gal. 3:25)?" The dominant Protestant approach has not merely misunderstood Paul's answer to this question; it has entirely misunderstood his question, and therefore *could* not answer it correctly. Paul was asking what purpose the Law had "*until* the coming faith would be revealed" (Gal. 3:23); Luther and Calvin were asking what uses it has *after* the coming faith was revealed. Framing a question rightly does not guarantee a right answer; but framing it wrongly ordinarily does. We cannot frame Paul's question differently than he did and make any sense of his answer.

Few people dispute the presence of synecdoche in the New Testament writings, and people routinely acknowledge that Paul employs "faith" as a synecdoche for the New Covenant in Galatians 3:23 and 25 ("before faith came…after faith came"). Systematic-theological concerns, however, appear to cause some interpreters to be nervous about Paul characterizing these three covenants as "promise," "law," and "faith," because they fear that doing so will imply too much discontinuity or difference between the various covenants. Were not some imperatives (e.g. circumcision) given to Abraham? And did not Moses encourage the Israelites to believe in Yahweh (e.g. to deliver them from the Egyptians)? Yes and yes; but the way synecdoche works is to describe a reality by a dominant or characteristic feature, without implying that said dominant feature is an exclusive feature. A covenant characterized by law-giving could also encourage faith, and could also remind of previous promises. Its dominant feature is not and need not be its exclusive feature. Much of the hesitance, I would argue, to acknowledge Paul's synecdoches in the Galatian letter has been due to this reluctance to suggest that the Sinai covenant is exclusively about law, or that the Abrahamic covenant is exclusively about promise, or that the New Covenant is exclusively about faith. But when synecdoche is employed to describe the prevailing or dominant feature of a thing, it does not necessarily exclude other, subsidiary characteristics. When we refer to police officers as "the law," for instance, this is because they do indeed enforce the law; but they also assist us when our automobiles break down by the side of the road, they escort us to the hospital during emergencies, they help us find lost children, etc. (though they do not help with treed cats).

When I attempt to unpack Paul's reasoning in chapters 3 and 4, I suggest that ὁ νόμος is used throughout Galatians as it is in Gal. 3:17, to refer to the (Israel-segregating, Gentile-excluding, obedience-demanding, curse-threatening) covenant God instituted at Sinai with the Israelites.[110] Much later, in the afterword, I will suggest that what is true of Galatians is largely true of Paul's other letters also. When ὁ νόμος is understood as a synecdoche for the Sinai covenant, much light is spread over Paul's letters and his thought.[111]

2. Covenant historical argumentation ("covenant" or "covenants")

Throughout my detailed discussion of Galatians 3 and 4, I argue that Paul's reasoning is covenant-historical. That is, he discusses the

---

[110] I also suggest later that this is Paul's ordinary use of νόμος in his other letters. Exceptions to this usage can appear (in Galatians and elsewhere), but ordinarily not when νόμος is used absolutely. When νόμος is followed by some qualifying genitive, that qualifying genitive can alter the ordinary referent of νόμος. So, e.g., in Gal. 6:2, τὸν νόμον τοῦ Χριστοῦ does not refer to the covenant made through Moses, because the qualifying genitive alters what the term ordinarily means otherwise. At Rom. 3:27, this is also the case with νόμου πίστεως, and this occurs also at Rom. 8:2, ὁ γὰρ νόμος τοῦ πνεύματος τῆς ζωῆς ἐν Χριστῷ Ἰησοῦ ἠλευθέρωσέν σε ἀπὸ τοῦ νόμου τῆς ἁμαρτίας καὶ τοῦ θανάτου. But without such qualification, νόμος ordinarily refers to the Sinai covenant in Paul's letters. In a separate work on Romans, I would suggest that, even in chapters 3 and 8, the Pauline association of νόμος and the Sinai covenant does not entirely recede, and the genitives in question probably distinguish the Sinai covenant from the New Covenant, which is characterized by such realities as faith, life, and the eschatological Spirit. So while the genitives in such texts change the referent from the Sinai covenant to something else, the "something else" is still a covenant-administration, but a different one.

[111] Using some of the simplest features of word processing, I prepare a few handouts for my students to illustrate this. First, I search for all of the 121 Pauline uses of ὁ νόμος. I then print them several times, once in which it is translated "God's moral will," once in which it is translated "legalism," and once in which it is translated "the Sinai covenant." I then ask them to read these over, marking "Y" or "N" or a question mark in the margin beside each, indicating whether the translation does, does not, or might make sense of the text. What they discover is they get far more "Y's" on their handouts for "Sinai covenant" than they do for the other renditions. They realize after this exercise that perhaps this should indeed be the controlling way of understanding the term in Paul's letters.

realities of church-life within the New Covenant by discussing the realities of the Abrahamic and Sinai covenants, respectively. He argues that the ceremonies of the Sinai covenant were/are temporary, because that covenant itself was temporary. There was a covenant before the Sinai covenant, with important differences. The Abrahamic covenant, while pledging to make Abraham's descendants numerous and give them a land, also pledged to bless all the nations of the world through a single descendant of Abraham (Gal. 3:16). That is, the Abrahamic covenant, unlike the Sinai covenant, comprehended the nations within its pledged blessings. More than four centuries before God made a (segregationist) covenant with a single nation, he had made a covenant that had pledged to bless *all* nations. Sinai, rightly understood, was temporary, a temporary covenant with Abraham's descendants that distinguished one nation *from* the other nations for a season of time, until the time would come when one of Abraham's descendants would bless all nations. If the Gentile-excluding Sinai covenant were permanent, it would prevent the fulfilling of what was pledged to Abraham; it was only temporary, "*until* (ἄχρις) the offspring should come to whom the promise had been made" (3:19). The Abrahamic covenant, in this sense, *temporalizes* and thereby *relativizes* the Sinai covenant. The Sinai covenant is secondary to it; and is only understood rightly as an instrument by which the earlier covenant reaches its fruition.[112]

Paul's language throughout Galatians 3 and 4 was/is remarkably temporal: the Abrahamic covenant preceded the Sinai covenant by 430 years; the Abrahamic covenant was "previously ratified by God." The Sinai covenant, therefore, comes *after* one covenant and *before* another. It (and its Gentile-excluding ceremonies) was only in place "*until* the offspring should come to whom the promise had been made" (3:20), "*until*

---

[112] Early covenant theologians recognized this, and some, such as Samuel Bolton (1605-1654), a commissioner to the Westminster Assembly, therefore referred to the Sinai covenant as a "*Foedus subserviens*," to what they called the covenant of grace. Referring to the Sinai covenant, Bolton said: "It was given by way of subserviency to the Gospel and a fuller revelation of the covenant of grace; it was temporary, and had respect to Canaan and God's blessing there, if and as Israel obeyed. It had no relation to heaven, for that was promised by another covenant which God made before He entered the subservient covenant. This is the opinion which I myself desire modestly to propound, for I have not been convinced that it is injurious to holiness or disagreeable to the mind of God in Scripture." *The True Bounds of Christian Freedom* (rpt. Edinburgh: Banner of Truth Trust, 1964), p. 99.

the coming faith would be revealed" (3:23), "*until* Christ came" (3:24). But in these passages Paul also indicated that the New Covenant realities are similar in kind to the Abrahamic realities; and dis-similar in kind to the Sinai covenant realities. The Abrahamic and New covenants comprehend Gentiles within their blessings; whereas the Sinai covenant is made with a single nation. The Abrahamic and new covenants are promissory, dependent for their fruition only on the faithfulness of the promising God (3:16-17); whereas the Sinai covenant is legal/conditional, dependent for its fruition on the obedience of the Israelites. In this sense, the Sinai covenant "is not of faith" (3:12). The Abrahamic and new covenants pledge to bless (3:6-9); the Sinai covenant threatens to curse (3:10-13). Much of what Paul argues in these chapters is that the Abrahamic covenant was different from, and preferable to, the Sinai covenant in many ways, and reaches its full expression and blessedness in the New Covenant. The differences between the Abrahamic covenant and the Sinai covenant are so stark, that Paul anticipated his readers raising the question: "Why then the Law?" (3:19). His answer to this was somewhat complex and somewhat difficult, but effectively he answers that there was a season in the history of redemption during which memory of the promise to Abraham (to bless the nations through one of his descendants) was in jeopardy of being forgotten, and during which time the integrity of Abraham's lineage was also threatened (by intermarriage with the *Am ha-aretz*). During this season, the Sinai covenant, precisely *by* its prohibitions of such inter-marriage (and other ceremonies that distinguished Jew and Gentile) preserved both the basic integrity of Abraham's lineage and memory of the pledge to bless the nations through that lineage's coming Seed. The Law, during this period, was a "guardian" (3:24-25); its Gentile-excluding ceremonies guarded Israel from her own tendency to be like the nations around her and to inter-marry with them.[113] The Sinai

---

[113] Cf. my "A Note on ΠΑΙΔΑΓΩΓΟΣ in Gal. 3. 24-25," in *New Testament Studies*, 35, no. 1, January, 1989, 150-54. In this, I acknowledged, with many others, that the "child-servant" had different functions in different households. In some, to be sure, the παιδαγωγὸς was, as Luther thought, disciplinary; and in others, the παιδαγωγὸς was, as Calvin thought, tutorial/instructive. But in yet others, the παιδαγωγὸς was manifestly a bodyguard, whose role was to protect or guard. In Galatians, therefore, it is this latter, protecting/guarding role, to which Paul refers by the analogy. Sinai's Gentile-excluding regulations protect/preserve both memory of the Abrahamic promise and the basic integrity of his biological lineage from the Israelite tendency to inter-marry with the *Am ha-aretz*.

covenant "guarded" Israel against her own prevailing tendency to intermarry with the *Am ha-Aretz* and follow their deities, forgetting her own covenant marriage to Yahweh. Of course, it guarded her only imperfectly, and some generations less well than others. But at least when the coming Seed of Abraham appeared, Matthew could trace his lineage back to Abraham. In this sense, the first chapter of Matthew's gospel, in which Christ's lineage is traced back to Abraham, testifies that the Law had fulfilled its "guardian" function adequately.

Precisely here James D. G. Dunn's various discussions of Paul are tantalizingly close to being exactly right. He rightly focuses on the Gentile-excluding dimensions of Torah as the primary reason for Paul's negative statements about ὁ νόμος. For the dominant Protestant approach, Paul's negative comments about ὁ νόμος were attributed to people's (alleged) attempts to justify themselves by obedience thereto; for Dunn's approach, Paul's negative comments about ὁ νόμος are attributed to how it separates Jew from Gentile. On this point, Dunn's contribution to Pauline scholarship[114] is, in my opinion, both substantial and salutary. But his "sociological" language suggests that the separation of Jew and Gentile was due to ordinary sociological, ethnic, or even xenophobic reasons. Paul's point is that ὁ νόμος *required* this separation, a separation which the Israelites, throughout much of their history, did not desire. Paul's point is that ὁ νόμος not only protected/guarded Israel from the *Am ha-aretz*; it protected Israel *herself* from her characteristic desire to intermarry with them.

3. Arguing *From* Justification or *For* Justification

Many competent and helpful authors have addressed Galatians in terms of Greco-Roman rhetoric, both generally and specifically. I make no attempt to address each of those here, though the literature is both erudite and fascinating. Rather, I merely wish to introduce one controlling feature of my understanding of the rhetoric of Galatians 3 and 4, in an extremely general and non-technical way.[115] As far as I can tell, after

---

[114] With a little assistance from Krister Stendahl's *Paul Among Jews and Gentiles* (Philadelphia: Fortress, 1976).

[115] By "non-technical," I mean that I ordinarily make no effort to interact with the secondary literature about Greco-Roman rhetoric, and the various technical terms and devices associated with such study, useful as it is. Nor do I distinguish "rhetorical"

thirty years of reading Galatians, Paul does not argue *for* the doctrine of justification by faith in the letter; rather, he argues *from* the doctrine of justification by faith. In ordinary rhetoric, whether Greco-Roman or otherwise, people attempt to settle disputed matters by appealing to some commonly shared, non-disputed matters. The nature of such reasoning is to draw out the implications or consequences of the non-disputed matters as a means of settling the disputed matters. Throughout the Galatian letter, I not only find no evidence that the Galatians misunderstood the doctrine of justification by faith in Christ, but to the contrary: I find express evidence that Paul refers to it as a settled doctrine, and a settled doctrine that enables him to address what is unsettled, namely: what ceremonies to require of Gentiles.

The issue is not one of refined, technical issues in rhetoric; it is simpler than that. There is a difference between a premise, an argument, and a conclusion. The dominant Protestant approach to interpreting Paul has conceived the doctrine of justification in Galatians as an argument or conclusion; I conceive it as a premise. Paul refers to the doctrine of justification as a settled matter (as a premise) upon which he makes arguments that lead to his conclusion (that the gospel, not just his mission,

---

analysis from "epistolary" analysis. Rather, I use "rhetoric" in its general sense, of understanding the logic employed in the letter: what case is Paul making, and how is he making that case? For an introduction to the more-technical study of Galatians in light of Greco-Roman rhetoric, cf. Hans Dieter Betz, "The Literary Composition and Function of Paul's Letter to the Galatians," *NTS* 21:3 (1975), pp. 353-79), and *Galatians: A Commentary on Paul's Letter to the Churches in Galatia* (Hermeneia, Philadelphia: Fortress, 1979); George A. Kennedy, *New Testament Interpretation through Rhetorical Criticism* (Chapel Hill, NC: University of North Carolina Press, 1984); David E. Aune, "Review of Galatians--Dialogical Response to Opponents," *CBQ* 46 (1984); Wilhelm Wuellner, "Where is Rhetorical Criticism Taking Us?, *CBQ* 49 (1987), pp. 448-63; Burton L. Mack, *Rhetoric and the New Testament* (Minneapolis: Augsburg/Fortress (1990), pp. 66-73; Walter B. Russell, Rhetorical Analysis of the Book of Galatians," *Bibliotheca Sacra* 150 (July-September, 1993), pp. 341-58; Carl Joachim Classen, *Rhetorical Criticism of the New Testament* WUNT 128, (Tübingen, Mohr Siebeck, 2000), esp. pp. 1-28; Thurén, Lauri, *Derhetorizing Paul: A Dynamic Perspective on Pauline Theology and the Law* (Tübingen, Mohr Siebeck, 2000); Ben Witherington III, "The Rhetoric of Galatians," in *Grace in Galatia: A Commentary on Paul's Letter to the Galatians* (New York: T. & T. Clark, 2004), pp. 25-36; D. Francois Tolmie, *Persuading the Galatians: A Text-Centred Rhetorical Analysis of a Pauline Letter*, Wissenschaftliche Untersuchungen zum Neuen Testament 2. Reihe 190 (Tübingen: Mohr Siebeck, 2005); Duane F. Watson, *The Rhetoric of the New Testament: A Bibliographic Survey* (Tools for Biblical Study; Blandford Forum, UK: Deo, 2006).

is νόμος-free), and its practical consequences (that no one—Jew *or* Gentile—needs to observe the Law).

Because the doctrine of justification by faith alone was unsettled in Luther's and Calvin's day, much Protestant interpretation of the Galatian letter has (erroneously, in my judgment) assumed that Paul's issue was the same as Luther's and Calvin's. But it was not. Paul's issue was quite different from that of Luther and Calvin. Paul's issue was virtually identical to the issue addressed at the Jerusalem council: Which, if any, of the ceremonies of the Mosaic Law are Gentiles required to observe in the New Testament church? Must they be circumcised? Shall they be required to observe the Jewish calendar or dietary laws? These were the questions the apostles addressed in Acts 15, and they were similar to the questions Paul addressed at Galatia, though Galatians adds the additional consideration of whether even Jews (such as Peter) *may* observe those aspects of the Mosaic law that require separation from table-fellowship with Gentiles. As Paul looked for a rhetorical lever in this circumstance, he selected (among others) the doctrine of justification by faith alone. If Abraham was justified by faith (even before he was circumcised; Genesis 15 precedes Genesis 17), then those who have faith are his spiritual progeny (Gal. 3:7, 9), regardless of whether they are circumcised. If Abraham was justified by faith 430 years before the Mosaic law (with its calendar and dietary laws) was given, then people can be justified apart from that calendar and apart from those dietary laws. And, if people can be justified apart from such ceremonies, perhaps it is not necessary to require them at all.

So, while Paul addresses and affirms the doctrine of justification by faith in Galatians, he does not argue *for* it as a doctrine disputed at Galatia. He argues *from* it, as a doctrine/premise as old as Abraham, as a doctrine/premise which Abraham--not Paul--originated. Some of the post-Sanders discussion of the nature of first-century Palestinian Judaism is, in this limited and particular sense, irrelevant. Is it possible that some first-century Jews had confused ideas about the relation between the Abrahamic promises and the Mosaic laws? Certainly; but Mr. Gallup was not around to take a poll to determine the matter, and even the relevant literature may only reflect the opinions of those first-century Jews who were familiar with that literature. And, in a prevailingly oral culture, in which written material was extremely rare and extremely expensive, we just do not and cannot ever know what Joe Israelite actually believed in the first century; nor do we need to know this. It does not matter to Paul. Paul, rhetorically, refers to the Abrahamic doctrine of justification by faith as a settled matter, without any speculation about whether his entire audience agrees with him or not (or had ever thought about the matter). This is a routine part of human rhetoric, whether ancient or modern. We routinely refer to ideas, attitudes or values that we judge to be well known and publicly recognized, without speculating as to whether 100% of our audience actually functions entirely consistently with the same. We say things such as: "As we all know, our founding fathers were committed to the idea of freedom of speech," without any consideration at all as to whether our audience may or may not contain a handful of bigots or parochials who actually do *not* believe in freedom of speech.[116]

I am not denying that the post-Sanders discussion of first century Palestinian Judaism is useful and important in its own right; it is both useful and important. I am merely denying that such study substantially illuminates the rhetoric of Galatians. That rhetoric can be discovered by the nature of the reasoning itself, with or without reference to our always-tentative historical judgments about an ancient culture. Paul reasoned with Peter (and therefore with his audience) by saying, "we who are Jews by birth, and not Gentile sinners, knowing (εἰδότες) that a man is not justified by observing the law..." As with virtually every use of οἶδα or γινώσκω in the first person plural in Paul's letters, the rhetoric here refers to the matter as settled. Whether it was actually settled, intellectually or psychologically, in the minds of every individual in Paul's audience was and is entirely irrelevant (as strange as that seems), because the nature of human rhetoric was and is always this way. No author and no speaker can actually know the contents of the minds of each individual member of the audience; all an author or speaker can know is what is publicly and widely acknowledged within the community that is being addressed. Paul therefore assumed, rhetorically, that his audience was familiar with father Abraham, and with the promises God made freely to him, which Abraham and Sarah received by faith (albeit imperfect faith in what Sarah regarded

---

[116] According to Mark Bauerlein, "In a 2003 survey on the First Amendment commissioned by the Foundation for Individual Rights in Education, only one in 50 college students named the first right guaranteed in the amendment, and one out of four did not know *any* freedom protected by it." Cf. *The Dumbest Generation: How the Digital Age Stupefies Young Americans and Jeopardizes our Future (Or, Don't Trust Anyone under Thirty)*. Tarcher Press, 2008, p. 10.

as risible promises). Paul also assumed, rhetorically, that his audience would not have regarded as a novelty his routine reference to Genesis 15:6, that Abraham "believed God, and it was counted to him as righteousness" (Gal. 3:6).

This is simply the nature of human rhetoric: we refer to well-known, publicly acknowledged ideas or values to settle unsettled matters. In doing so, we assume nothing about the actual ideas or values of each of the particular members of our particular audience. When we refer to Lincoln's Gettysburg address, or his (more eloquent) Second Inaugural address, we know perfectly well that there may be some Southern sympathizers in our audience; but we don't care (at least not rhetorically). We refer to Lincoln's sentiments as sentiments that are widely known and publicly acknowledged as an important part of our cultural ethos and history, without any concern for the particular opinions of, in this case, the descendants of John Wilkes Booth. Indeed, part of the skillful use of rhetoric is to refer to some matters as settled matters even if we know or suspect that there are a few dissenting opinions within our audience. When Christian clergy refer to Holy Scripture in a sermon, for instance, they do not assume that every individual in the audience knows or believes in every sentence in the Scriptures; but the Scriptures, in that context, are regarded as religiously authoritative, and can be referred to as such, employing the adjective "holy."

Paul's reasoning with Peter, then, is very significant, because Paul articulated as a *settled* matter between them exactly the opposite thing that the dominant Protestant view had long taught. The dominant Protestant understanding had taught that first century Judaism commonly or routinely taught that people are justified by observing the Mosaic Law, rather than by faith. But Paul said precisely the opposite of this: "We who are Jews by nature, and not sinners of the Gentiles, knowing that a man is not justified by the works of the law…" (Gal. 2:15-16, KJV). Many ETs (e.g. RSV, ESV) obscure this somewhat, by translating *"yet* we know," but the original is fairly straightforward: Ἡμεῖς φύσει Ἰουδαῖοι καὶ οὐκ ἐξ ἐθνῶν ἁμαρτωλοί· εἰδότες ὅτι οὐ δικαιοῦται ἄνθρωπος ἐξ ἔργων νόμου. While the "yet" may suggest that Paul's beliefs were contrary to ordinary Jewish belief, the "yet" depends on two very thin lines of evidence. First, it must assume that the δὲ following εἰδότες is in fact genuine, despite considerable evidence to the contrary.[117] And second, it must assert an aggressively adversative meaning *to* the disputed δὲ. My search program counts 636 uses of δὲ in Paul's letters (if we include the disputed epistles). Yet a translation such as the ESV only translates 8 of those 636 as "yet." In only seven other places, out of 636, is the δὲ translated with the strongly adversative "yet."[118] Even if we granted the textually suspect δὲ to be original, and even if we approved this extremely rare adversative translation of it, this would still not undo the rhetorical power of the participle itself, εἰδότες. However we attempt to evade/avoid what Paul said, it cannot be disputed that he says at Gal. 2:16--that Jews know/knew that a person was not justified by observing the law.[119] All of the rhetorical power of that clause would be lost if the clause following εἰδότες were debated. Paul asserted in this passage that one thing Jews knew (in contrast to "Gentile sinners") was that an individual was not justified by observing the law.[120]

---

[117] I regard the textual evidence as a virtual dead-heat here: the δὲ is included by ancient and diverse textual traditions such as ℵ, B, C, D*, F, and some Latin versions, omitted by P46, A, D2 Ψ, the Majority texts, and the Syriac versions.

[118] 1Cor. 2:6 *Yet* among the mature we do impart wisdom…
1Cor. 7:28 *Yet* those who marry will have worldly troubles, and I would spare you that.
1Cor. 7:40 *Yet* in my judgment she is happier if she remains as she is.
1Cor. 12:20 As it is, there are many parts, *yet* one body.
2Cor. 6:10 as sorrowful, *yet* always rejoicing…
Gal. 2:4 *Yet* because of false brothers secretly brought in…
Gal. 2:16 *yet* we know that a person is not justified by works of the law…
1Tim. 2:15 *Yet* she will be saved through childbearing…

[119] And it is entirely irrelevant to my purposes whether 2:15-18 contains Paul's reasoning with Peter or Paul's reasoning with his fellow Jews at Galatia; either way he asserts that "We…Jews" know perfectly well that the Law does not justify, as a means to his pre-arguing his point that the non-law-observing Gentiles are not thereby going to be helped any by observing the Law.

[120] It is even theoretically possible that Paul was mistaken; that he projected his view onto others whose beliefs differed from his. Even if this were so, it would not alter my thesis: Even if Paul were entirely delusional, to understand the epistle of a delusional individual we must understand rightly what *he* regards as axiomatic; even if no one else regards it as such. In his apology, for instance, Socrates regarded pantheism as axiomatic; as did his accusers. We might regard both Socrates and Meletus as being mistaken, but to make sense of their respective arguments, we must rightly understand their premises. The correspondence of those premises to *reality* is an entirely different matter than the correspondence of those premises to their *reasoning*.

Some have attempted to deflect this clause by another effort. They have suggested that the "we" who know that a person is not justified by observing the law are Christian believers. While, as a pure conjecture, it might be plausible for a Pauline "we" to refer to believers, this passage does not do so; it refers to those who are Jews-and-not-Gentiles: "We who are Jews by nature/training and not Gentile sinners, having known that a man is not justified by observing the law..." (my own free translation of Ἡμεῖς φύσει Ἰουδαῖοι καὶ οὐκ ἐξ ἐθνῶν ἁμαρτωλοί εἰδότες [δὲ] ὅτι οὐ δικαιοῦται ἄνθρωπος ἐξ ἔργων νόμου). That is, Paul does not say, "we who are by nature Christians," or "we who are by nature believers," but "we who are by nature Jews." Further, his negative clause does not say "and not unbelievers," but "and not Gentile sinners." Nothing, it seems, but our predetermined belief that first century Judaism was meritorious causes us to misconstrue Paul's reasoning. Paul appears to be observing a commonplace Jewish recognition, that could be paraphrased something like this:

> "Peter, you and I who know the Jewish Scriptures--unlike those *meshugina* Gentiles--have read example after example of the prophets bringing judgment on our fathers because of their disobedience to the commandments of the Torah, and we know perfectly well that the Torah, for all its moral wisdom, never produced the moral wisdom it commended, and therefore was an instrument of condemnation, not justification. Now, if it always brought condemnation (rather than justification) upon us to whom it was given, why on earth would we saddle the hapless Gentiles with it? If we ourselves longed for the blessedness that would come one day through Abraham's Seed, and if many Gentiles join us in believing that Jesus of Nazareth was and is that Seed through whom both they and we are blessed, isn't it enough that we are all baptized into his name?"

Further, throughout chapter 3 and 4, Paul argues *from* the canonical OT scriptures; not from sayings from Jesus or other apostolic letters (or even, remarkably, the Jerusalem Council). That is, the nature of his reasoning in chapters 3 and 4 is to demonstrate that the Jewish Scriptures themselves teach justification by faith-and-not-the-Law, and the temporary nature of the Law.

When we arrive at the exposition of Paul's reasoning in chapters 3 and 4 (and even when we discuss briefly his reasoning in chapters 1 and 2), my exposition will be guided by these three controlling realities: That ὁ νόμος was regularly employed in Galatians as a synecdoche for the Sinai covenant-administration in its entirety; that Paul's reasoning was covenant-historical (and therefore poly-covenantal rather than mono-covenantal); and that he argued not *for* justification by faith but *from* justification by faith. Readers are invited to judge for themselves whether such a reading of Galatians is more adequate than alternative readings.

Galatians as Examined by Diverse Academics

Historical Questions Pertinent to Galatians

Several historical questions are pertinent to the interpretation of Galatians, some more than others. It is no purpose of mine in this book to address all of them. I will express virtually no opinion, for instance, about the North Galatia/South Galatia question, and will intentionally offer no new arguments or speculations about that matter. For the narrow purposes of this work, which is to assess the nature of Paul's theological reasoning in Galatians 3 and 4, several other historical matters must be briefly addressed, some more general and some more specific. I do little more than introduce those matters here, as a means of permitting the reader to understand the method to my madness later. Whether my tentative conclusions on these matters contributes to a more-successful reading of Galatians will only be determined later, after the pericope-by-pericope survey of Paul's reasoning in those chapters.

General

Biblical studies might proceed in a more helpful manner if graduate programs required more study of the concept and methodologies of historical research, rather than jump right in to resolve specific historical questions or challenges. "History" is not merely a subject-matter (e.g., "The War of 1812"); it is a mode of inquiry, a manner of asking questions about how certain dynamics and events influenced or caused others. Its closest analogous discipline is probably Archaeology. Both disciplines ordinarily begin with some givens: In the case of Archaeology it is, ordinarily, artifacts. Artifacts are discovered at a site, and then, based on what we can know about those artifacts, archaeologists attempt to reconstruct the character of the culture. Archeological knowledge is always tentative or provisional, because its conclusions are limited twice: once by the available artifacts, and again by the conjectures drawn from them.

These available artifacts limit us not merely because we ordinarily wish we had more of them, but because, in many situations, the artifacts discovered may be misrepresentative of their culture. If a given city were razed by marauders, for instance, the marauders would likely have made off with everything valuable, leaving behind only matters of comparatively little value. Archaeologists, discovering this "impoverished" artifactual heritage, do not always know whether the remaining artifacts accurately reflect life in the former community, or whether (because of theft or looting) they misrepresent that life. In addition to this artifactual limitation, archaeologists are limited by their imaginative ability to reconstruct a culture on the basis of the available artifacts. So, Archaeology is a fascinating discipline, but also a difficult one, whose "results" are hardly ever final.[121]

History is not substantially different from Archaeology. Both disciplines attempt to understand a past moment in light of the existing evidence. Prior to the printing press, however, the documentary evidence for civilizations was much more scanty, and much less likely to be representative of the culture as a whole. Since the materials on which manuscripts were written were expensive, comparatively few documents exist from such cultures, and we cannot always know how widely known those documents were.[122] The percentage of individuals who actually read or wrote manuscripts was probably smaller than the percentage of those who teach at the college or university level today, and who would suggest that our academic writings are necessarily representative of our culture? So historians function in a similar fashion to archaeologists, doing the best they can to reconstruct a circumstance by evaluating the evidence that exists, and by speculating about how to make sense of it. What we ordinarily call "historical knowledge," therefore, is substantially speculative or theoretical.

As it pertains to biblical studies, the point is this: What we actually have before us is the text (itself sometimes mildly disputed, depending on the manuscript evidence). The text, that is, has a certain "fact-ness" or "given-ness" to it, and I judge that the text, which is not a theoretical construct, should have veto power over all the theoretical

---

[121] Some disciplines appear very different to outsiders than to insiders. Outsiders to Physics and Archaeology probably think of both disciplines as very factually based. In truth, some of the most flexible, ingenious minds appear in these disciplines, minds that attempt to make comprehensive sense of a fairly limited amount of data. This is a very high level of intelligence that integrates both right brains and left brains, both rationality and imagination.

[122] There are occasional exceptions to this. If Milman Parry was right, the Homeric "literature" first existed orally; and, as such, may well have been widely known before it was reduced to writing. Cf. Parry, "Studies in the Epic Technique of Oral Verse-Making. II: The Homeric Language as the Language of an Oral Poetry." *Harvard Studies in Classical Philology* Vol. 43 (1932), 1–50.

constructs surrounding it. If the text, that is, conflicts with our various speculations about its historical surroundings, the evidence of the text should be given more weight than speculations about the culture that produced it, at least in the act of interpreting the text. That is, some interpretations are not only more or less plausible in terms of speculations about the historical circumstances, some are more or less plausible in terms of the text itself. I tend to favor, for instance, an interpretation that is more plausible in terms of the text, even if it is less plausible in terms of my reconstruction of the historical situation. If there are several historically plausible ways of reading the text, I prefer the one that conforms to the most plausible reading of the text itself, the reading that accounts best for the data of the text itself, as it were.

To illustrate this, some years ago I argued that the ellipsis in Romans 9:32 was better supplied by adding the copula than by repeating a verb ("pursued") that had appeared earlier in the text.[123] By supplying the ellipsis differently, the interpretation differs in answering Paul's rhetorical question:

> "What shall we say, then? That Gentiles who did not pursue righteousness have attained it, that is, a righteousness that is by faith; but that Israel who pursued a law that would lead to righteousness did not succeed in reaching that law. Why?"

Paul wonders why Israel did not attain the law, and in his answer, the Greek has an ellipsis: ὅτι οὐκ ἐκ πίστεως ἀλλ' ὡς ἐξ ἔργων: "because not by faith but as by works." In English, the two possible answers to this "Why?" would be as follows:

> Option A: "Because (they did not pursue it) by faith, but as (if it were) based on works"
>
> Option B: "Because (the Law is) not by faith, but as by works"

In each case, the supplied ellipsis is indicated by parenthesis marks. Now, every translation must supply the ellipsis somehow, and students of Greek

---

[123] "Why Israel Did Not Obtain Torah-Righteousness: A Translation Note on Romans 9:32." *Westminster Theological Journal* 54 (1992): 163-66.

know that when a verb is missing, it can be supplied either by the copula or by repeating some other, already-mentioned verb. Almost all translations take Option A, above, and I was proposing Option B. On two grammatical grounds, this is preferable to me. First, the alternative translation skips over the more-proximate verb ("succeed in reaching," ἔφθασεν in Greek), reaching back behind it to a less-proximate verb ("pursued", Greek διώκων). Second, the comparative particle (ὡς), which normally is merely comparative ("like" or "as" something), would, on the first translation above, need to bear the weight of creating a condition contrary to fact (or "unreal condition"), which ordinarily requires a secondary tense in the protasis, a secondary tense in the apodasis, and ordinarily the particle ἄν in the apodasis, none of which is present. Now, since the verb is missing, one could supply a verb in the secondary tense. Further, since by the Koiné period the particle ἄν is not *always* necessary in conditions contrary to fact, it is possible, grammatically, to supply the ellipsis as many English translations do, even though it requires a substantial reach to create a condition contrary to fact on as little ground as the comparative particle ὡς.

Contextually, there is also a Pauline ground for my preference, because this is precisely what he says in Galatians 3:12: "for the law is not of/by faith" (ὁ δὲ νόμος οὐκ ἔστιν ἐκ πίστεως). That is, the reading that I prefer grammatically also has the virtue of at least being identical to what Paul expressly *says* elsewhere. Since he elsewhere says that the law is "not of faith," it is not at all a *risky* speculation to suggest that this is what he means at Romans 9:32; whereas the alternative translation is risky, and does indeed require a speculation that is otherwise unsubstantiated by Paul's other writings. Further, the alternative translation has Paul faulting Israel for pursuing the Law "*as if* it were *not* by faith," when in Galatians 3:12 he expressly says that the law is indeed "*not* by faith." Why would Paul fault Israel for pursuing the Law "*as if* it were not by faith" when elsewhere he says that the Law *is* "not by faith"? Just a few verses later, he says: "For Moses writes about the righteousness that is based on the law, that the person who *does* the commandments shall live by them," and contrasts such righteousness with "righteousness by faith" (Rom. 10:4-5). So why does almost every translation prefer what I consider to be the weaker translation? Because, prior to E. P. Sanders, the dominant historical reconstruction of first century Judaism believed there was good historical evidence that some (if not most) Jews pursued religion wrongly, legalistically: "as if it were based on works." So, on the basis of what was mere historical conjecture, an inferior translation (on grammatical and contextual grounds, to my mind) was preferred to a superior translation. The translation and interpretation of the text were "bent," as it were, in the direction of the historical conjecture, rather than the other way around. It remains entirely plausible, and in my opinion much more likely, that Paul's answer to his own rhetorical question in Romans 9 is that Israel did not attain unto the Law because the Law required works, not faith, works beyond the reach of any group of sinners, Jew or Gentile, a point he also made in Romans 2, when he asserted that the Law hypothetically justifies only its *doers*, not its hearers (Rom. 2:13), and saying shortly thereafter that no one will be justified by observing the Law (ἐξ ἔργων νόμου οὐ δικαιωθήσεται πᾶσα σάρξ, Rom. 3:20).

Thus, my own prejudice, regarding historical questions pertinent to biblical interpretation, is that I am self-consciously somewhat agnostic. I prefer historical doubt to historical confidence, because I am aware of the power of our theoretical reconstructions of history to injure our ability to understand the various texts well. The texts are givens; Galatians 3 and Romans 9 are givens, for instance, and if Romans 9 has an ambiguity in it, that ambiguity can be resolved better by reference to what is less disputable (Galatians 3) than to what is merely suppositional and therefore more disputable. As we shall see below, this means for me that the benefit of E. P. Sanders is not necessarily that his vision/version of first century Palestinian Judaism is now a fixed construct that guides our interpretive labors, but that his reconstruction is sufficiently persuasive to call into *doubt* our confidence in the previously dominant reconstruction. The effect of that doubt drives interpreters back to the text, which is, in my judgment, the best place for them to be anyway.

Put in a more straightforward manner: I prefer to read the lines rather than read between the lines. If two interpretations of a text are equally plausible, but one requires our reading between the lines some historical thing the lines themselves do not say, I prefer the reading that reads the lines themselves. This preference, in the study of Galatians, is hermeneutically consequential (albeit, of course, possibly erroneous). From Calvin to the present, the assumption of the dominant approach to Galatians has been this: On the surface, Paul appears to be arguing about Jewish ceremonies, but there is a deeper issue, beneath the surface, that is Paul's (allegedly) real concern. As Calvin put it: "We must remark, however, that he does not confine himself entirely to Ceremonies, but argues generally about Works, otherwise the whole discussion would be trifling."[124] For Calvin, taken at face value, Paul's Galatian concern is "trifling." Therefore, because Calvin believed that such a trifling concern could not occupy Paul, Calvin read between the lines, as it were, and conjectured that Paul was *really* concerned about something else, in this case, justification by works.[125] But, as much recent scholarship has demonstrated, since the ceremonies of the Mosaic Law separated Jew and Gentile, to observe those ceremonies that declare Gentiles to be strangers to God's covenanting purposes (Eph. 2:12) was an enormous problem for the apostle to the Gentiles. We, living two millennia after the apostle, may take it for granted that God is now covenanting with Gentiles as well as with Jews; but it was not taken for granted in Paul's generation. Further, as we shall see in some detail later, Paul argued that proclamation to the Gentiles was itself a fulfillment of the third promise God had made to Abraham, to bless all the nations of the world through Abraham's single descendant, whom Paul identifies as Christ (3:16). For Paul, there was nothing "trifling" about God's fulfilling the third pledge he made to Abraham. It was not trifling when God multiplied Abraham's descendants greatly; it was not trifling when (with some assistance by Joshua and the judges) God gave his descendants their own land. Similarly, it was not and is not trifling that God, in Christ and Paul's proclamation about Christ, blessed all the nations of the world through Abraham's descendant.

Calvin, steeped in Renaissance appreciation for history, might have known better. Though for his own generation, disputes about Jewish ceremonies may have appeared merely trifling, there was ample evidence that the matter was not so in Paul's day. Calvin was not unaware of Paul's comments in Romans 3: "Or is God the God of Jews only? Is he not the God of Gentiles also? Yes, of Gentiles also, since God is one" (Rom. 3:29-30). Similarly, Calvin was not unaware of Paul's thoughts in Ephesians 2

---

[124] *Commentaries on the Epistles of Paul to the Galatians and Ephesians* (Grand Rapids: Baker, 1979) p. 18.

[125] Perhaps the most interesting irony about the dominant Protestant approach to Paul is that it has ordinarily been promoted by those (such as Calvin) who also promote a so-called "high" doctrine of the inspiration of Holy Scripture. But does a "high" doctrine of Scripture promote our regarding as "trifling" its evident concern? Does a "high" doctrine of Scripture encourage reading "between the lines" of said Scripture, rather than Scripture itself?

(nor did his generation have any qualms about attributing Ephesians to Paul):

> Therefore remember that at one time you Gentiles in the flesh, called "the uncircumcision" by what is called the circumcision, which is made in the flesh by hands— remember that you were at that time separated from Christ, alienated from the commonwealth of Israel and strangers to the covenants of promise, having no hope and without God in the world. But now in Christ Jesus you who once were far off have been brought near by the blood of Christ. For he himself is our peace, who has made us both one (τὰ ἀμφότερα ἓν) and has broken down in his flesh the dividing wall of hostility by abolishing the law of commandments and ordinances (τὸν νόμον τῶν ἐντολῶν ἐν δόγμασιν καταργήσας), that he might create in himself one new man (ἕνα καινὸν ἄνθρωπον) in place of the two, so making peace…(Eph. 2:11-15).

Calvin's training in Renaissance humanism, a humanism that virtually invented the notion of anachronism,[126] should have and could have been more wary about reading his own circumstances back into Paul's.

Ironically then, Calvin's position actually strengthens mine. He as much as conceded that the lines themselves (unless we read *between* them) taught that the problem at Galatia was requiring Gentiles to observe Jewish ceremonies. It was only Calvin's failure of imagination that required him to read between the lines, as it were, and posit that something *else*, something not said in the lines themselves, *must* have been the problem. I am suggesting a different hermeneutical posture than that of Calvin: a posture that reads the lines themselves whenever doing so provides a plausible explanation of the text. My reading may be right,

---

[126] "Perhaps the most important result of this shift in the scholarly interest and emphasis was the development of a new sense of historical perspective, the birth (or rebirth) of the sense of anachronism. The medieval Schoolmen's preoccupation with timeless and abstract truth reflected the underdeveloped historical sense of the Middle Ages." E. Harris Harbison, *The Christian Scholar in the Age of the Reformation* (New York: Charles Scribner's Sons, 1956), pp. 36-37.

wrong, or (more likely) partially right; but I will present it below, and merely here candidly state my hermeneutical bias and why I embrace it.[127]

Specific: Paul, the Law, and E. P. Sanders

The "problem" of Paul and the Law is the problem of reconciling his positive statements about the law with his negative statements about the law. Paul can as easily say that the Law is "holy" or "good" (Rom. 7:12,13) as that the law "brings wrath" (Rom. 4:15), or that "the power of sin is the law" (1 Cor. 15:56). Prior to E. P. Sanders, this conundrum was rather easily solved: Paul's positive statements contain his true thinking about the Law *itself*, as delivered at Sinai, and his negative statements about it express his thinking about a later meritorious/legalistic *abuse* of it in the first century. This "solution" required, even before Sanders, a certain willingness to self-deceive; after all, in Galatians 3 (as we shall see), it is the Law itself, that "came 430 years after the promise," that Paul contrasts with Abrahamic faith (Gal. 3:17), not some alleged later abuse of the Law. And when Paul contrasts the Abrahamic covenant with the Sinai covenant in Galatians 3, he cites texts in the Law itself (Deut. 27:26, Lev. 18:5), not Second Temple Jewish texts. Nonetheless, for a human race prone to self-deception, this was not a grave difficulty, and we went merrily along with the self-deception (pausing occasionally to make flattering observations about the Emperor's wardrobe), content that this self-deception at least cleaned up the messy problem of Paul and the Law. Paul's brain-teasing paradox--"The very commandment that promised life proved to be death" (Rom. 7:10)--was rather breezily dismissed by reference to an alleged meritorious/legalistic abuse of the Law.

And then E. P. Sanders appeared, re-iterating arguments that had been made before, challenging the consensus that the religion of Second Temple Judaism could justly be accused of meritorious legalism. Many of the substantial arguments had been made before: Jewish scholars had also made the "patterns of religion" argument, that Jewish texts had often been wrested from their over-all religious context; and scholars such as W. D.

---

[127] My brief explanation here is not designed to be convincing. I do not expect many or any of my readers to concur, on the grounds mentioned here, in my preference of the text over speculative historical reconstruction. I merely intend to be candid about my minority view on the matter, and candid about how/why that influences my interpretation of Galatians. At a minimum, another monograph could be devoted to defending/promoting this minority thesis.

Galatians as Examined by Diverse Academics

Davies had demonstrated that Second Temple Judaism was not at all unaware of a merciful God. But for Sanders, the timing was right. The post-Holocaust interpreters of Paul were finally (though belatedly) wary of appreciating Paul at the expense of Judaism, finally willing (perhaps eager) to read his letters free from assumptions that were unflattering and unfair to Second Temple Judaism. As Peter Stuhlmacher has said, regarding the New Perspective: "We must also keep in mind the apparent goal of these authors to make a new beginning in Pauline interpretation, so as to free Jewish-Christian dialogue from improper accusations against the Jewish conversation partners."[128]

In what follows, what will be apparent is that I join Sanders in concluding that the dominant Protestant understanding of Second Temple Judaism prior to him was a distorted caricature of what the (reliably-dated) literature presents, and that I concur with those interpreters of Paul who, as Stuhlmacher said, desire to free Jewish-Christian dialogue from such improper accusations against the Jewish conversation partners. At the same time, it will become apparent that I do this in a different manner than most. Most of the post-Sanders interpreters of Paul, in an appropriate effort to free Palestinian Judaism from charges of meritorious legalism, have had a tendency to conflate several covenant-administrations into a single covenant, and a gracious one at that. But to understand Palestinian Judaism, and to understand the third and fourth chapters of Galatians correctly, one must recognize that both parties were attempting to make sense of a Hebrew Bible that contains a number of covenant-administrations, some more promissory and some more legal. Indeed, I will argue that the Abrahamic covenant is so promissory that Paul ordinarily refers to it by the synecdoche ἡ ἐπαγγελία, and that the Sinai covenant is so legal that Paul ordinarily refers to it by the synecdoche ὁ νόμος. Yahweh simply promised, or pledged, to bless Abraham and his

---

[128] Peter Stuhlmacher, Donald A. Hagner, *Revisiting Paul's Doctrine of Justification: A Challenge to the New Perspective: With an Essay by Donald A. Hagner*, p. 34. Stuhlmacher's judgment is surprisingly similar to what George Foot Moore had said nearly a century earlier in the opening sentence of an influential article: "Christian interest in Jewish literature has always been apologetic or polemical rather than historical." The same may be the case in the present day, even though the apologetic is an ecumenical apologetic, and the polemic is directed against overt suggestions that Christianity may be superior to some forms of Judaism, at least in some respects. Moore, "Christian Writers on Judaism," *Harvard Theological Review* Vol. 14, No. 3 (Jul., 1921), pp. 197-254.

seed, and indeed to bless all the families of the earth through his seed. But through Moses, the same Yahweh said,

> "But if your heart turns away, and you will not hear, but are drawn away to worship other gods and serve them, I declare to you today, that you shall surely *perish*. You shall *not live long* in the land that you are going over the Jordan to enter and possess. I call heaven and earth to witness against you today, that I have set before you life *and* death, blessing *and* curse" (Deut. 30:17-19).

Abraham had learned of a deity who pledged to *bless* freely, generously, and sovereignly. Moses learned that the same deity could and would also *curse*, under certain circumstances. Moses learned that Yahweh, at least as regarded temporal blessings in the land of Canaan, would condition such blessings upon Israel's obedience. Both Second Temple Judaism, therefore, and Paul, had to wrestle with the *multiple* covenants existing side by side in the Hebrew Bible, and both had to wrestle with how, if at all, Jesus of Nazareth figured into expectations arising from that Bible.

E. P. Sanders (and George Foote Moore, and W. D. Davies, for that matter) had found many pertinent Second Temple texts that reflected belief in a gracious and merciful God. Sanders's critics have found some pertinent texts that appear to condition blessing on Israel's obedience. Neither Sanders nor his major critics, to my knowledge, have adequately accounted for this matter as I will attempt to account for it. I account for this the way I judge that Paul did: within the Hebrew Bible there are several covenants (at a minimum, two with Noah, one with Abraham, one with the Israelites through Moses, one with Phinehas, and one with David).[129] What appears to be tension, therefore, between some Second Temple texts and others is likely due to the varying character of the several covenants that informed Second Temple Judaism, and to the

---

[129] I say "at a minimum," because I am myself persuaded that the Adamic material is covenantal also. But this one is so at a more implicit level, and though Paul appears to regard it as covenantal at Romans 5:12-21, he makes no reference to it in Galatians (nor does he refer to the Noahic covenants, nor to those with Phinehas nor David, in Galatians). Cf. Byron Curtis's chapter on Hos. 6:7 in *The Law is Not of Faith: Essays on Works and Grace in the Mosaic Covenant*, ed. Bryan Estelle, J. V. Fesko, and David VanDrunen (P&R, 2009).

responsible efforts of Second Temple Judaism to make sense of those several covenants.

Both the New Perspectives on Paul and their critics, however, often make a crucial mistake at this point: at an implicit level, if not explicitly, they regard these various covenants in an aggregate manner, as though they are pieces of the puzzle that constitute Second Temple Judaism. And, indeed, in some senses, they are such pieces to an historical puzzle. But in another sense, a theological sense, they are not pieces to a common puzzle; each is its own puzzle. Each of these covenants has its own integrity and its own purpose. They cannot and do not meld over into one another regarding their parties, their stipulations, or their benefits. Regarding the parties, for instance, only David's lineage could build the house for Yahweh, only the lineage of Phinehas could serve as priests, and only a portion of Abraham's lineage (not Ishmael, and not Esau) would be the vehicle by which God would one day bless all the families of the earth. So also the benefits differ: Through the covenant with Phinehas, a sacramental priesthood was given to the Israelites, to teach them (and the world) the theological concept of atonement (though the blood of the animals there sacrificed was not actually efficient to atone for human sin). Through the Davidic covenant, a "permanent" house for Yahweh could be built. Through the Sinai covenant, temporal prosperity could be secured for the Israelites in the land of Canaan. And through the Abrahamic covenant, eschatological blessings would eventually come to all the nations of the earth through his seed.[130]

When either proponents or opponents of the New Perspective on Paul, therefore, describe the realities of Second Temple Judaism in terms of "the covenant" (in the singular), they are prevented from the outset from making sense of an historic religion that was itself shaped and formed by its efforts to relate properly several distinct covenants. And indeed, it is entirely possible that some of the parties to Second Temple

---

[130] It may not be self-evident that the pledges to Abraham are ultimately eschatological, but there are clues that this will be the case, such as the references to his seed being as numerous as the sands of the sea (hinting at cosmological renewal) or as numerous as the stars of heaven, a more overt eschatological hint. And in Romans 4, Paul likened the provision of a child to (old) Abraham and (barren) Sarah to giving "life from the dead" (4:17), and noting that Abraham's body was, at that point "as good as dead" (4:19); so Paul, at least, appears to have regarded the pledges to Abraham as reversing the mortality-curse of Genesis 3, which makes them eschatological in character.

Judaism made the same mistake, though I am an agnostic on that point. But Paul's reasoning in Galatians takes another approach. Speaking through both chapters 3 and 4 of the five differences between the Abrahamic and Sinai covenants, he creates a figure of speech in his concluding verses of chapter four, discussing Hagar and Sarah, and says of the two women, "These are two covenants" (Gal. 4:24). Throughout Galatians, Paul self-consciously refers to the realities of a new covenant in Christ by referring to other covenants that antedated it. Paul does not refer to Israel's heritage in the singular, as "the covenant," but in the plural, as "the covenants" (cf. Rom. 9:4, and Eph. 2:12).

My approach then, if it succeeds, accomplishes two things. First, and most importantly, it provides a way of understanding the covenant-historical argumentation of Galatians better than other proposals. But secondly, in the post-holocaust discussions, it enables us to recognize why both E. P. Sanders and his opponents appear to be able, at times, to muster textual evidence for their point of view. Second Temple Judaism, like Paul, was attempting to make sense of a canon that contained several different covenants, each of which came from the same God while containing distinctive parties, distinctive stipulations, and distinctive benefits. Any responsible wrestling with such a poly-covenantal Hebrew Bible will reflect the same tensions and distinctives that appear in those several covenants themselves.

Specific: Jewish problems/Christian problems

One semi-hidden assumption that has influenced Pauline studies significantly is the assumption that if there is a problem in the Christian churches it must reflect an antecedent problem in Jewish synagogues: If there were Judaizers of some sort at Galatia, there must have been similar Judaizers in the Jewish synagogues that were the source of the problem. *Prima facie*, this is a rather curious line of reasoning. After all, Paul writes to the "*churches* of Galatia (ταῖς ἐκκλησίαις τῆς Γαλατίας)," not to "the *synagogues* of Galatia." Is it not at least possible that the early Christian assemblies generated their own errors, whether behavioral or doctrinal? Does not Paul routinely address other errors in his letters that no one would dream of attributing to Jewish influence? Does anyone blame the synagogues, for instance, for the man who had sexual relations with his stepmother, in 1 Corinthians 5? To raise the question is to answer it.

Galatians as Examined by Diverse Academics

What makes this assumption more plausible (though still, in my judgment, unwarranted), is that Paul discusses in Galatians so many realities associated with God's covenanting with the Israelites: circumcision, the dietary laws, the Mosaic law itself, etc. And indeed, Paul uses the language of "Judaizing" at 2:14. It is therefore understandable that interpreters of Galatians would inquire as to whether there might have been an antecedent problem within Second Temple Judaism that was analogous to the problem Paul encountered at Galatia. It is *understandable* that interpreters might look for this, but it would also be understandable for them to have not done so, to have intentionally considered an alternative: that the problem at Galatia was *sui generis*, just as the immoral Corinthian was, to our knowledge, *sui generis*, and not attributable to some antecedent error in Second Temple Judaism.

That is, I propose an alternative: Rather than base our interpretation of Galatians on the constantly-shifting reconstructions of the nature of first century Palestinian Judaism, we might at least *consider* the possibility that the problem at Galatia was a Christian error in its origins, with no corresponding error in Palestinian Judaism.[131] Is it not possible to reconstruct the problem at Galatia from the evidence of the text itself? Is it not possible that the text itself describes what the problem is, regardless of whether the problem existed elsewhere in Jewish or early Christian circles? Is it not at least theoretically possible that the erroneous belief or practice at Galatia was generated by *Christian* misunderstandings of the Mosaic Law and not by alleged *Jewish* misunderstandings thereof? When the question is stated so acutely, it is difficult to regard it as anything but rhetorical. But the question is not unimportant. If, as Peter Stuhlmacher observed, many of us are attempting to understand Paul without misconstruing Palestinian Judaism, we could, theoretically, accomplish this in either of two ways: First, as Sanders and many others have done, we could pore over the reliably dated texts from the era and conclude that

---

[131] I am not unaware that the term "judaize" appears outside of Galatians. Some might be inclined to believe that this demonstrates that there was a fairly well-established Jewish error known as "judaizing." But the verb only appears once in the LXX (Esth. 8:17), once in the inter-testamental writings (Theodotus 4:1), once in Paul (Gal. 2:14), and once, later, in the apostolic fathers (Ignatious to the Magnesians 10:7-8), which is hardly enough evidence to suggest a common or well-known problem. Further, in some of those other texts, it denotes a virtue, not a vice. Cf. below, my discussion of the lexical issues surrounding this uncommon verb.

those texts do not warrant a legalistic/meritorious understanding of Second Temple Judaism. But second, as I propose, we could also discuss Paul's problem at Galatia without the assumption that it must have been spawned by Temple Judaism at all: the early Christian churches may have had their own creative genius for inventing behavioral or doctrinal errors without any assistance from the Jewish synagogues. I propose that, barring any evidence that Paul attributes the Galatian error to a common Second Temple synagogue error, there is no need for us to speculate about the matter at all.[132]

One fairly common objection to the re-assessment of Palestinian Judaism provoked by E. P. Sanders is that it is novel. The objection is put like this: "If Judaism of the first century was not, in fact, meritorious, why did almost everyone from Luther and Calvin until E. P. Sanders believe that it *was* meritorious?" Such questions place the burden of proof on Sanders (et al.) to account for why the novel view should be embraced over an older view. To such questions, I propose several answers. First, in point of fact, Sanders's view is not novel; many Jewish scholars had suggested similar things for many years, and even some notable Christian scholars of the preceding generation (George Foot Moore, David Daube, W. D. Davies) had said similar things. Second, the "dominant" Protestant understanding from Luther until Sanders was largely based on the assumption that the Talmudic literature accurately reflected the Palestinian Judaism of Paul's day, an assumption that few would concede today. The writing *Tannaim* came well over a century after the destruction of the Temple, and their writings are not necessarily an accurate reflection of the Temple Judaism that antedated them. And some of the intertestamental literature available to us now (certainly, e.g., the Dead Sea Scrolls) was not known to Luther. That is, Sanders did not merely read the same literature *differently* than did Luther and Calvin; he read *different* literature altogether. The view of Luther and Calvin was based upon their reading of a literature (the Babylonian Talmud) that they judged to be an accurate reflection of first century Palestinian Judaism; a view we simply do not share today. Third, while it is not inappropriate to refer to the pre-Sanders approach as the "dominant" Protestant approach, we can only call it

---

[132] And, had this proposal been embraced forty years ago, thousands of pages of such speculation might never have been written, which surely would have been a welcome boon to many graduate students.

"dominant;" we cannot call it "confessional," because, in point of fact, the Protestant confessions make no comment at all about the character of Palestinian Judaism. That is, there is nothing at stake, in terms of Protestant confessional orthodoxy, in this conversation. No Protestant body was ever so confidant of its speculative reconstruction of Palestinian Judaism as to record a word about the matter in any of its confessional or catechetical literature.

Specific: "Judaize"

Those who troubled the Galatians have often been called "Judaizers." To the unwary, this expression may suggest a standing, well-known idea or practice, associated with a particular, well-known movement, such as Pharisaism, Sadduceeism or Essenism. As we shall see, such a suggestion would be wrong; the term is remarkably rare in the extant literature, and is only employed by Pauline scholars because Paul uses the expression in his conversation with Peter: "If you, though a Jew, live like a Gentile and not like a Jew, how can you force the Gentiles to *live like Jews* (εἰ σὺ Ἰουδαῖος ὑπάρχων ἐθνικῶς καὶ οὐχὶ Ἰουδαϊκῶς ζῇς, πῶς τὰ ἔθνη ἀναγκάζεις ἰουδαΐζειν)?" This requirement that Gentiles ἰουδαΐζειν, then, is the source of our term, "Judaize." What constitutes "Judaizing?"

Specifically, we raise this question: Is the problem at Galatia behavioral or doctrinal? The assumption, by so many Pauline interpreters, is that the problem is doctrinal; the "errorists" at Galatia have frequently been referred to as those who "taught x." But such a determination cannot be made as a mere assumption; it must be the result of some evidence or reasoning, because Paul, in his letters, corrected both doctrinal problems and behavioral problems. Among the things Paul corrected at Corinth, for instance, were incest (5:1-13), vexatious lawsuits (6:1-11), immorality (6:12-20), celibacy versus marriage (7:1-24), eating food that had been sacrificed to idols (8:1-11:1), headcoverings (11:2-16), mispractice of the Lord's Supper (1:17-34), misuse of spiritual gifts (12:1-14:40), collections for the relief of saints (16:1-11), and the doctrine of the resurrection (15), only the last of which was a doctrinal error. The majority of the letter addressed behavioral issues; and only one (important) chapter addressed a doctrine.

It is perfectly fair, and perfectly in accord with the evidence from other Pauline epistles, to inquire as to whether the problem at Galatia is doctrinal or behavioral. In doing so, I do not intend to exclude the middle, or to frame the question erroneously. It is entirely possible, *prima facie*, that the problem will disclose itself to be both doctrinal and practical, and if the evidence for that third, mediating position is substantial, that mediating position should be embraced. What we cannot do, however, is assume before investigation that the problem is doctrinal in part or whole. The error could be entirely behavioral or partly behavioral, and we must raise the question openly and fairly.

I recognize that it is entirely possible that any behavioral error *implies* a doctrinal one. Any erroneous behavior, that is, implies at least the *idea* that the behavior is acceptable. The behavior of the man at Corinth who had relations with his stepmother, for instance, had implications for the doctrine of marriage, the doctrine of human sexuality, etc. However, Paul said nothing about these doctrines in his refutation, nor did he object to the behavior *because* of its potential doctrinal implications. The behavior itself was wrong, so shamefully wrong, Paul said, that it even would have embarrassed the pagans. Paul expressed no concern that this behavior would lead to doctrinal error; to the contrary, he feared that tolerating it might cause similar *behavioral* error to spread (1 Cor. 5:6).

So what does the term "Judaize" mean? Well, we note from the language of Gal. 2:14, that the expression is parallel to the expression "live like/as a Jew," and indeed, most English translations translate ἰουδαΐζειν just as they translate the parallel expression Ἰουδαϊκῶς ζῇς (from which, as a simple matter of word-formation, it appears to be derived). The English translations assume that the two expressions mean essentially the same thing, since the word-formation of the verb ἰουδαΐζειν consists of the two separate words of the expression Ἰουδαϊκῶς ζῇς. We note then, *prima facie*, that Paul does not say anything here about "*believing* like a Jew" but about "*living* like a Jew." And indeed, Paul has indicated what constitutes "living like a Jew" two verses earlier: "For before certain men came from James, he was eating with the Gentiles; but when they came he drew back and separated himself, fearing the circumcision party." Peter had relaxed the requirement of *Kashrut* and eaten with Gentiles; he had, in doing so, "lived as a Gentile, and not as a Jew." When representatives from Jerusalem came down, and out of fear of their reaction, Peter separated himself from the Gentiles, in conformity with the dietary laws. If we knew nothing else from Galatians but this contextual information, we would determine that "to live as a Jew" meant to observe the dietary laws of Moses, which was/is a behavioral error. That is, the *prima facie* contextual evidence, unless the usage of the term in the extant literature of Paul's day is otherwise or technical, suggests that the term designates a practice, not a doctrine. To that extant literature we now turn.

The first thing one notices in researching ἰουδαΐζειν is how rare the term is. It is a New Testament *hapax*, occurring only in Galatians 2:14. This itself is significant. If the term designated some well-known existing party or viewpoint within Judaism, one might have expected that party to have appeared more frequently in the New Testament. "Pharisee" occurs 98 times in the New Testament, by comparison, and "Sadducee" appears fourteen times. The term is even more rare in the LXX, since it only appears there, in a vaster literature, one time also, in the Book of Esther:

> Esth. 8:15-17 Then Mordecai went out from the presence of the king in royal robes of blue and white, with a great golden crown and a robe of fine linen and purple, and the city of Susa shouted and rejoiced. The Jews had light and gladness and joy and honor. And in every province and in every city, wherever the king's command and his edict reached, there was gladness and joy among the Jews, a feast and a holiday. And many from the peoples of the country declared themselves Jews (καὶ πολλοὶ τῶν ἐθνῶν περιετέμοντο καὶ ἰουδάιζον διὰ τὸν φόβον τῶν Ἰουδαίων), for fear of the Jews had fallen on them.

We initially note that many English translations have one verb ("declared themselves Jews," RSV and ESV, "became Jews," KJV), though the LXX has two: περιετέμοντο καὶ ἰουδάιζον. The English translations follow the Hebrew, which has a single verb (מתיהדים, itself a *hapax* in the Hebrew Bible). The LXX translators chose to translate the single Hebrew verb with two Greek verbs, electing to employ hendiadys to represent the meaning of the original. It is not without significance, especially for Galatians, that a literal translation of the LXX rendering would be "*were circumcized* and lived as Jews." That is, if the hendiadys is accurate, the later ETs such as RSV and ESV are preferable to the KJV. Where the King James translated "*became* Jews," the RSV and ESV translated "*declared* themselves Jews," indicating that the behavior referred to being *marked* by circumcision as a Jew and not a Gentile.

We also note another matter significant to interpreters of Galatians. Why did these people of the land mark themselves as Jews by the rite of circumcision? Because "*fear* of the Jews had fallen upon them" (διὰ τὸν φόβον τῶν Ιουδαίων). Similarly, when Paul objected to Peter's behavior of withdrawing from Gentile table fellowship, Paul accused him of the identical motivation: "For before certain men came from James, he was eating with the Gentiles; but when they came he drew back and separated himself, *fearing* the circumcision party." (φοβούμενος τοὺς ἐκ περιτομῆς). Note especially that these people of the land were not attempting to be justified before God, nor was their spiritual condition at stake in any way. They "feared" not God's judgment, but the Jews; the way Peter feared the circumcision party. In each case, the error was behavioral; in each case it consisted of observing those Mosaic laws that distinguished Jew from Gentile, and in each case it was motivated by concern about status before other (Jewish) human beings, not status before God.

Not surprisingly, this term that is a hapax both in the NT and in the LXX is also rare in the Intertestamental literature, where I find it only in Theodotus.[133]

> He says that Jacob came from the Euphrates to Hamor in Shechem, and that he welcomed him and gave some of the region to him. He apportioned the land to Jacob, and Jacob's sons --there were eleven of them --tended sheep, while his daughter, Dinah, and his wives worked with the wool. Dinah, still a virgin, wanting to see the city, went to Shechem during a festival. When Shechem, the son of Hamor, saw her, he fell in love with her: taking her as though she was his own, he carried her off and defiled her. But the next day, he came with his father to Jacob and asked to be joined to her in marriage. [Jacob] said he would not give [his consent], until all the inhabitants of Shechem *became like the Jews, by being circumcised* (πρὶν ἂν ἢ

---

[133] The stem (יהד) from the Hebrew of Esther 8:17 does not appear in Qumran. Qumran does not appear to use the expression.

πάντας τοὺς οἰκοῦντας τὰ Σίκιμα περιτεμνομένους Ἰουδαΐσαι), and Hamor said that he would persuade them [to do so]. And, concerning the necessity of them being circumcised, Jacob said, "For it is certainly not lawful for Hebrews to bring sons-in-law or daughters-in-law in from elsewhere, to lead them into the house; rather, [they are allowed to bring only] someone who boasts of being from the same race." (Theodotus. 4:0-3).

Here ἰουδαΐζειν is translated "became like the Jews," as the KJV translated Esther 8:17. And note here that, as in Galatians and in the LXX, the verb appears with circumcision, possibly as hendiadys. The residents of Shechem "became like the Jews *by being circumcised.*" Note also that the behavior was undertaken not out of regard to God, but out of regard for Jews (in this case, Jacob). The term is unusually rare, appearing only once in the LXX, once in the Intertestamental literature, and once in the NT.[134] In none of the examples is anything explicitly said about salvation, justification, or any other doctrinal matter at all. It appears to mean something like this: "Identify oneself as a Jew by performing the requisite marking ceremonies, to appease those Jews who would be scandalized otherwise."[135]

Negative evidence may also be significant here. In all of Galatians, of the ordinary four Greek words for "teaching" (διδάσκαλος, διδάσκω, διδαχὴ, διδασκαλία), only one appears, and that only one time, when Paul refers to his own Damascus instruction at 1:12: "For I did not receive it from any man, nor was I taught it (οὔτε ἐδιδάχθην), but I received it through a revelation of Jesus Christ." Think of how often the language of "false *teachers* at Galatia" or "false/erroneous *teaching* at Galatia" appears in New Testament studies, and yet Paul never says any such thing in the letter, not even once. He never employs any of the ordinary Greek

---

[134] Similarly, in the early church fathers it appears only in Ignatius to the Magnesians 10:3: "It is monstrous to talk of Jesus Christ and to practise Judaism. For Christianity did not believe in Judaism, but Judaism in Christianity, wherein {every tongue} believed and {was gathered together} unto God" (ἄτοπόν ἐστιν Ἰησοῦν Χριστὸν λαλεῖν καὶ ἰουδαΐζειν. ὁ γὰρ χριστιανισμὸς οὐκ εἰς ἰουδαϊσμὸν ἐπίστευσεν, ἀλλ᾽ ἰουδαϊσμὸς εἰς χριστιανισμόν, ᾧ πᾶσα γλῶσσα πιστεύσασα εἰς Θεὸν συνήχθη.).

[135] That is, curiously enough, it means largely what James D. G. Dunn thinks "works of the law" means.

doctrinal vocabulary to describe the problem at Galatia. To the contrary, he uses almost everything *but* such language:

> 1:7 but there are some who trouble you (ταράσσοντες ὑμᾶς)
> 2:4 Yet because of *false brothers* secretly brought in—who slipped in *to spy out our freedom* that we have in Christ Jesus
> 2:13 And the rest of the Jews *acted hypocritically* along with him, so that even Barnabas was led astray by their hypocrisy.
> 4:10-11 You *observe* (παρατηρεῖσθε) *days and months and seasons and years*! I am afraid I may have labored over you in vain.
> 5:8-9 This *persuasion* (ἡ πεισμονὴ) is not from him who calls you. A little *leaven* leavens the whole lump.
> 5:12 I wish those who *unsettle* you (οἱ ἀναστατοῦντες) would emasculate themselves!
> 5:15 But if you *bite and devour* one another, watch out that you are not consumed by one another.
> 6:12 It is those who want to *make a good showing in the flesh* who would force you to be circumcised, and only in order that they may not be persecuted for the cross of Christ.
> 6:17 From now on let no one cause me *trouble* (κόπους), for I bear on my body the marks of Jesus.

Paul referred to the Galatian Judaizers by almost every expression shy of Jude's "waterless clouds" (Jude 12). Couldn't Paul have just said "teach," "doctrine," or "teacher" one time? Instead he uses language such as "unsettle," "bite and devour," "make a good showing in the flesh," etc., as though he were bending over backward to avoid/evade any appearance that the problem at Galatia was doctrinal. It is, I concede, entirely possible that any behavioral error has doctrinal implications. Early in the first chapter, Paul said: "I am astonished that you are so quickly deserting him who called you in the grace of Christ and are turning to a different gospel— not that there is another one, but there are some who trouble you and want to distort (μεταστρέψαι) the gospel of Christ" (Gal. 1:6-7). So, the purity of the gospel is indeed at stake at Galatia, but is this "distortion" the result of erroneous teaching or the result of erroneous behavioral requirements?

Galatians as Examined by Diverse Academics

Paul employed no doctrinal language to describe the error at Galatia; but he did employ behavioral language to describe it, referring to circumcision, observing the Jewish calendar, and withdrawing from Gentile table-fellowship. If we "read the lines" of Galatians itself, rather than read between them, we find that the error of "Judaizing" was a behavioral error, an error that consisted of the specific behavior of continuing to observe the various Mosaic ceremonies that separated Jews from Gentiles. Further, if we read Galatians itself, and the fairly miniscule lexical evidence elsewhere, we note that the Judaizing behavior was motivated by a desire to win *Jewish* approval, not *divine* approval. If you wish to marry Jacob's daughter, you must be circumcised; if the *Am ha-Aretz* wish to join in Jewish celebrations, they must be circumcised; if Peter desires the approval of the Jerusalem apostles, he must avoid table-fellowship with the uncircumcised Gentiles.

A final observation about "Judaize" should be made here. It is entirely possible that ιουδαΐζειν refers not to Jewish behavior but to Gentile behavior. As counter-intuitive as that may seem, the lexical evidence is compelling. At Galatians 2:14, it is unmistakable: "how can you force *the Gentiles* to live like Jews?" Similarly, in both Esther and in Theodotus, as we observed earlier, it was Gentiles who performed the action denoted by this verb. With entire justification, therefore, Stephen G. Wilson has said: "L. Gaston more sensibly argues that we should use the term 'judaizer' only in its ancient and technical sense, i.e. of non-Jews who chose to live like Jews. A judaizer was by definition a Gentile and it is Christian Gentiles of this sort on whom we shall focus."[136] Similarly, James D. G. Dunn has said: "'To judaize' was a quite familiar expression, meaning 'to adopt a (characteristically) Jewish way of life'. The fact that many *Gentiles* in the ancient world 'judaized', that is adopted Jewish customs, attended Jewish synagogues, identified themselves in some measure with Jews, is well attested."[137] While a "Judaizing" Gentile's

---

[136] "Gentile Judaizers." *New Testament Studies* 38, no. 4 (1992), p. 605.

[137] *The Epistle to the Galatians*, Black's New Testament Commentary (Peabody, MA: Hendrickson, 1993), p. 129. I do not concur with Dunn's reference to the verb as "quite familiar," or even "well attested," since the term is so rare. But he is certainly correct in observing that many Gentiles "judaized," despite his earlier comment, "That the 'troublemakers' or 'agitators' were Jews is also fairly obvious. It is implicit in the very fact that circumcision was their primary demand" (p. 9). I still think it is possible that even the "troublers" themselves were Gentiles, though indeed every act of "judaizing"

behavior had reference to winning the *approval* of law-abiding Jews, the behavior itself was a Gentile behavior, and it is even possible that the troublers at Galatia themselves were Gentiles who had already "Judaized," and were now urging their fellow-Gentiles to do the same. My interpretation of Galatians does not depend upon this possibility in any substantive manner, but it also does not preclude the possibility.

My reading of Galatians, therefore, is self-consciously suspicious of much of the "reading between the lines" interpretation that has gone before. My interpretation, while largely agnostic on most of the historical issues, is perfectly compatible with a reconstruction that says the problem at Galatia had no antecedents outside of the churches. To the contrary, it could quite possibly be a Christian error alone, not a Jewish one. Those Jews who chose not to follow Christ would necessarily remain disciples of Moses, and would enjoin obedience to his commandments. Only Christian churches would be capable of the error of requiring unnecessary rites of their members, the error may have been entirely self-generated by the early churches, and it may have been entirely committed by Gentiles. It is, of course, also possible that Jewish Christians were "troublers" also, but my reading of Galatians requires no resolution to this issue.

---

has reference to Jewish approval, as Dunn rightly notes: "In short, though there were clear boundary lines between Jew and Gentile, marked out, not least, by the food laws and the complex of traditional attitudes and practices gathered round them, there were many Gentiles who were eager to cross these boundaries, to at least some extent, and who were welcomed by Jews when they did so" (p. 120).

A Cinderella Story:
The Role of Galatians within a Gospel Canon[138]

Paul Landgraf
St. John Lutheran Church

1. Introduction

The scholar whose name is synonymous with a canonical perspective, Brevard S. Childs, within his very last book, put forward his reasoning to focus on both Romans and the Pastoral Epistles of the Pauline corpus.

> The structure of these books at the beginning and end of the corpus sets the canonical context for its interpretation. They address the crucial hermeneutical issue of the interpretation of Paul, namely, how are his letters in

---

[138] The paper given at the *Paul's Letter to the Galatians and Christian Theology* conference at St Andrews Divinity School in July of 2012 was an earlier version of this paper. This author is grateful for all the input received thus far but is solely responsible for all its (many) errors.

their highly particularized, time-conditioned, historical settings to be used by future generations of Christians?

The initial hermeneutical key is offered by the letter to the Romans, which covers the same topics dealt with in the earlier letters in a lengthy and profound reformulation. Romans and the Pastorals represent two very different literary genres from the highly particularized letters that form the bulk of Paul's missionary message. How are they to be related? The solution is not one of harmonization. Nor is the proper hermeneutical approach one that blunts the particularity of the letters within the corpus by various appeals to creedal abstraction. Rather, the canonical structure sets up a dialectical interaction within the context of the corpus between the general and the specific, between the universal content of the gospel and the unique needs of each congregation, between the sound doctrine of Paul and the particularity of its application by the apostle who labored to target the continuing theological crises with the gospel of Jesus Christ.[139]

So what about the Epistle to the Galatians? One reviewer of Child's work wrote in response that this methodology to understanding the Pauline corpus makes the Epistle to the Galatians, the fourth epistle, "a poor stepchild."[140]

This paper agrees with that reviewer and will argue that the Epistle to the Galatians serves a more critical role, specifically due to its placement as the fourth epistle within the New Testament. The Epistle to the Galatians is not a poor stepchild, but it is arguably a Cinderella story and has gone from "rags to riches" in the part that it plays within the New Testament canon.[141] The role of fourth place for a Pauline epistle is not a

---

[139] Brevard S. Childs, *The Church's Guide for Reading Paul: The Canonical Shaping of the Pauline Corpus* (Grand Rapids, Mich.: Eerdmans, 2008), 76.

[140] Jeffrey Kloha, "The Problem of Paul's Letters: Loss of Authority and Meaning in the 'Canonical Approach' of Brevard Childs," *Concordia Journal* 35, no. 2 (Spring 2009): 161.

[141] The definition of canon here is that of the final form of the New Testament. The word is used so that some thought would be given to the way in which those twenty-

negative one but a critical one especially if the New Testament canon is understood to have a gospel theme and emphasis. To be more specific, this paper will propose the thesis that the Epistle to the Galatians, in its placement as the fourth epistle within the New Testament, forms a closure for a deliberate fourfold epistolary structure that supports a fourfold gospel.[142]

Such a thesis will admittedly be difficult to support. The Pauline epistles are usually considered as a whole, and the thought that often predominates is that they were put together according to their length.[143] For there to be some evidence of a deliberate, fourfold, epistolary structure, there should also be some significant and early evidence for a fourfold gospel structure, since the usual understanding is that the epistles were written first.[144] Perhaps the most significant point is that the gospel and epistle sections of the New Testament are not thought to have many connections; therefore there is no clear theme.[145] It is important to deal with all these issues, and essentially any question dealing with the canon involves a large number of factors.[146]

What will add to the difficulty is that the overall emphasis for the biblical scholarship has been on the historical nature of the documents

---

seven books eventually came to be known as the New Testament while other writings were left out.

[142] From this point on, abbreviated names for all the epistles will be given (Romans, etc.). For more information about the fourfold gospel, see Martin Hengel, *The Four Gospels and the One Gospel of Jesus Christ* (Harrisburg, Penn: Trinity International, 2000).

[143] Kloha, "The Problem of Paul's Letters," 161. See David E. Aune, *The New Testament in Its Literary Environment* (Philadelphia: Westminster, 1987), 205.

[144] I. Howard Marshall, *New Testament Theology: Many Witnesses, One Gospel* (Downers Grove, Ill.: InterVarsity, 2004), 22.

[145] David Wenham, *Paul: Follower of Jesus or Founder of Christianity?* (Grand Rapids, Mich.: Eerdmans, 1995), 3-33. For a larger overview, see Gerhard F. Hasel, *New Testament Theology: Basic Issues in the Current Debate* (Grand Rapids, Mich.: Eerdmans, 1978); cf. James D. G. Dunn, *Unity and Diversity in the New Testament: An Inquiry into the Character of Earliest Christianity* (3rd ed., London: SCM, 2006); Childs, *The Church's Guide for Reading Paul*, 223.

[146] Harry Y. Gamble, "The New Testament Canon: Recent Research and the Statis Quaestionis," in *The Canon Debate* (Lee Martin McDonald and James A. Sanders, eds., Peabody, Mass.: Hendrickson, 2002), 294.

rather than their literary structures.[147] Recent efforts have focused more on the literary nature of the texts, and noticeable advancements have been made.[148]

The hope is that by putting forward a basic understanding of what is meant by a *gospel* canon that there would be a clearer perspective when dealing with the complex idea of the canon. The hope is also that this particular perspective, when applied to only one aspect of the New Testament canon—that of the placement of Galatians—may constrain this paper to an adequate length.

This connection between gospel and canon is not new. Martin Luther (1483-1546) made a distinction between those New Testament writings which he thought had more to do with the gospel or the message of salvation than the others, and this is usually termed negatively as "a canon within the canon."[149] Some have defended the action and phrase, stating that essentially equal significance within a group of various writings is neither possible nor the intention of the writings.[150]

---

[147] This was Childs' concern. Childs, *The Church's Guide for Reading Paul*, 76-78. Hans W. Frei, *The Eclipse of the Biblical Narrative: A Study in Eighteenth and Nineteenth Century Hermeneutics* (New Haven, Conn.: Yale University, 1974); see Sir Edwyn Hoskyns and Noel Davey, *The Riddle of the New Testament* (London: Faber and Faber, 1958), 12; C.F.D. Moule, *The Birth of the New Testament* (Black's New Testament Commentaries, 3rd ed., London: Adam & Charles Black, 1981), 1-18.

[148] N.T. Wright, *The New Testament and the People of God* (Minneapolis: Fortress, 1992). E.g., Robert Alter, *The Art of the Biblical Narrative* (New York: Basic Books, 1981); John W. Welch, ed., *Chiasmus in Antiquity: Structures, Analyses, Exegisis* (Provo, Utah: Research Press, 1981).

[149] Inge Lønning, *'Kanon im Kanon': Zum dogmatischen Grundlagenproblem des neutestamentlichen Kanons* (Oslo: Universitets Forlaget, 1972). Others themes have been proposed, e.g., William R. Farmer and Denis M. Farkasfalvy, *The Formation of the New Testament Canon* (New York: Paulist, 1983), 31-43.

[150] Ultimately the purpose of the complex writings is to point to the complex person of Jesus. Thomas Söding, *Einheit der Heiligen Schrift? Zur Theologie des biblischen Kanons* (Freiburg: Herder, 2005), 103-110; Lee Martin McDonald, "Identifying Scripture and Canon in the Early Church: The Criteria Question," in *The Canon Debate*, 428-30; H.C. Kingsley Barrett, "The Centre of the New Testament and the Canon," in *Die Mitte des Neuen Testaments: Einheit und Vielfalt neutestamentlicher Theologie, Festschrift für Eduard Schweizer zum siebzigsten Geburtstag* (Ulrich Luz and Hans Weder, eds., Göttingen: Vandenhoeck & Ruprecht, 1983), 18-19.

It is important to remember that a canon with a gospel theme or emphasis need not have that word as prominent within all its writings. The so-called "catholic epistles" do not focus on the gospel, but they certainly value the authority of the Lord's words and

Galatians as Examined by Diverse Academics

The basic progression of the paper will be as follows. First there will be an overarching analysis of this gospel theme within the first four epistles, especially examining some of the pertinent parts of Galatians, particularly Paul's distinctive use of the word "canon" at the end of the work (6:16). Second, there will be a brief proposal of the resulting sets that occur within the Pauline corpus as a result of this paper's thesis. The third main section of the paper will strengthen the connections between the epistles and the fourfold gospel, mainly by proposing a much earlier appearance of the fourfold gospel based upon the gospel theme mentioned earlier. A brief conclusion will finish the paper.

These three sections could easily be at least three separate papers—perhaps three books! Unfortunately only a limited amount of the current scholarship on each of these topics will be included so that this work could still be considered a *short* paper.[151] The hope is that by combining the above sections into one, the reader may find more than one area of interest and that the weight of evidence would influence the reader to see Galatians as a Cinderella story in its placement as fourth. The hope is also that, even if this particular perspective and proposal are not believed, the reader would, in the end, have a greater appreciation for the Epistle to the Galatians, the complex structure of the Pauline corpus, and especially the gospel.

2. Gospel Theme

This first section will look at the gospel theme present within the four epistles. This is a huge topic and will only be manageable because this part of the paper will essentially focus on the use of the word "gospel" in the texts and its close relations with other words.

It will be helpful to remember that the word "gospel" as a noun has a significant history even within the Old Testament, though the word there is extremely rare.[152] In the Old Testament "gospel" signifies the

---

actions as authoritative (see, e.g., 2 Pet 1:17; 1 John 1:1). These writings are not in decreasing length. Anything not said in direct contradiction may be seen as supportive. As it was with the Old Testament, so it is with the New. The same God is behind it all.

[151] The number of works which *could* be referenced within this paper is legion.

[152] The title "Old Testament" will be used throughout this paper although there are less-anachronistic ways to describe it, e.g., Hebrew Bible. The Hebrew root *bśr* occurs only thirty times.

messenger (of good news or bad) that goes from one significant place or person to another.[153] The reason for its importance in the Pentateuch is that the original situation of Adam and Eve had a close connection with Yahweh, but then after their rebellion, Yahweh was at a distance, and the face of Yahweh is never seen again, even during the various theophanies of the Old Testament.[154] The rest of the Old Testament, in light of what is to come, is a preparation for a divine messenger of good news. It should be no surprise, therefore, that Jesus uses the word "gospel" very early in his ministry.[155]

The word obviously occurs much more frequently in the New Testament. Within the first four epistles the word "gospel" as a noun appears thirty-two times and only thirty times after that.[156] It is used almost immediately in the first epistle's salutation. What follows are the phrases made with the word within the first four epistles:[157]

Rom 1:1   having been separated to *gospel* of God
       1:9   whom I serve ... in the *gospel* of the Son of him
       1:16   for I am not ashamed of the *gospel*
       2:16   God judges the hidden things of men according to the *gospel* of me
       10:16   not all followed the *gospel*
       11:28   according to the *gospel*, they are, on the one hand, enemies because of you

---

[153] Ludwig Koehler et al., *HALOT, Volume 1, 'Aleph – heth* (Leiden: Brill, 2001), 163-64; Schilling, "בשׂר *bśr*," in *TDOT, Volume 2 bdl-galah* (G. Johannes Botterweck and Helmer Ringgren, eds., Grand Rapids, Mich.: Eerdmans, 1975), 313-316; see esp. the first occurrence of the word in 1 Sam 4:17 where the significant place was the battlefield and the significant person was Eli.

[154] Cf. Gen. 1:2 (20, 29) and 2:6. Gen 4:16; Exod 24:10-11; 33:20; Deut 34:10; Isa 6:1; Ezek 1, 10.

[155] Mark 1:15; cf. Matt 4:23; Luke 4:18. The word never appears as a noun in Luke-Acts until Acts 15:7.

[156] Eph 1:13; 3:6; 6:15, 19; Phil 1:5, 7, 12, 16, 27(2); 2:22; 4:3, 15; Col 1:5, 23; 1Thess 1:5; 2:2, 4, 8, 9; 3:2; 2 Thess 1:8; 2:14; 1 Tim 1:11; 2 Tim 1:8, 10; 2:8; Phlm 13; 1 Pet 4:17; Rev 14:6.

[157] All translations within this paper are by the author and are purposefully more literalistic to give the reader a sense of the original. Any translation is ultimately an interpretation. The extent of the quotation depends on what appears in Moulton and Geden, *Concordance to the Greek New Testament* (I. Howard Marshall ed., 6th ed., New York: T & T Clark, 2002).

15:16 sacrificing the *gospel* of God
15:19 until Illyricum to have fulfilled the *gospel* of the Christ
16:25 to the one being able to establish you according to the *gospel* of me[158]

1 Cor 4:15 for in Christ Jesus through the *gospel* I begat you
9:12 lest we give to anyone an obstacle to the *gospel* of the Christ
9:14 thus also the Lord ordained to the ones announcing the *gospel*
9:14 to live from the *gospel*
9:18 in order that, evangelizing, I place without charge the *gospel*
9:18 so as to not use to the full the my authority in the *gospel*
9:23 but I do all things because of the *gospel*
15:1 and I make known to you … the *gospel* which I evangelized to you

2 Cor 2:12 but coming into Troas into the *gospel* of the Christ
4:3 but if indeed the *gospel* of us is being hidden
4:4 to not shine forth the enlightenment of the *gospel* of the glory of the Christ
8:18 of whom the praise in the *gospel* is throughout all the churches
9:13 on the submission of your confession into the *gospel* of the Christ
10:14 for as far as even you, we preceded in the *gospel* of the Christ
11:4 a different *gospel* which you did not receive
11:7 freely the *gospel* of God I evangelized to you

Gal 1:6 thus quickly you are removing … to another *gospel*
1:7 wishing to pervert the *gospel* of the Christ
1:11 and I make known to you … the *gospel* which was evangelized by me

---

[158] This is a doubtful text. See Bruce M. Metzger, *A Textual Commentary on the Greek New Testament* (2nd ed., Stuttgart: Deutsche Bibelgesellschaft, 2002), 470-77.

2:2   I put before them the *gospel* which I proclaim
2:5   in order that the truth of the *gospel* might continue with you
2:7   I have been entrusted with the *gospel* of the uncircumcision
2:14 they were not walking straight with the truth of the *gospel*

This author will not dispute the progression from the general or the universal to the specific noted by Childs at the beginning of this paper. What should be noted is that a progression to the specific happens earlier than the Pastoral Epistles. The connections to the gospel are to God, then to the Son or the Christ, then to Paul, in that order, both at the beginning and ending of Romans.[159] This close connection between the gospel and Paul within Romans is eventually put to the test very near to the start of Galatians where the debate regarding the gospel and its ramifications are being discussed. The phrase, "the truth of the gospel" appears twice within the epistle, and the second time, the final time within these four epistles, the entire phrase is that "they were not walking straight (*orthopodoúsin*) with the truth of the gospel." This was Paul's accusation against Peter, and the claim was of course that Paul *was* walking properly.[160]

This last use of the word "gospel" has a significant connection to at least one part of Acts. After the Jerusalem Council, when Paul arrived back in Jerusalem in Acts 21, James and all the elders give Paul a plan to have the Jews who were now believers to support Paul, so that, in their words, "everybody will know ... that you yourself conform (*stoicheís*), guarding the Torah (*nómon*)."[161]

At first glance it does not seem that one can simultaneously walk in these two ways—straight with the truth of the gospel and also by guarding the Torah or law. This disunity has been typified by the phrase,

---

[159] For more details regarding the genitive, see Daniel B. Wallace, *Greek Grammar Beyond the Basics: An Exegetical Syntax of the New Testament* (Grand Rapids, Mich.: Zondervan, 1996), 72-136. To delve further into the issues of Paul and "his" gospel, see Seyoon Kim, *Paul and the New Perspective: Second Thoughts on the Origin of Paul's Gospel* (Grand Rapids, Mich.: Eerdmans, 2002).

[160] The structure of Galatians is such that, even before the "Thanksgiving" that Paul usually has for the congregation, he brings up the topic of the gospel. The first use of the word in Eph (1:13) is to those who listen to the gospel, and the first use in 2 Thess (1:8) is for those who do not listen. More will be mentioned about this possible "set" later in the paper. Cf. 1 Cor 15:1 and Gal 1:11. Although Galatians does not contain the phrase, "the gospel of me," it does come very close.

[161] Acts 21:24; cf. Acts 15:13-21.

"Jesus vs. Paul" and was hinted at above.[162] To see a resolution between these two, a broader understanding of the word "gospel" which incorporates the foundational themes within the Pentateuch mentioned above will be necessary.

Both these texts have a significant connection to one of the few times that the word "canon" is mentioned within the New Testament: "For neither circumcision nor uncircumcision is anything, but a new creation. And as many as those who will conform (*stoichỳsousin*) to this canon, peace be upon them, and mercy, and upon the Israel of God."[163] The word "canon" *could* be connected to law or Torah and normally means a standard or rule, but here it is connected to "a new creation."[164]

This seemingly weak connection between Torah and gospel is significantly strengthened by the use of a much "larger" phrase, that of "a new creation." Recent research regarding this phrase has been helpful. It is deliberately broad so that all, both Jews and Gentiles, have connections to it.[165] The phrase is used only within these first four epistles, and this is not surprising because of the predominance of the closely connected word "gospel."[166] Although within these first four epistles this word "gospel" has specific connections to Paul, it also has a connection to every individual through the idea of "a new creation." Such a duality may be

---

[162] Kloha, "The Problem of Paul's Letters," 159: "And, in the present context, Paul's letters retain a central role, whether Paul is construed as the 'founder of Christianity' or trumpeted as the clearest articulator of 'justification by faith,' over and against both James and Jesus(!)." One place to start on this topic would be Dunn, *Unity and Diversity in the New Testament*.

[163] Gal 6:15-16; cf. 2 Cor 10:13, 15, 16. See William R. Farmer, "Reflections on Jesus and the New Testament Canon," in *The Canon Debate*, 321-40.

[164] Eugene Ulrich, "The Notion and Definition of Canon," in *The Canon Debate*, 21-35; "νόμος," BDAG (Chicago: University of Chicago Press, 2000), 677-78. The previous two uses of the word "uncircumcision" (2:7 and 5:6) are connected to the prior mention of the word "gospel" and to being "in Christ Jesus."

[165] T. Ryan Jackson, *New Creation in Paul's Letters: A Study of the Historical and Social Setting of a Pauline Concept* (WUNT vol. 272, Tübingen: Mohr Siebeck, 2010); cf. François Bovon, "L'homme nouveau et la loi chez l'apôtre Paul," in *Die Mitte des Neuen Testaments*, 22-33.

[166] The phrase is only here and in 2 Cor (5:17). The first epistle uses the word "creation" as many times as the other epistles combined (Rom 1:20, 25; 8:19, 20, 21, 22, 39; Col 1:15, 23; Heb 4:13; 9:11; 1 Pet 2:13; 2 Pet 3:14; Rev 3:14).

seen as complementary and not contradictory. Certainly much more could be said, but thus ends the part of the paper on the gospel theme.[167]

3. Sets of Epistles

The paper will now turn to examine the sets that occur within the rest of the Pauline epistles because of this proposed fourfold gospel-related structure at the beginning. As was mentioned before, much of the previous scholarship viewed the epistles historically, as a whole, since they were originally seen to come from essentially one author. Also the original situation of both the writer and the congregation is usually thought to influence the content of the letter and therefore both its length and also its placement.[168]

A scholar who proposed the same first set based more on literary purposes is David Trobisch. His proposal was that Paul himself put together Romans through Galatians in an effort to help organize the collection for the poor in Jerusalem.[169] Murphy-O'Conner took this another step and proposed the three partial collections of the Pauline corpus that were hinted at above, but these collections were based more on

---

[167] Connections have already been made by others between the so-called "pillars" in Gal 2:9 and the so-called "catholic epistles." See, e.g., Farmer and Farkasfalvy, *The Formation of the New Testament Canon*, 153. An interesting direction for future study is the connections within these first four salutations to the other parts of the New Testament. Within the first part of the salutation of the first epistle, there are connections to Jesus being born of the seed of David and being called the Son of God at his resurrection (Rom 1:3-4), and these are the titles used at the beginning and the ending of the fourfold gospel (Matt 1:1; John 20:31). This part of the salutation is also extremely long, while the last part of the salutation of the fourth epistle is also extremely long. Cf. Jerome Murphy-O'Conner, *Paul the Letter-Writer: His World, His Options, His Skills* (Collegeville, Minn.: Liturgical Press, 1995), 45-109.

[168] This has recently been questioned because of the diverse style and vocabulary of some of the writings. For a recent summary and proposal based on some of the latest research, see Stanley E. Porter, "Paul and the Process of Canonization," in *Exploring the Origins of the Bible: Canon Formation in Historical, Literary, and Theological Perspective* (Craig A. Evans and Emmanuel Tov eds., Grand Rapids, Mich.: Baker Academic, 2008), 173-202.

[169] David Trobisch, *Paul's Letter Collection: Tracing the Origins* (Minneapolis: Fortress, 1994), 55-98; cf. David Trobisch, *The First Edition of the New Testament* (New York: Oxford University Press, 2000), 60-61.

the historical details rather than the literary content.[170] The lack of an addressee within some manuscripts of both Romans and Ephesians supports these divisions if the thought would have been that only a minimum needs to be changed to make the text applicable for others.[171]

With the content of Galatians having a reference to both new creation and the collection, while Ephesians having references to neither, perhaps it is not surprising that Galatians is ahead of Ephesians. It will be noted here—and probably should have been noted sooner—that, if length were the *only* factor, Galatians should switch places with Ephesians. Galatians is shorter than Ephesians by about two hundred words.

Murphy-O'Conner, for one, sees no problem in saying that Galatians and Ephesians are essentially the same length. He points out that in at least one manuscript the two epistles have an equal number of lines, and since this is the standard used for scribes to be paid, he dismisses the order of Galatians and then Ephesians as "an insignificant error."[172] While this may be true, the placement of Galatians as fourth may have also been a way of pointing to a fourfold set with a particular emphasis, perhaps that of the collection or the gospel (of Paul but for all).

An interesting pattern appears when the use of both "Christ Jesus" and "Jesus Christ" in the beginning of the salutations is laid out essentially according to these divisions. A case could be made for some of the earlier

---

[170] Murphy-O'Conner, *Paul the Letter-Writer*, 120-30.

[171] See Metzger, *A Textual Commentary on the Greek New Testament*, 446, 478, 532. What makes the literary content of this middle set (Eph through 2 Thess) interesting is that there is a discernible, chronological progression. Very near the beginning of Eph, even before the typical thanksgiving, the text emphasizes what God did before time (Eph 1:4-5), and the theme that is well known in both 1 and 2 Thessalonians is the end of time (e.g., 1 Thess 4:15 – 5:2). Was this meant to be an early timeline of God's involvement with the world and circulated as another individual set? This division may *possibly* be supported by the content of P92 which only has a part of Eph 1 and a part of 2 Thess 1. See Kurt Aland and Barbara Aland, *The Text of the New Testament: An Introduction to the Critical Editions and to the Theory and Practice of Modern Textual Criticism* (Erroll F. Rhodes, trans., 2nd ed., Grand Rapids, Mich.: Eerdmans, 1989), 369. It may also be said that the progression within this set is from the general to the specific.

[172] P46, a very early manuscript, has Eph ahead of Gal. Sinaiticus has Gal to be the same stichoi as Eph. Phil and Col are switched in some manuscripts, and they too have a similar length. Murphy-O'Conner, *Paul the Letter-Writer*, 120-24. A person whose writings have been compared with scripture (2 Pet 3:16) would have had his words closely studied and compared.

writings to have "Jesus Christ," instead of "Christ Jesus."[173] Looking at the texts in a more literary fashion, the use of the two terms forms a discernible chiastic (ABBA, or, in this case, CJJC) pattern which Paul has used elsewhere.[174]

Romans	1 Corinthians	2 Corinthians	Galatians
CJ	CJ	CJ	---- JC
Ephesians	Philippians	Colossians	1 Thessalonians
2 Thessalonians			
CJ	CJ	CJ	---- JC
JC			
	1 Timothy	2 Timothy	Titus
	CJ	CJ ----	JC
		Philemon	
		CJ[175]	

Although the following comment would have been more appropriate in the following section, the point will be made here that this pattern has the primary emphasis on Christ Jesus and therefore makes a much larger chiastic pattern with the gospel accounts, three of which emphasize Jesus Christ in their introductions.[176] What follows now is a discussion regarding the fourfold gospel.

4. Early Fourfold Gospel

For there to be a predetermined theme to the epistles, one which reflected a fourfold gospel, it would be helpful for there to be an early and significant emphasis of the fourfold gospel. The next part of the paper is the longest part of the paper and will propose a much earlier appearance of

---

[173] See, e.g., Frank Thielman, *Theology of the New Testament: A Canonical and Synthetic Approach* (Grand Rapids, Mich.: Zondervan, 2005), 10.

[174] See John W. Welch, "Chiasmus in the New Testament," in *Chiasmus in Antiquity*, 211-30.

[175] There are some textual variants for some of these. See, e.g., Metzger, *A Textual Commentary on the Greek New Testament*, 446, 478. It is also interesting to note that Paul designates himself as a slave within the first, sixth, and twelfth epistles (Rom 1:1; 1 Tim 1:1; Titus 1:1).

[176] Matt 1:1; Mark 1:1; John 1:18.

the fourfold gospel based upon the gospel theme mentioned earlier. This part of the paper will also seek to establish an even greater connection between the gospel and epistle sections of the New Testament.

This idea of how the four gospel accounts came together and how they relate to one another is another huge topic essentially known as the Synoptic Problem.[177] In a way today's scholarship has very limited evidence when dealing with the historical record of how the accounts came together. There are few quotations from the early church fathers regarding the origin of the four accounts, and these have been variously interpreted and sometimes even seen as contradictory.[178] In another way today's scholarship has an overwhelming amount of evidence simply because of the actual existence of the four accounts. Many blanks need to be filled in, and the options for answers are usually not multiple choice.

David Dungan started out his massive work, *A History of the Synoptic Problem*, by connecting the diversity within the four gospel accounts to the missionary expansion.[179] Moule in his book, *The Birth of the New Testament*, gave the theory that the gospel Paul preached was combined with the historical details of Jesus' life because his followers simply wanted to know more about him.[180] The eventual differences among the four accounts are explained by both chronological and geographical distances.[181] Does this make the earliest account the most important because it is closest to the actual events, or is what was passed on and therefore what remains to have been considered the most important

---

[177] See David Laird Dungan, *A History of the Synoptic Problem: The Canon, the Text, the Composition, and the Interpretation of the Gospels* (New York: Doubleday, 1999). Regarding the Gospel according to John and its place in the Synoptic Problem, see David L. Dungan, ed., *The Interrelations of the Gospels: A Symposium* (BETL vol. 95, Leuven: University Press, 1990), 609; cf. T.K. Heckel, *Von Evangelium des Markus zum viergestaltigen Evangelium* (WUNT vol. 120, Tübingen: Mohr & Siebeck, 1999).

[178] One issue is whether the Gospel according to Matthew was written in the Hebrew language or a Hebrew style. For an argument in support of the latter, see J. Kürzinger, "Das Papiaszeugnis und die Erstgestalt des Matthäusevangeliums," *Biblische Zeitschrift* 4 (1960): 19-38. For the debate regarding the order in which the gospel accounts were written, see Stephen C. Carlson, "Clement of Alexandria on the 'Order' of the Gospels," *New Testament Studies* 47, no. 1 (2001): 118-25.

[179] Dungan, *A History of the Synoptic Problem*, 11.

[180] Moule, *The Birth of the New Testament*, 123.

[181] See Chris Forbes, "The Historical Jesus," in *The Content and Setting of the Gospel Tradition* (Mark Harding and Alanna Nobbs eds., Grand Rapids, Mich.: Eerdmans, 2010), 231-38.

to the followers?[182] Ultimately it is both. Any amount of evidence may be helpful when solving an immensely complex question.

Also like in the last section, some recent scholarship has headed in a slightly different direction. The work of Richard Bauckham, *The Gospels for all Christians*, proposed that all four accounts were ultimately written for all Christians.[183] *Four Gospels, One Jesus?* is a similar, somewhat-less scholarly work by another British scholar, Richard Burridge. The latter work is based firmly on the vision of God's throne in the first chapters of Ezekiel and Revelation.[184] The proposal that all four accounts are to work together, not in contradiction but to support each other, is a significant step.

That direction may also be seen with this Old Testament understanding of the word "gospel" described earlier. It is often forgotten that, in ancient cultures, the symbolism of a (four-sided) throne was significant.[185] Also the position of being seated is today not considered to be anything special, but in ancient times it was the position of authority, and inscribed upon the throne were those things over which the king had authority and which portrayed his glory.[186]

---

[182] "When Matthew wrote his gospel, he did not intend to supplement Mark: his incorporation of most of Mark's Gospel is surely an indication that he intended that his gospel should replace Mark's, and that it should become *the* Gospel for Christians of his day." Graham N. Stanton, *Jesus and Gospel* (Cambridge: Cambridge University Press, 2004), 87.

[183] Richard Bauckham, *The Gospels for All Christians* (Richard Bauckham, ed., Grand Rapids, Mich.: Eerdmans, 1998); cf. Edward W. Klink III, ed., *The Audience of the Gospels: The Origin and Function of the Gospels in Early Christianity* (LNTS vol. 353, New York: T & T Clark, 2010).

[184] Ezek 1; 10; Rev 4. Burridge's work begins with an excellent illustration of the complex man, Winston Churchill, who was pictured in four very different ways. Richard A. Burridge, *Four Gospels, One Jesus? A Symbolic Reading* (2nd ed., Grand Rapids, Mich.: Eerdmans, 2005).

[185] Numbers were also significant in the Old Testament since the Hebrew language had a close connection between words and numbers. See, e.g., E.W. Bullinger, *Number in Scripture: Its Supernatural Design and Spiritual Significance* (London: Eyre & Spottiswoode, 1894).

[186] O. Schmitz, θρόνος, TDNT vol. 3 (Gerhard Kittel and Geoffrey W. Bromiley, eds., Grand Rapids, Mich.: Eerdmans, 1965), 160-67.

Galatians as Examined by Diverse Academics

The foundational message of the Pentateuch, as was mentioned above, is that Yahweh's face can no longer be seen.[187] If therefore this theme of the gospel is in both the Old and New Testaments, then the position of Yahweh on his throne is a significant one and the messenger who goes out from that throne has a significant amount of authority, essentially the same authority as Yahweh.[188] The question is whether or not the messenger's authority relates to the signs of authority on Yahweh's throne. Are these signs of authority connected to creation or redemption? Ultimately it is both. The four living creatures in Revelation first sing a song that deals with creation, and later they sing a new song having to do with redemption.[189]

T.C. Skeat and others have proposed that the idea of the fourfold gospel went back to the four living creatures on Yahweh's throne in Ezekiel, but since this emphasis does not seem to appear within Acts, the connection is usually thought to have been imposed upon the text.[190] But it may also have been the case that too obvious of an emphasis in Acts may have distracted people from the content of the message.

The presence of this divine messenger has been previously connected to the Pentateuch and to the rest of the Old Testament. In the same way that there is very little direct, literary interaction between the Pentateuch and the parts of the Old Testament that follow, the same thing

---

[187] Another connection to the Pentateuch may be in the following passage: "Let every word be confirmed in the presence of two or three witnesses (Deut 19:15)." Choosing the latter option within the verse would make a total of four accounts. The first few words of the Gospel according to Luke seem to indicate the need for multiple, reliable witnesses. The idea of a witness is very important within this account and within the Gospel according to John as well. The four things that Jesus promises the Paraclete will do are the following: teach, remind, witness, and convict (John 14:25; 15:26; 16:8).

[188] The arrival of that divine messenger to his final destination is a significant enough event for a new "era" to begin. No other event in the history of the world may be compared to it. The departure of that messenger would also be a significant event; the long-awaited, important message from Yahweh himself has just been delivered. That special "era" would have ended. Any authoritative writings having their source in that "era" would be a gospel canon.

[189] Rev 4:11; 5:9-14.

[190] T.C. Skeat, "The Origin of the Christian Codex," *Zeitschrift für Papyrologie und Epigraphik* 102 (1994): 263-68.

should be said regarding the New.[191] An expectation for Jesus to "predict" Paul's authority or of Paul to quote Jesus and thus show his close connection would be to miss the element of divine authority which supports the entire gospel message. Nowhere does Paul describe himself as a prophet, but by what he does certainly implies that he is, and his writings are similar to the prophets of the Old Testament.[192] If Paul would have been too obvious with his authority, that would have distracted from the important message. If Paul had been identified in Acts as a writer to churches, this again would be too distracting. Some basic details are given because the epistles are not anonymous. The gospel accounts, on the other hand, are. To have Acts describe in detail the gospel accounts being written would certainly focus on the accounts being written and not on their authoritative message. Enough information is given in all the parts of the Old or New Testaments to realize that a significant event is occurring without undue focus on the secondary issues. Even though the connections between gospel accounts and epistles are infrequent, with this gospel perspective the understanding is that there is one divine messenger with one important message.

The final question to be asked is whether or not this one important message has an early fourfold manifestation and if this even appears in Acts. One possibility will be laid out in the following paragraphs.

A geographical and chronological gap has been attributed to the writing of the four gospel accounts, but could this gap be descriptive of the time when the accounts were finished? Could the four accounts have been started much earlier? William Farmer points out that the first evident need for writing down the words of Jesus may have been in connection with the need for the oral word to be translated in a reliable way.[193] This may have happened in the unfortunate circumstance of the Hellenistic widows being overlooked in the so-called "daily service" of Acts 6:1. This is usually

---

[191] Vogels considered the gospel accounts to be in parallel with the Pentateuch. Walter Vogels, "La Structure Symetrique de la bible Chretienee," *The Biblical Canons* (BETL 163): 295-304.

[192] See Karl Olav Sandnes, *Paul – One of the Prophets? A Contribution to the Apostle's Self-Understanding* (WUNT vol. 43, Tübingen: Mohr Siebeck, 1991).

[193] Farmer, *The Formation of the New Testament Canon*, 50: "The first evident need for writing down the words of the Lord may have been in connection with the need for the oral tradition to be translated in a reliable way into languages other than that spoken by Jesus, or other than that spoken by Christian prophets speaking in the spirit and name of Jesus."

understood that they were not receiving food and that the seven who were appointed eventually helped with the further spread of the gospel.[194] The so-called "New Perspective" may help to point out another issue involved.[195] After Acts 6 the issue with eating with Gentiles is still a prominent one.[196] It may have been that the Twelve still had a problem with going through the doorway of a Gentile and eating with a Gentile; this may have been a part of "the daily service."[197] The Jewish disciples could have easily filled the role of the man of the house for the Jewish widows, but to do the same thing with the Hellenistic widows may have seemed to them as if they were "leaving the Word of God to serve tables (6:2)." Therefore they could have been just dropping off the food at the door. The Greek widows may have been taken care of in terms of receiving food, but they may have been overlooked in receiving a word about Jesus.[198] So these seven, all Greek and all male, may have begun their work of visiting the Hellenistic widows with the understanding that they would be doing their work in place of the Twelve, speaking to the widows about Jesus. The collection of the poor in Jerusalem could have helped support these expensive writings. Even if the poor are those who are economically disadvantaged, they could have considered themselves helped by hearing accounts of Jesus' actions.[199]

Having stories about Jesus is one thing, but having a fourfold gospel is another. When was a fourfold gospel discussed? Martin Hengel, in his book, *The Four Gospels and the One Gospel of Jesus Christ*, pointed out that there were very few events in the first centuries that were

---

[194] F.F. Bruce, *The Acts of the Apostles: The Greek Text with Introduction and Commentary* (London: Tyndale, 1952), 150-54. The word "overlooked" is a *hapax*. See παραθεωρέω, BDAG; cf. θεωρέω, BDAG. The word, because of Old Testament influence, can mean to see someone's face or to see someone in person.

[195] See Kim, *Paul and the New Perspective*, 2-4.

[196] Acts 11:2; cf. 15:1.

[197] The NIV translates this as the "daily distribution of food."

[198] See Acts 4:34-35; cf. 6:7. The summary statement is that the "Word of God increased" and "the number of disciples in Jerusalem was multiplied exceedingly." It should also be noted that Stephen gets into trouble because of what he has said (although he has false witnesses speak against him; Acts 6:10-14). Acts 5:42; cf. 15:35.

[199] See πτωχός, BDAG. If the collection functioned in this way, it would be an important thing for Paul. As was mentioned above, the topic appears especially in the first four epistles (Rom 15:25-33; 1 Cor 16:1-4; Gal 2:9-10). For a recent survey of the issues surrounding the collection, see David J. Downs, *The Offering of the Gentiles* (WUNT vol. 248, Tübingen: Mohr Siebeck, 2008).

authoritative enough to authorize a fourfold gospel collection.[200] What about the Jerusalem Council as an *initial* decision for the fourfold gospel collection? The difficulty is of course that there's no literal mention of the decision to write four accounts, but, as was mentioned above, such a decision would have focused attention on the accounts and not on the message that they contain. An attempt at a brief proposal of this point follows.

The Jerusalem Council is a central event to the early church.[201] What may be significant to note is that this is the first occurrence of the word "gospel" as a noun within all of Luke-Acts. Up to this point the verb form has been used. Given the topic of discussion, whether or not Gentiles must be circumcised, that word is at the heart of the matter. Obviously much which was said at that council was not recorded.[202]

One possible connection may be made between the four accounts and the four so-called "prohibitions" given first by James and then in the letter which was written. The first time these "prohibitions" are given, this statement follows: "for Moses from ancient generations has in every city those who proclaim him, being read in the synagogues on every Sabbath."[203] If at this council it was proposed to have four gospel accounts, the emphasis within this verse may have meant that these accounts would be read in the synagogues after the reading from the

---

[200] Hengel writes: "It can therefore also by no means be assumed that at some time in this dark period, before Irenaeus or even more before Justin, there had been a kind of general 'council' of a number of churches in a province at which the four hitherto anonymous writings gained recognition, were given their titles, and were then brought together as a 'four-Gospel canon.' Such an idea would be completely anachronistic. The first local synods known to us are only in connection with the origin of Montanism towards the end of the second century, in the province of Asia, and did not concern themselves with the questions of the canon. Far less could the 'four-Gospel collection' be the work of a single Christian authority or school, because no person, school, or even community in the early second century possessed the authority and power to establish its own Gospel collection throughout the church by one decisive action." Hengel, *The Four Gospels and the One Gospel of Jesus Christ*, 53.

[201] "The Book of Acts, and especially chapter 15, serves as an important link between the Gospels and the Epistles." Charles H. Savelle, "A Reexamination of the Prohibitions in Acts 15," *Bibliotheca Sacra* 161 (Oct-Dec 2004): 449.

[202] Acts 15:1, 7.

[203] Acts 15:21. For the importance of Scripture reading for Paul, see Guy Waters, *The End of Deuteronomy in the Epistles of Paul* (WUNT vol. 221, Tübingen: Mohr Siebeck, 2006).

Pentateuch. The intention would probably have been that these accounts would have been seen as supportive of the Pentateuch.[204]

There is also a much more "gospel-understanding" within these four "prohibitions" than with the previous understanding because the Greek word to "abstain" may also mean to "receive in full."[205] With the latter sense of the word, these four topics within these chapters of the Pentateuch may be "received in full" by hearing about Jesus who was the fulfillment of the Old Testament promises.[206]

---

[204] The center was seen as an important part of the text (see Gen 2:4-7; cf. Ps 1:1-4). The center of the entire Pentateuch is, according to the Masoretes, Lev 11:42 according to letters and Lev 10:46 according to words. Page H. Kelley et al., *The Masorah of Biblia Hebraica Stuttgartensia* (Grand Rapids, Mich.: Eerdmans, 1998), 108. If the first section from Genesis (1:1-11:26) is not included, then the center point is much closer to the Day of Atonement chapter. These prohibitions follow immediately after that chapter and applied to both Jew and foreigner (17:8, 10, 12, 13, 15)

[205] The letter contains the only two uses of the word in Acts (15:20, 29), but in Luke the word occurs four times (6:24; 7:6; 15:20; 24:13), the first occurrence having the meaning of "receive" and the rest to be "distant,"

[206] Interesting enough, these four words (idolatry, fornication, things strangled, and blood) connect to the four gospel accounts since Jesus, at the moment he is described as being put on the cross, is described with four significantly different emphases in these four accounts. Matt 27:35-37: "And having crucified him, they divided his garments, casting a lot, and sitting, they kept him there." Mark 15:24: "And they crucify him and divide his garments, casting a lot upon them, what each might take." Luke 23:33: "And when they came upon the place called 'Skull,' there they crucified him and the criminals, one on the right and one on the left." John 19:17-18: "And himself carrying the cross, he went forth to the place called 'Of a Skull,' which is called in Hebrew 'Golgotha,' where they crucified him, and with him two others, on this side and that, and in the middle, Jesus." At the point of crucifixion, the first two accounts emphasize the soldiers and the last two, the criminals with Jesus. The first one is different from all the rest in that the soldiers are described as sitting, a position of authority. The last account is different in that the writer is describing the situation from what seems to be an eyewitness account. The four topics are most closely connected in the way they are given first in their normal order: idolatry, fornication, things strangled, and blood. The first two deal with relationships with others (God and man), and the second two deal with death. The first (idolatry) deals with taking God's place, and the seated position is that of a king, and a king is usually thought to have authority from the divine. The last (blood) is given as part of the eyewitness account when blood and water are seen to come out of Jesus' side after he was pierced. See John 19:35 (Note that only in the Gospel according to Luke are the criminals described as hanging. See Luke 23:39). Several connections can also be made to the different ways Jesus' death is described in the four sermons in Acts which are before the Jerusalem Council (Acts 2, 3, 10, 13).

Galatians as Examined by Diverse Academics

It is important to note that prophets accompany this letter which contains the list of four and that, after the letter was read, the followers in Antioch rejoiced upon what was given (*paraklÿsei*), and what was given could be translated as comfort or exhortation. Since the word could essentially be understood as either positive or negative, perhaps the message was different and depended on whether the listeners were Jew or Gentile. The text also states that Judas and Silas, those who were prophets, comforted or exhorted (*parekálesan*) with many words (Acts 15:35).[207] As in the previous situations, many blanks are being filled. One more speculation will occur, and this will be regarding the second mention of the word "gospel."

This second and final occurrence of the noun "gospel" is one of the closest to the event of the formation of the New Testament.[208] The context for that use is Paul's speech to those in Ephesus who are overseers. Here would be the potential for laying out a guide to the future "New Testament" if it were actually discussed at the Jerusalem Council, but again that would be too obvious and distract from the message. Paul's words, as recorded, are the following:

> But I do not consider my life of any account as precious to myself, so as I may finish my course and the ministry which I received from the Lord Jesus, to witness solemnly to the gospel of the grace of God. And now, behold, I know that all of you, among whom I went about proclaiming the

---

Blass-Debrunner compares Luke 1:1-4 with the so-called "Apostolic Decree" (Acts 15:24-27) . "The prologue to the Gospel of Luke is a beautiful period; Luke elsewhere forsakes this device, it is true, and the introduction to Acts is not a period but a series of clauses strung together; only the introduction of the apostolic decree in Acts 15:24-26 forms a genuine period." Blass-Debrunner, *A Greek Grammar of the New Testament and Other Early Christian Literature* (Chicago: University Press, 1961), 242. Cf. Josep Rius-Camps and Jenny Read-Heimerdinger, *The Message of Acts in Codex Bezae (Vol. 3): A Comparison with the Alexandrian Tradition: Acts 13.1-18:23* (LNTS vol. 365, London: T & T Clark, 2007), 223-24.

What could certainly be called a coincidence is that, if the two lists of "prohibitions" are compared, the difference is that of the order of the four accounts normally (Matt, Mark, Luke, John) and that of the so-called "Western Order" (Matt, John, Luke, Mark).

[207] παράκλησις, BDAG, 766. παρακαλέω, BDAG, 764-65.

[208] In Johannine literature the word only appears one time, in Rev. 14:6, where an angel is carrying an eternal gospel.

kingdom, will see my face no more. Therefore I witness to you on this day that I am clean from the blood of all, for I have not held back to declare to you all the counsel of God.[209]

The most obvious connection is back to Acts 15(:11), after Peter mentions the gospel, he finishes his speech by saying that "we believe that we are saved through the grace of the Lord Jesus, just as they also are." In light of what has previously been said regarding the idea of "gospel" within the Old Testament, the phrases of "kingdom", "to see someone's face," and "the whole counsel of God" are quite significant. They seem to point, albeit in a hidden way, to the gospel theme and emphasis previously described. Since Paul's very last words in this message are a quote from Jesus, "It is more blessed to give than to receive," it is quite appropriate for his very *last* words to be a direct quote from Jesus' mouth. The message was not meant to be historically based, but divine-messenger based.

Obviously the previous assumption was that there were multiple gospel accounts and that four were picked at the time the entire canon was formed. C. Stephen Evans, for one, has pointed out the possibility of an extremely early authority to the writings of the New Testament, even to the time of their writing.[210] What has been suggested here is that four accounts were authorized at the Jerusalem Council and were later—

---

[209] Acts 20:24-27. The entire speech is Acts 20:18-35. Much could be said regarding this speech. For more detail, see C.K. Barrett, *A Critical and Exegetical Commentary on the Acts of the Apostles* (Vol. 2: Acts 15-28, Edinburgh: T & T Clark, 1998), 961-84.

[210] C. Stephen Evans, "Canonicity, Apostolicity, and Biblical Authority: Some Kierkegaardian Reflections," in *Canon and Biblical Interpretation* (Craig G. Bartholomew et al., eds., Scripture and Hermeneutics Series vol. 7, Grand Rapids, Mich.: Zondervan, 2006), 164: "The principle I am relying on here does not imply that the writers of the New Testament thought of themselves as writing what would later be thought of as the New Testament, a particular collection of books constituting a closed canon. Such a claim would certainly be anachronistic. The claim I am defending is that it is plausible that the writers of what we call the New Testament thought of themselves as apostles who had the authority to speak a word from God, and that this enabled both these writers and others who accepted their apostolic status to understand at least some of their writings as having a scriptural status from the beginning."

perhaps much later—finished at the various places where they have been known to be (Rome, Syria, etc.).[211]

This concludes the proposal for an early fourfold gospel. What follows is a brief conclusion.

5. Conclusion

William Farmer saw a theological reason behind Marcion's canon with his "adjustment" of Galatians as the first of his epistles.[212] This is perhaps a "true *fairy tale* Cinderella story." Galatians is not Romans, nor is it Ephesians, nor is it any of the other epistles. It has its own, unique and critical role as fourth.

Perhaps this author lost the reader right in the first section when the paper put forward the possibility of a gospel theme and emphasis which pervades both Old and New Testaments. Hopefully seeing the progression within the first four epistles and the gospel's connections to God, then to Paul, but then to all creation, was helpful in seeing the immense significance of that special word "gospel."

The second section not only assumed the coherence of the first four epistles but brought up a couple points of coherence for the next five. Perhaps this is where the reader was lost.

The third and final section is in all probability where *all* the readers were lost, since it proposed a "hidden," early fourfold gospel structure that was significant enough to predate the epistles. Obviously crucial to this proposal is the point that, if such a structure were obvious, more attention would be devoted to the structure rather than to its purpose and message. But since the structural evidence is not so obvious, such a conclusion will remain of a dubious nature.

Wherever the reader was lost, perhaps he or she has gained a slightly greater appreciation for the complexity of Galatians and, of course, the Pauline corpus. Hopefully both the gospel and the fourfold gospel will also be more greatly appreciated. This author will continue to hold on to the slight possibility of at least another "believer" (not his godmother!) that, because Galatians is the fourth epistle with several distinct characteristics, it is a "true Cinderella story" for the New

---

[211] See Hengel, *The Four Gospels and the One Gospel of Jesus Christ*, 208-9.
[212] Farmer, *Formation of the New Testament Canon*, 79-81.

Testament canon. Whatever the result, if the reader has made it to the end, this author hopes for some feedback in some form (preferably before midnight).

Galatians as Examined by Diverse Academics

Bibliography

Aland, Kurt and Barbara Aland. *The Text of the New Testament: An Introduction to the Critical Editions and to the Theory and Practice of Modern Textual Criticism*. Translated by Erroll F. Rhodes. 2nd ed. Grand Rapids, Mich.: Eerdmans, 1989.

Alter, Robert. *The Art of the Biblical Narrative*. New York: Basic Books, 1981.

Aune, David E. *The New Testament in Its Literary Environment*. Philadelphia: Westminster,1987.

Barrett, C.K. *A Critical and Exegetical Commentary on the Acts of the Apostles*. 2 vols. Edinburgh: T & T Clark, 1998.

----------. "The Centre of the New Testament and the Canon." In *Die Mitte des Neuen Testaments: Einheit und Vielfalt neutestamentlicher Theologie, Festschrift für Eduard Schweizer zum siebzigsten Geburtstag*. Edited by Ulrich Luz and Hans Weder. Göttingen: Vandenhoeck & Ruprecht, 1983: 5-21.

Bauckham, Richard. *The Gospels for All Christians*. Edited by Richard Bauckham. Grand Rapids, Mich.: Eerdmans, 1998.

Bauer, Walter et al. (BDAG). *A Greek-English Lexicon of the New Testament and Other Early Christian Literature*. Revised and edited by Frederick W. Danker. 3rd ed. Chicago: University of Chicago Press, 2000.

Blass, F. and A. Debrunner. *A Greek Grammar of the New Testament and Other Early Christian Literature: A Translation and Revision of the ninth-tenth German edition incorporating supplementary notes of A. Debrunner by Robert W. Funk*. Chicago: University Press,1961.

Bovon, François. "L'homme nouveau et la loi chez l'apôtre Paul." In *Die Mitte des Neuen Testaments: Einheit und Vielfalt neutestamentlicher Theologie, Festschrift für Eduard Schweizer zum siebzigsten Geburtstag*.

Edited by Ulrich Luz and Hans Weder. Göttingen: Vandenhoeck & Ruprecht, 1983: 22-33.

Bruce, F.F. *The Acts of the Apostles: The Greek Text with Introduction and Commentary*. London: Tyndale, 1952.

Bullinger, E.W. *Number in Scripture: Its Supernatural Design and Spiritual Significance*. London: Eyre & Spottiswoode, 1894.

Burridge, Richard A. *Four Gospels, One Jesus? A Symbolic Reading*. 2nd ed. Grand Rapids, Mich.: Eerdmans, 2005.

Carlson, Stephen C. "Clement of Alexandria on the 'Order' of the Gospels." *New Testament Studies* 47, no. 1 (2001): 118-25.

Childs, Brevard S. *The Church's Guide for Reading Paul: The Canonical Shaping of the Pauline Corpus*. Grand Rapids, Mich.: Eerdmans, 2008.

Downs, David J. *The Offering of the Gentiles*. WUNT vol. 248. Tübingen: Mohr Siebeck, 2008.

Dungan, David Laird. *A History of the Synoptic Problem: The Canon, the Text, the Composition, and the Interpretation of the Gospels*. New York: Doubleday, 1999.

----------, ed. *The Interrelations of the Gospels: A Symposium*. BETL vol. 95. Leuven: University Press, 1990.

Dunn, James D. G. *Unity and Diversity in the New Testament: An Inquiry into the Character of Earliest Christianity*. 3rd ed. London: SCM, 2006.

Evans, C. Stephen. "Canonicity, Apostolicity, and Biblical Authority: Some Kierkegaardian Reflections." In *Canon and Biblical Interpretation*. Edited by Craig G. Bartholomew, Scott Hahn, Robin Parry, Christopher Seitz, and Al Wolters. Scripture and Hermeneutics Series vol. 7. Grand Rapids, Mich.: Zondervan, 2006: 146-66

Farmer, William R. and Denis M. Farkasfalvy. *The Formation of the New Testament Canon*. New York: Paulist, 1983.

Forbes, Chris. "The Historical Jesus." In *The Content and Setting of the Gospel Tradition*. Edited by Mark Harding and Alanna Nobbs. Grand Rapids, Mich.: Eerdmans, 2010: 231-62.

Frei, Hans W. *The Eclipse of the Biblical Narrative: A Study in Eighteenth and Nineteenth Century Hermeneutics*. New Haven, Conn.: Yale University, 1974.

Gamble, Harry Y. "The New Testament Canon: Recent Research and the Statis Quaestionis." In *The Canon Debate*. Edited by Lee Martin McDonald and James A. Sanders. Peabody, Mass.: Hendrickson, 2002: 267-94.

Hasel, Gerhard F. *New Testament Theology: Basic Issues in the Current Debate*. Grand Rapids, Mich.: Eerdmans, 1978.

Heckel, T.K. *Von Evangelium des Markus zum viergestaltigen Evangelium*. WUNT vol. 120. Tübingen: Mohr & Siebeck, 1999.

Hengel, Martin. *The Four Gospels and the One Gospel of Jesus Christ*. Harrisburg, Penn: Trinity International, 2000.

Hoskyns, Edwyn and Noel Davey. *The Riddle of the New Testament*. London: Faber and Faber, 1958.

Jackson, T. Ryan. *New Creation in Paul's Letters: A Study of the Historical and Social Setting of a Pauline Concept*. WUNT vol. 272. Tübingen: Mohr Siebeck, 2010.

Kelley, Page H., Daniel S. Mynatt, and Timothy G. Crawford. *The Masorah of Biblia Hebraica Stuttgartensia: Introduction and Annotated Glossary*. Grand Rapids, Mich.: Eerdmans, 1998.

Kim, Seyoon. *Paul and the New Perspective: Second Thoughts on the Origin of Paul's Gospel*. Grand Rapids, Mich.: Eerdmans, 2002.

Klink III, Edward W., ed., *The Audience of the Gospels: The Origin and Function of the Gospels in Early Christianity*. LNTS vol. 353. New York: T & T Clark, 2010.

Kloha, Jeffrey. "The Problem of Paul's Letters: Loss of Authority and Meaning in the 'Canonical Approach' of Brevard Childs." *Concordia Journal* 35, no. 2 (Spring 2009): 156-69.

Koehler, Ludwig and Walter Baumgartner. *Hebrew-Aramaic Lexicon of the Old Testament (HALOT)*. 4 vols. Leiden: Brill, 2001.

Kürzinger, J. "Das Papiaszeugnis und die Erstgestalt des Matthäusevangeliums." *Biblische Zeitschrift* 4 (1960): 19-38.

Lønning, Inge. *'Kanon im Kanon': Zum dogmatischen Grundlagenproblem des neutestamentlichen Kanons*. Oslo: Universitets Forlaget, 1972.

Marshall, I. Howard. *New Testament Theology: Many Witnesses, One Gospel*. Downers Grove, Ill.: InterVarsity, 2004.

McDonald, Lee Martin. "Identifying Scripture and Canon in the Early Church: The Criteria Question." In *The Canon Debate*. Edited by Lee Martin McDonald and James A. Sanders. Peabody, Mass.: Hendrickson, 2002: 416-39.

Metzger, Bruce M. *A Textual Commentary on the Greek New Testament*. 2nd ed. Stuttgart: Deutsche Bibelgesellschaft, 2002.

Moule, C.F.D. *The Birth of the New Testament*. Black's New Testament Commentaries. 3rd ed. London: Adam & Charles Black, 1981.

Moulton and Geden. *Concordance to the Greek New Testament*. Edited by I. Howard Marshall. 6th ed. New York: T & T Clark, 2002.

Murphy-O'Conner, Jerome. *Paul the Letter-Writer: His World, His Options, His Skills*. Collegeville, Minn.: Liturgical Press, 1995.

Porter, Stanley E. "Paul and the Process of Canonization." In *Exploring the Origins of the Bible: Canon Formation in Historical, Literary, and Theological Perspective*. Edited by Craig A. Evans and Emmanuel Tov. Grand Rapids, Mich.: Baer Academic, 2008.

Rius-Camps, Josep and Jenny Read-Heimerdinger. *The Message of Acts in Codex Bezae*. 4 vols. London: T & T Clark, 2007.

Sandes, Karl Olav. *Paul – One of the Prophets? A Contribution to the Apostle's Self-Understanding*. WUNT vol. 43. Tübingen: Mohr Siebeck, 1991.

Savelle, Charles H. "A Reexamination of the Prohibitions in Acts 15." *Bibliotheca Sacra* 161 (Oct-Dec 2004): 449-68.

Schilling. "בשר *bśr*." In *Theological Dictionary of the Old Testament (TDOT), Volume 2 bdl-galah*. Edited by G. Johannes Botterweck and Helmer Ringgren. Grand Rapids, Mich.:Eerdmans, 1975.

Schmitz, O. θρόνος. *Theological Dictionary of the New Testament (TDNT), Volume 3*. Edited by Gerhard Kittel and Geoffrey W. Bromiley. Grand Rapids, Mich.: Eerdmans, 1965.

Skeat, T.C. "The Origin of the Christian Codex." *Zeitschrift für Papyrologie und Epigraphik* 102 (1994): 263-68.

Söding, Thomas. *Einheit der Heiligen Schrift? Zur Theologie des biblischen Kanons*. Freiburg: Herder, 2005.

Stanton, Graham N. *Jesus and Gospel*. Cambridge: University Press, 2004.

Thielman, Frank. *Theology of the New Testament: A Canonical and Synthetic Approach*. Grand Rapids, Mich.: Zondervan, 2005.

Trobisch, David. *Paul's Letter Collection: Tracing the Origins*. Minneapolis: Fortress, 1994.

----------. *The First Edition of the New Testament*. New York: Oxford University Press, 2000.

Ulrich, Eugene. "The Notion and Definition of Canon." In *The Canon Debate*. Edited by Lee Martin McDonald and James A. Sanders. Peabody, Mass.: Hendrickson, 2002: 21-35.

Vogels, Walter. "La Structure Symetrique de la bible Chretienee." *The Biblical Canons*. BETL vol. 163. Edited by J.M. Auwers and H.J. DeJonge. Leuven: University Press, 2003: 295-304.

Wallace, Daniel B. *Greek Grammar Beyond the Basics: An Exegetical Syntax of the New Testament*. Grand Rapids, Mich.: Zondervan, 1996.

Waters, Guy. *The End of Deuteronomy in the Epistles of Paul*. WUNT vol. 221. Tübingen: MohrSiebeck, 2006.

Wenham, David. *Paul: Follower of Jesus or Founder of Christianity?* Grand Rapids, Mich.: Eerdmans, 1995.

Wright, N.T. *The New Testament and the People of God*. Minneapolis: Fortress, 1992.

Welch, John W. "Chiasmus in the New Testament." In *Chiasmus in Antiquity: Structures, Analyses, Exegisis*. Edited by John W. Welch. Provo, Utah: Research Press, 1981: 211-49.

Sola Scriptura and Galatians 1:8-9:
Galatians' Prejudice against Alternative Interpretation[213]

Heerak Christian Kim
Asia Evangelical College and Seminary

The principle of the Reformation was premised on the idea that the Bible is the sole authority for Christian doctrine and practice. Thus, the Reformers coined the phrase, "Sola Scriptura" to emphasize the primacy of the Bible as the authoritative text to adjudicate theological debates and ecclesiastical decision. But the concept of Sola Scriptura is not exclusive in the Protestant domain. Since the earliest Christianity, there have been

---

[213] This was first presented as a shorter paper at the Paul's Letter to the Galatians & Christian Theology conference held on 10-13 July 2012 in St. Andrews, Scotland, at the University of St. Andrews. There were significant expansion and revision. I would like to thank the participants at the conference for their friendship and valuable comments. I would particularly like to thank Professor Mark Elliott, who is a very warm Christian person and a great scholar, for his kindness and generosity as the host of the conference. Prof. Elliott was instrumental in making everyone feel welcome and happy in St. Andrews, Scotland.

efforts to define the authority of the canon and enforce it as a guide in canon law and theological discourse. In my paper, I will identify the "Gospel" that is to be authoritative even over angels and describe the "another gospel" that is a "perverted Gospel" (Galatians 1:7) in the framework of the book of Galatians. I will describe the literary device of "Key Signifier" that is identifiable in the rhetoric of the writer of the Galatians and evaluate its effectiveness as a rhetorical tool. "Key Signifier" is a literary device that I have coined at the International Society of Biblical Literature Conference in Singapore, and its enumeration can be found in the book, *Key Signifier as Literary Device: Its Definition and Function in Literature and Media* (Edwin Mellon Press, 2006).

Simply put, the authoritative Gospel that St. Paul is espousing in the Epistle to Galatians[214] is the claim that salvation[215], or regeneration, is possible only[216] through faith in Christ Jesus[217], who is divine. This

---

[214] Bas Van Os argues that Galatians was carried to different Jewish communities and read aloud as oratory as if St. Paul were present. Like at Antioch, Galatians was meant to elicit a decision from Jewish Christians, whose identity is attested by the use of first person plural pronoun in Galatians 2:15 (Bas Van Os, "The Jewish Recipients of Galatians," in *Paul: Jew, Greek, and Roman*, ed. Stanley E. Porter {Leiden: Brill, 2008, pp. 51-64}, pp. 59-60). But Van Os admits the possibility that "we" can refer to Peter and Paul, and not the audience.

[215] Michel Foucault argues that in the first two centuries of the common era, the traditionally Platonic idea that individual salvation was integrally linked to the salvation of the city-state was inverted. Thus, whereas for Plato the salvation of the city-state was primary, in the Hellenistic era and in the Roman Empire, the salvation of the self (or the individual) was seen as primary. The Hellenistic logic was that one has to save oneself in order to be able to save others. Foucault explains: "The benefit for others, the salvation of others, or that way of being concerned about others that will make their salvation possible or help them in their own salvation, comes as a supplementary benefit of, or, if you like, follows as what is no doubt a necessary, although only correlative effect of the care you must take of yourself, of your will and application to achieve your own salvation" (Michel Foucault, *The Hermeneutics of the Subject: Lectures at the College de France, 1981-82*, trans. Graham Burchell {New York: Palgrave Macmillan, 2005}, p. 192). On one level, St. Paul is a product of his times; St. Paul is trying to save himself from the Judaizers, so that he would be able to save others.

[216] Wayne Meeks argues that emphasizing the oneness of God is characteristic of Paul's theology. Thus, by emphasizing one faith, St. Paul was affirming the oneness of God. Thus, St. Paul viewed Judaizers as deviating from the oneness of God. Meeks states: "We shall pass over Paul's *tour de force* in Galatians, in which he draws an analogy between the 'Judaizing' practices being urged by the latter-day missionaries and pagan

faith[218] involves the belief that Jesus Christ is God who can save. In a sense, therefore, St. Paul was forwarding the divine nature of Jesus Christ in the Epistle to Galatians. This is accomplished primarily through linking the unity of the means of salvation, or regeneration, in the Old Testament[219] and the New Testament.[220] St. Paul argues, in effect, that

---

polytheism (Gal. 4:8-11). Paul even sets the oneness of God against the multiplicity of mediation by which the Torah itself was given (3:19f.)" (Meeks, *The First Urban Christians*, p. 166).

[217] Jerry L. Sumney states: "There is no reason to think that their gospel does not include Christ..." (Jerry L. Sumney, *'Servants of Satan', 'False Brothers' and Other Opponents of Paul* {Sheffield: Sheffield Academic Press, 1999}, p. 137). See also Nikolaus Walter, "Paulus und die Gegner des Christusevangeliums in Galatien," in *L'apôtre Paul: Personnalité, style, et conception du ministère*, ed. A. Vanhoye {Leuven: Leuven University Press, 1986}, p. 351). But it is important to see that it is possible to see the arguments of the opponents through St. Paul's own apologetics.

[218] Panayotis Coutsoumpos states: "It is reasonable to assume that the apostle Paul is not attacking those who think that salvation derives from keeping the law, but those who insists on retaining those aspects of the law that separate Jews from Gentiles" (Panayotis Coutsoumpos, "Paul's Attitude towards the Law," in *Paul: Jew, Greek, and Roman*, ed. Stanley Porter {Leiden: Brill, 2008, pp. 39-50}, p. 45). The problem is that it is not reasonable to assume this. Galatians clearly describes an opposition between law and faith that cannot be glossed over.

[219] Panayotis Coutsoumpos states: "Consequently, the Judaism of Jerusalem, rather than the paganism of Tarsus, seems to be the root for Paul's approach to the problem of law" (Coutsoumpos, "Paul's Attitude towards the Law," p. 46). But this does not take into consideration the nature of Paul's radical conversion experience; there was a traumatic paradigm shift. Alan F. Segal states: "Paul does not forget his Jewish past; rather, he inverts the values of his past in a way that is consonant with his new commitments" (Alan F. Segal, *Paul the Convert: The Apostolate and Apostasy of Saul the Pharisee* {New Haven: Yale University Press, 1990), p. 125}. The important word to remember is "apostasy." The Twelve Benedictions show Judaism's fear of apostates and prescribes excommunication for them. Jewish self-identity marker was poignantly in motion at that time, and this cannot be ignored. See Heerak Christian Kim, *The Jerusalem Tradition in the Late Second Temple Period: Diachronic and Synchronic Developments Surrounding Psalms of Solomon 11* (Lanham: University Press of America, 2007) to understand better developments in the "Judaism of Jerusalem."

[220] Vern Poythress states: "The whole Old Testament finds its focus in Jesus Christ, His death, and His resurrection" (Vern S. Poythress, *The Shadow of Christ in the Law of Moses* {Phillipsburg: P. & R. Publishing, 1991}, p. 5). From the earliest strata of Christianity, the Old Testament was appropriated by early Christians for themselves. Galatians provides a concrete example of how St. Paul wrested the Old Testament away from Judaizers/Judaism.

those who received salvation, or regeneration, in the Old Testament era also received salvation by the same means that the New Testament era people do; namely, by faith.[221] And this faith is assumed to be the faith in Jesus Christ.

Merely by emphasizing the unity of the means of salvation in the Old Testament and the New Testament, that of faith in Jesus Christ, St. Paul is assuming the divinity of Jesus Christ.[222] This can be seen as a rhetorical[223] tool, employed by St. Paul. St. Paul does not argue explicitly that Jesus Christ existed at the time of Abraham. St. Paul merely assumes, and St. Paul expects his listeners to simply agree with this assumption.[224]

---

[221] Philip Esler states: "In the face of solidly based claims that Israelite righteousness and the Mosaic law were inextricably connected, he proposes an alternative mode of access – from faith in Christ, not from the law" (Philip F. Esler, *Galatians* {London: Routledge, 1998}, p. 171).

[222] G. Walter Hansen writes: "The phrase *God sent his Son* is taken by some interpreters as merely a reference to the prophetic mission of Jesus. As the prophets of old were sent by God, so Jesus was sent by God for a special redemptive mission. The background may be found in the parable Jesus told about the wicked tenants of the vineyard (MK 12:1-12): the owner of the vineyard (God) first sent messengers (prophets), who were killed by the tenants (Jewish leaders); then he sent his own son (Jesus), who was also killed. But in light of Paul's other references to the preexistence of the Son (see 1 Cor 8:6; Phil 2:5-8; Col 1:15-17), we may also see here an affirmation of the deity of Jesus. Before the incarnation, the preexistent Son was commissioned by God to set slaves free and make them children of God" (G. Walter Hansen, *Galatians* {Downers Grove, IL: InterVarsity Press, 1994}, p. 118). In other words, the assumption of the pre-existence of Jesus of Nazareth is claim to his divinity.

[223] Rhetorical tools must be distinguished from classical rhetoric, which was often attached to the law courts. Philip H. Kern writes: "This, to be sure, begs the question of Paul's use of classical rhetoric; and we will argue from several lines of evidence that he did not employ it – forcing the conclusion that some scholars impose handbook categories upon texts which result from other types of rhetoric. In other words, the boundaries distinguishing various levels of rhetoric, and segregating rhetoric of the same level, are being overlooked or ignored. What can readings based on such oversight offer other than a distorted and anachronistic readings?" (Philip H. Kern, *Rhetoric and Galatians: Assessing an Approach to Paul's Epistles* {Cambridge: Cambridge University Press, 1998}, p. 21).

[224] Leander E. Keck argues that there is a need for a renewal of the study of Christology from a theological perspective. Keck states: "'Christology' is a comprehensive term for the statement of the identity and significance of Jesus. .... Accordingly, the subject matter of Christology is really the syntax of relationships or correlations. In developed Christology this structure of signification is expressed in relation to God (the theological

Galatians as Examined by Diverse Academics

This assumption points to the established and accepted notion of the deity of Christ and his pre-existence, which in fact functions as the proof of his divinity. For St. Paul, faith that saves is the faith in Jesus Christ, who is divine.

In the Galatians passage, St. Paul argues that it was by faith that Abraham was saved, or regenerated. St. Paul makes the link with Abraham for several reasons. First, because the only coherent written body of religious text available to the new converts to Christianity was the Old Testament, most likely propagated in the Greek translation, or the Septuagint, it could have been possible for converts to Christianity from paganism to mistake the value of Judaism and Jewish interpretation[225] in the Christian religion. Judaizers were Jews[226] who joined Christianity[227],

---

correlation proper), the created order (the cosmological correlation) and humanity (the anthropological correlation); each of these impinges on the others whether or not this impingement is made explicit" (Leander E. Keck, "Toward the Renewal of New Testament Christology," in *From Jesus to John: Essays on Jesus and New Testament Christology in Honour of Marinus de Jonge*, ed. Martinus C. De Boer {Sheffield: Sheffield Academic Press, 1993, pp. 321-340}, pp. 322-323). A question that must be raised is whether the assumption that Christology developed later in early Christianity is accurate; it is possible that there was a form of Christology within the ministry of Jesus of Nazareth as there was messianism in the earliest Qumran documents. The possibility of a well-developed Christology at the time of Jesus of Nazareth gains greater currency in light of Qumran's 4Q246, better known as the "Son of God" text. In this text, the messiah is identified as "Son of God" (John J. Collins, "The *Son of God* Text from Qumran," in *From Jesus to John: Essays on Jesus and New Testament Christology in Honour of Marinus de Jonge*, ed. Martinus C. De Boer {Sheffield: Sheffield Academic Press, 1993, pp. 65-82}, pp. 65-66).

[225] Kjell Arne Morland states that St. Paul customarily stood against Jewish interpretation of the Old Testament. Morland writes: "Undoubtedly, almost every time Paul cites the Hebrew Bible to support his understanding of righteousness, law, and faith, he is in opposition to Jewish exegesis (Koch 1986:299-300). Thus a Hebrew Bible citation also involves a dispute about its true meaning, and we are virtually every time cast into a discussion relating to the stasis presented above" (Kjell Arne Morland, *The Rhetoric of Curse in Galatians: Paul Confronts Another Gospel* {Atlanta: Scholars Press, 1995}, p 126).

[226] James D. G. Dunn agrees that the agitators in Galatia were Jewish and that they were an identifiable, distinct group. Dunn writes: "But the fact that Paul always refers to the troublemakers in the third person, while addressing his converts in the second person, strongly suggests that the two groups are distinct. Moreover, the emphasis throughout the letter indicates that the terms of the dispute were Jewish through and through, and

who emphasized that Jewish laws[228] must be kept in the manner that was exposited by leaders in Judaism.[229] These Judaizers emphasized the value

---

probably so perceived through Jewish eyes. .... Most commentators therefore conclude that the agitators were Jews" (James D. G. Dunn *The Theology of Paul's Letter to the Galatians* {Cambridge: Cambridge University Press, 1993}, p. 8)

[227] Dunn agrees that these were Jews who had converted to Christianity. Dunn writes: (p. 9) – "It is even clearer that the 'troublemakers' were, like Paul, Christian Jews, that is, believers in Jesus as Messiah and followers of his 'way' (Acts 24.14, 22). This is obvious inference from the fact that Paul acknowledges, however grudgingly, that they claimed to preach the 'gospel of Christ' (1.6-9), since the word 'gospel' was already a distinctively Christian term" (Dunn, *The Theology of Paul's Letter to the Galatians*, p. 9). However, "another Gospel" could function like the "anti-Gospel" in the same way that "anti-Christ" is a foil for "Christ" in the New Testament.

[228] William N. Wilder states: "That the phrase 'under the law' ... should refer to a condition of bondage with particular reference to law-observing Jew is, even before any contextual considerations, suggested by the phrase itself. The preposition [*hupo*] conveys, if not the idea of bondage *per se*, at least the hegemony of the law over those in its realm. The word [*nomos*], on the other hand, is most naturally a reference to the Mosaic law, itself an exclusive covenant between God and the Jewish people. The simplest interpretation of the phrase, therefore, is one which emphasizes the authority of the law over the Jewish people. Only if this interpretation cannot be sustained in a given passage should recourse be made to extending or universalizing its meaning" (William N. Wilder, *Echoes of the Exodus Narrative in the Context and Background of Galatians 5:18* {New York: Peter Lang, 2001}, p. 77).

[229] Philip Esler states that there was pressure from leaders in Judaism on Jewish converts to Christianity to alienate the Gentiles. Esler writes: "That the gentile members believed, or were at risk of believing, that righteousness was obtained in this way must have resulted from persuasion by Israelite Christ-followers, since these were the Israelites with whom they had the closest dealings. Yet these Israelite members were themselves under pressure from other Israelites to end their anomalous boundary violation with gentiles (Gal. 6.12-13). This means that righteousness must have been at home in the wider Judaic community. The discussion of the law in the *Letter of Aristeas* which we examined in Chapter 3 brings out this position quite unambiguously; there righteousness was depicted as essential in designating the condition of Israelites *vis-à-vis* the gentiles" (Esler, *Galatians*, p. 143). In other words, because of peer-pressure from Jews in Judaism to stay away from the Gentiles, Jewish converts to Christianity sought to judaize Christians, so that they might become acceptable for association in the eyes of Jews of Judaism. Esler writes: "For Israelites in the first century, as we saw in Chapter 3, the Mosaic law played a leading role in the operation of the boundary which preserved their distinctive identity in relation to the gentiles among whom they lived. The Israelite push for the circumcision of gentile Christ-followers in Galatia stemmed from a sense of anomy – and anomaly – provoked by the breach of one aspect of this law, namely, a

of circumcision[230] and Jewish law observance that mirrored the emphasis of Jewish leaders in Judaism,[231] particularly the Pharisees.[232] These

---

proscription on table-fellowship between Israelites and gentiles (In the full sense), which was under threat from the Eucharistic practice of Paul's congregations" (Esler, *Galatians*, p. 178).

[230] Hansen notes: (p. 15) – "But not long after Paul planted the churches in Galatia, some Jewish Christians taught these new believers that it was necessary to belong to the Jewish people in order to receive the full blessing of God. Therefore they required the marks of identity peculiar to the Jewish people: circumcision, Sabbath observance and kosher food (see 2:12-14; 4:10; 5:2-3; 6:12-13). No doubt they used the story of Abraham's willingness to be circumcised to persuade the Galatian believers that without membership in the Jewish people by circumcision they could not participate in the covenantal blessings promised to Abraham. Evidently they also preempted Paul's authority by claiming support from the higher authority of the original apostles in the Jerusalem church. They probably pointed out that the mother church in Jerusalem still faithfully followed Jewish customs" (Hansen, *Galatians*, p. 15). In other words, Judaizers were espousing the view that Gentiles had to become a member of Judaism to be saved, thereby blurring the distinction between Judaism and Christianity.

[231] Esler states that Jewish identity distinction in Late Antiquity is historically significant. Esler writes: "From a social-scientific perspective, the existence of groups of people who called themselves *Israelitai* after a putative ancestor, Israel, and who were referred to by their contemporaries as *Ioudaioi* ('Judeans') from the geographic area of the eastern Mediterranean – Judea – from which they were thought ultimately to hail, living among gentiles in places as far from Palestine as Galatia, demands attention be paid to the whole question of ethnicity. This factor contributed significantly to their distinctiveness as a group and must be taken into account in considering how they related to other groups" (Esler, Galatians, p. 78). Obviously, if Jews militantly guarded their distinctive identity and refused assimilation, then such an identity protection would play a significant role within those who stay in the group as well as those who join another group. In the case of the Judaizers, who are Jewish converts to Christianity, their Jewish group identity dominated.

[232] Ronald Y. K. Fung states: "It was zeal for this ancestral law, an intense personal concern for its fulfillment, which provided both the inspiration and the vehicle of expression for Paul's progress in the Jewish religion, and it would seem that his 'advance' had to do, primarily and especially, with 'the achievement of righteousness according to the standards and ideals of Pharisaism.' It was the same zeal, moreover, which led to his implacable hostility towards Christianity and intense persecution of the Church, for a direct relation is clearly implied between vv. 13b and 14b. The parallel construction of the two clauses is seen most clearly in the Greek but remains recognizable in a more literal rendering like the RV.... This parallelism serves to enhance the thought that Paul's hostility to the Church was the outcome of his devotion to the law (cf. Phil. 3:5f.; Acts 22:3f.). From this it would appear that even before he turned to Christ Paul had

Galatians as Examined by Diverse Academics

Judaizers made it seem as if such Jewish law observance was necessary even for Christian salvation.[233] Certainly, such interpretation of Judaizers assumed that the faith in Jesus Christ was not sufficient for salvation, or regeneration.[234] Thus, for St. Paul, linking Christian salvation with the salvation of Abraham was important in bypassing and contradicting the

---

realized distinctly the essential incompatibility between Christianity and Judaism, and in particular the threat which the new faith posed to the supremacy of the law" (Ronald Y. K. Fung, *The Epistle to the Galatians* {Grand Rapids: William B. Eerdmans Publishing Company, 1988}, p. 57).

[233] Dunn agrees that these Judaizers were trying to impose Judaism on Christians. Dunn writes: "If then the opponents were Christian Jews who had come to the Galatian churches from outside, who were they and how should we refer to them? 'Troublemaker' is, of course, Paul's own way of referring to them and hardly provides an unbiased description, rather the irascible response of one who felt his authority under threat. Traditionally they have been called 'judaizers', meaning those who attempt to bring others within Judaism. This is unfortunate since the word is drawn directly from the Greek, *ioudaizein*, which means 'to live like a Jew, according to Jewish customs,' *not* to impose Judaism on *others*. Furthermore, the latter, inaccurate meaning reinforces a view of Judaism as strongly evangelistic at this time, which although also widely held, is again almost certainly false, at least as an appropriate generalization" (Dunn, *The Theology of Paul's Letter to the Galatians*, p. 10). Dunn might be mistaken about the proselytizing nature of Judaism. There were God-fearers, who were Gentiles who had taken upon themselves observance of Jewish laws at the time, which would not have been possible if there had not been proselytizing effort of sorts. Furthermore, Professor Jon Levenson, who is the Albert List Professor of Jewish Studies at Harvard University, has told me in conversation that *The Genesis Apocryphon* shows that Jewish proselytism was active in this time period because Abraham and Sarah are portrayed as proselytizing in the Jewish primary source composed in the Late Antiquity.

[234] This is why J. Gresham Machen differentiates between the Judaizers and the Early Christian church. Machen states: "But in the early period, in Jerusalem, before it had become evident that the Jewish people as such was to reject the gospel message, the apostles continued to observe the Law. And by doing so, they gave the Judaizers some color of support. Thus if Judaizers did appeal to the original apostles in support of their legalistic claims, the appeal does not establish any real unity of principle between them and the original apostles, or any divergence of principle between the original apostles and Paul. But as a matter of fact it is by no means perfectly clear that the appeal was made; it is by no means clear that the Judaizers appealed to the original apostles for the content of their legalistic message rather than merely for their attack upon the independent apostleship of Paul (J. Gresham Machen, *The Origin of Paul's Religion* {Grand Rapids: Wm. B. Eerdmans Publishing Company, 1925}, p. 128).

version of Old Testament salvation as offered by Judaism,[235] and by extension, by the Judaizers.[236] Those within the Jewish religion[237]

---

[235] John J. Gunther states: "His insistence that he himself was not under the law of Moses witnesses to his break with Judaism" (John J. Gunther, *St. Paul's Opponents and Their Background: A Study of Apocalyptic and Jewish Sectarian Teachings* {Leiden: E. J. Brill, 1973), p. 62}. Trying to force St. Paul into Judaism when St. Paul exerted so much effort against it seems historically unethical.

[236] Esler emphasizes the social dimension of St. Paul's rhetorical strategy. St. Paul homogenized means of salvation as by means of faith in the Old Testament and the New Testament in order to drive a wedge between Judaism and Christianity. Esler writes: "In common with many other group leaders then and since, Paul engages in stereotyping to achieve this end. His aim is to help his audience learn to perceive and interpret a complex reality in a certain simplified way. He does this by insisting that the members of the two relevant groups have the same qualities in critical areas, favourable ones in the case of the ingroup and unfavourable ones in ... the outgroup. Accordingly, just as he has previously affirmed that those who depend on faith are the sons of Abraham (3.7) and share his blessing (3.9), now he proceeds immediately to insist that those who rely on law are under a curse (3.10). This is an example of extreme and rigid stereotyping, of the type mentioned in Chapter 2 as flourishing in conditions, as here, where the ingroup has a limited repertoire of positive social identities and must seek fiercely to preserve them, and where their low status is regarded, at least by their leaders, as illegitimate and capable of modification" (Esler, Galatians, p. 185). Thus, St. Paul intentionally portrays Jewish Law as evil, so that us-versus-them would be clearly established against Judaism for the early Christians.

[237] The friction between Christianity and Judaism seems to be a constant, and there is great sensitivity even among academics teaching in universities. One good example is found in the voice of the Director of the United Methodist Church's Boston University's Division of Religious and Theological Studies, which combines Boston University's Department of Religion and Boston University's School of Theology, which trains seminary students for ordination in the United Methodist Church and students from other Christian denominations who opt to receive their theological training at the United Methodist Church institution. The Director's name is Jonathan Klawans, who is Jewish. Professor Klawans writes: "Indeed, scholars of ancient Judaism in particular can exhibit a heightened form of anxiety with theology, one that has been understandably hardened by the clearly anti-Semitic descriptions of ancient Judaism by, especially, certain influential European seminarians. Julius Wellhausen, for instance, praised Christian faith (that is, Protestant faith) and denigrated rabbinic 'legalism" and "intellectualism" (in a word, Judaism)" (Jonathan Klawans, *Josephus and the Theologies of Ancient Judaism* {Oxford: Oxford University Press, 2012}, pp. 1-2). If praising Christianity and calling Judaism as legalistic is "anti-Semitic," then most Americans are "anti-Semitic"; clearly, if Professor Klawans' *ad hominem* attack is true, then Jesus of Nazareth and St. Paul are "anti-Semitic."

presumed that believers in the Old Testament were saved by keeping the law.[238] St. Paul was arguing that this was not the case.[239] Those in the Old Testament were saved, or regenerated, by faith in Jesus Christ,[240] just as the people in the New Testament time.[241] This assumed the divinity of Jesus Christ because such faith presupposes pre-existence of Jesus Christ. This was a conscious effort by St. Paul to drive a wedge between Judaism and Christianity.[242] St. Paul wanted Christians, both Jew and Gentile, to

---

[238] Eduard Lohse encapsulates the dominant Jewish perception at the beginning of the common era: "While the Torah was already existent in heaven, before it was delivered to Moses without any human collaboration, the other writings were written down by men under divine inspiration. Therefore the Law unequivocally deserves the highest rank, and all other scriptures only receive their authority from it. Canonical recognition is ascribed to them solely on the basis of their agreement with the Torah" (Eduard Lohse, *The New Testament Environment*, trans. John E. Steely {Nashville: Abingdon Press, 1976}, p. 167). Such an emphasis on the Law explains why early Christians and St. Paul were odious to Judaizers and Judaism.

[239] Franz From warns: "Because we simply see what people do, and because the experience of intention and purpose is not the result of a conscious process of deduction from the events we perceive but is something immediately apparent, it has been possible to make the peculiar mistake of regarding behavior with its inherent purpose as something belonging to a sphere of objective facts. And in making this mistake, which might be called the 'behavioristic fallacy,' the important task of elucidating how we experience behavior has in my opinion been grossly neglected" (Franz From, *Perception of Other People*, trans. Erik Kvan and Brendan Maher {New York: Columbia University Press, 1971}, p. 2).

[240] Vern Poythress explains what it meant for Israelites in the Old Testament to be saved by faith in Jesus Christ: "Israelites had genuine communion with God when they responded to what He was saying in the tabernacle. They trusted in the Messiah, without knowing all the details of how fulfillment would finally come. And so they were saved, and they received forgiveness, even before the Messiah came. The animal sacrifices in themselves did not bring forgiveness (Hebrews 10:1-4), but Christ did as He met with them through the symbols of the sacrifices" (Poythress, *The Shadow of Christ*, p. 11).

[241] Marinus de Jonge explains: "Early Christians recognized that a radical discontinuity between the Christ of their faith and the man Jesus would be fatal to their kerygma" (Marinus de Jonge, *Jesus, The Servant-Messiah* {New Haven: Yale University Press, 1991}, p. 28).

[242] St. Paul argued vehemently for the guilt of the Jews in the killing of Jesus of Nazareth. Marinus de Jonge states regarding 1 Thessalonians 2:15-16: "In this passage, a small digression in the letter, Paul draws on traditional material to link the killing of Jesus, who is named first and is expressly called 'the Lord,' with the killing of the prophets and the persecution of Jesus' followers" (De Jonge, *Jesus, The Servant Messiah*, pp. 34-35). De

make a clean break with Judaism and Jewish interpretation,[243] which emphasized salvation through keeping of the Jewish law.[244] Thus, for St. Paul, another Gospel is the emphasis that people can be saved by keeping the law,[245] including past people in the Old Testament.

Thus, it was natural for St. Paul to emphasize that the salvation of Abraham was through faith, rather than through the law.[246] St. Paul

---

Jonge identifies this idea to the oldest strata of early Christianity (p. 33). This can be seen as St. Paul's effort to define group identity at the expense of another group. Galatians presents a similar effort at group identity, but from another angle.

[243] Seyoon Kim argues that E. P. Sanders, Bruce Longenecker, and Heikki Räisänen agreed that it was St. Paul's conversion experience to Christianity (through faith in Christ) that led St. Paul to condemn Judaism and its legalism (Seyoon Kim, *Paul and the New Perspective: Second Thoughts on the Origin of Paul's Gospel* {Grand Rapids: William B. Eerdmans Publishing Company, 2002}, p. 144). Indeed, this represents the consensus position on Galatians research.

[244] Gunther states: "Propagators of the false gospel apparently were teaching that the privileges accruing to the seed of Abraham could be received by Gentiles only by obeying the law..." (Gunther, *St. Paul's Opponents and Their Backgrounds*, p. 74). This illustrates that the "false gospel" was a form of Judaism. Gentiles, or God-Fearers, at the time could join Judaism in the exact same manner of observing the Torah. Thus, the espousers of the "false gospel" could have been Jewish leaders who wanted to win Jews back to Judaism (and Gentiles for Judaism), and they might not have necessarily been Jewish Christians.

[245] What characterized Jewish groups in the first century is an effort to validate the Jewish law. Gerd Theissen states: "The various groupings and movements within Jewish society in the first century C.E. can be understood as different attempts to secure validity for this Law, whether by means of an interpretive adjustment to the manifold and altered circumstances of life (Pharisees), or by means of a consistent implementation of the Law in an unusually disciplined community cut off from society (Qumran), or by means of the political implementation of radicalized first commandment which authorizes acts of terrorism against those seen as violating it (Zealots). In each case we have an intensification of the Law" (Gerd Theissen, *The Social Setting of Pauline Christianity*, Trans. John H. Schütz {Philadelphia: Fortress Press, 1982}, pp. 32-33). In contrast, St. Paul takes a hostile attitude towards the Law.

[246] Daniel Boyarin refers to Richard Hays's argument against supersessionist nature of Paul's theology to argue that St. Paul regarded the Christian community as being in continuity with the historical Israel (Daniel Boyarin, *A Radical Jew: Paul and the Politics of Identity* {Berkeley and Los Angeles: University of California Press, 1994}, p. 31). The problem is that the definition or the nature of "the historical Israel" is not universally agreed, either at St. Paul's time or in ours. In fact, that is precisely the point for St. Paul. For St. Paul, Abraham was saved by faith and not by the law, in the same way that the Galatian Christians are saved by faith and not by the law. Certainly, St. Paul

Galatians as Examined by Diverse Academics

assumes that this faith was faith in Jesus Christ as God. And there is another reason why St. Paul explicitly makes the link to Abraham. In the Gospels, Jesus of Nazareth himself makes the link to Abraham. Jesus of Nazareth claims that Abraham was saved by faith. And the Gospel pericope makes it clear that this faith is the faith in Jesus Christ, who existed before the time of Abraham. John 8:58[247] establishes the pre-existence of Christ in the words of Jesus of Nazareth: "'Very truly I tell you,' Jesus answered, 'before Abraham was born, I am!'"[248] This pre-existence obviously is a claim to the divinity of Jesus Christ[249], since

---

argues for continuity between the Old Testament and the New Testament, but not in the same way that Daniel Boyarin assumes.

[247] Marinus de Jonge recognizes the early dating of Mark and Q, but states: "Of course, some material found only in Matthew and Luke, and even individual pieces of tradition recorded only in the Fourth Gospel, may also go back to an earlier date" (De Jonge, *Jesus, The Servant Messiah*, p.2). But D. Moody Smith argues that the Gospel of John is dependent historically on the Synoptic Gospels, but finds "I am" sayings as "historically suspect" since it contrasts with the Synoptics, in which "Jesus can scarcely be coaxed into talking about himself" (D. Moody Smith, "Historical Issues and the Problem of John and the Synoptics," in *From Jesus to John: Essays on Jesus and New Testament Christology in Honour of Marinus de Jonge*, ed. Martinus C. De Boer {Sheffield: Sheffield Academic Press, 1993,pp. 252-267}, p. 255). But this superficial conclusion must be reassessed. Since Jesus of Nazareth engaged in three years of ministry, in which he mostly spoke, it is possible that John records accurately the sayings of Jesus of Nazareth.

[248] The pre-existence of Christ, which is necessary for Abraham's salvation through faith in Christ, should not be seen as merely Pauline theology impacting Johannine Christology. The concept of pre-existence of Christ is multiply attested also in Luke 20:41-44, in which King David is described as having known Christ. The question is: Did Jesus of Nazareth claim to be pre-existent? The multiply attested passages In Galatians, John, and Luke seem to answer, "Yes." Thus, there is high probability that this claim goes back to the earliest strata of Jesus sayings.

[249] Matthew 26:64-68 describes Jewish High Priest accusing Jesus of Nazareth of blasphemy, because he claimed to be divine. Claiming to be a messiah is not blasphemy, but claiming to come back on the clouds of heaven is theophany and claim to divinity. See Deuteronomy 31:15 and Exodus 34:5. Since God appeared in or on the cloud, Jesus of Nazareth's use of the clouds was a key signifier that triggered the collective memory of the Jewish High Priests and the members of the Jewish Supreme Court (Sanhedrin) and then second-triggered a response, that of wanting to kill Jesus of Nazareth on charge of blasphemy. F. F. Bruce states: "Not only so; in speaking of the Son of Man as coming with the clouds of heaven he applied to himself the language of Daniel 7:13f. There is evidence for certain strands of Jewish interpretation of Daniel's reference to 'one like a

Galatians as Examined by Diverse Academics

humans cannot be pre-existent. Thus, there was a rhetorical strategy of emphasizing salvation through faith in Jesus of Nazareth as God in the earliest Christian communities.

It is important to note that sayings of Jesus Christ was pro-actively propagated within early Christian communities and utilized as evangelization tools. Thus, the Gospel pericope in which Jesus of Nazareth claims that Abraham was justified by faith was widely known among early Christians,[250] as most Americans know the story of Count Dracula. St. Paul makes a link to Abraham's salvation by faith because he knows that his listeners and readers would be familiar with the story of how Jesus of Nazareth taught that Abraham was saved, or regenerated, by faith in Him. Thus, the concept that Abraham was saved by faith can be seen as a key signifier for early Christians. Key Signifier is a literary device that I coined in the book, *Key Signifier as Literary Device: Its Definition and Function in Literature and Media* (Edwin Mellon Press, 2006).

Key signifier has a double trigger function. Key signifier triggers the collective memory[251] of readers, or listeners, because the story, concept, word, or phrase used is imbedded in the collective memory of the audience.[252] The second trigger is cause to action. After the collective

---

son of man' which viewed this figure as almost the peer of God" (Bruce, *New Testament History*, p. 198). Certainly, early Christians appropriated divine attributes to Jesus Christ: "Yet they also accord to the crucified and resurrected Messiah, Jesus, some titles and functions that in the Bible and Jewish tradition were attributed only to God" (Meeks, *The First Urban Christians*, p. 190). The claim of Jesus of Nazareth to divinity can be traced to the earliest strata of the Jesus movement and to the sayings of Jesus.

[250] In fact, Philip Esler dates the Epistle to the Galatians within about a decade or two from the death of Jesus of Nazareth on the cross. Esler writes: "Paul wrote his letter to the congregations of Galatia (located in Turkey) some time in the period from the late 40s to the mid-50s of the first century CE. It is a short document, comprising six chapters and totaling only 149 verses, yet packed with historical, social and theological material of the highest significance" (Esler, *Galatians*, p. 1). Thus, there were many eye witnesses to the preaching of Jesus of Nazareth, and they were shared among Christian believers.

[251] Esler writers: "Effective rhetorical discourse presupposes that the speaker and his or her audience share a basic understanding of the facts at issue and some measure of communality as far as beliefs and values are concerned" (Esler, *Galatians*, p. 18). Another way to describe this is with the phrase, "collective memory."

[252] Wayne Meeks notes that St. Paul's arguments in Galatians presuppose common collective memory/consciousness. Meeks writes: "The Letter to Galatians illustrates

memory is triggered, the audience reacts or acts in a certain way because of the manner in which the collective memory was triggered or because of the *Sitz im Leben*[253] of the audience[254] itself. In the case of the book of Galatians, both are operative in the second triggering process. The audience had been bombarded with Jewish propaganda that it was through the law that a person is saved, or regenerated. This Jewish propaganda was disseminated by so-called Christian leaders in their midst. This created confusion among early Christians.[255] It is in this Sitz im Leben, St.

---

another way as well in which Paul's innovations resemble the model of a millenarian prophet. He defines and defends the radically new order in terms drawn from the old. Not only does his argument presuppose familiarity with the notion of the one God who controls the future in accord with his promises, make revelations, judges the world, and so on; it also draws its proofs from the scripture and traditions of Israel" (Meeks, *The First Urban Christians*, p. 176).

[253] Esler emphasizes: "As noted above, the overall view I take to the New Testament documents is that they are communications from our ancestors in faith to their contemporaries on matters they deemed of great moment. In this context it can be argued (and I do not put it higher than this) that we are under an ethical obligation to seek, at some stage in the process of interpretation, to hear and understand their own voices in the historical context in which they were uttered, rather than rejecting such meaning in favour of the meanings we might produce from a text alleged to exist autonomously in relation to the circumstances of its creation" (Esler, *Galatians*, p. 24). The historical context should, therefore, be deemed significant in any analysis.

[254] Kern argues that the textual reflection of the conflict as it relates to the immediate audience is more significant. Kern writes: "Indeed if one chooses to pursue historical questions, Galatians can be thought to relate to two contexts. First, the immediate 'rhetorical situation' of the letter, the exigency which led Paul to write, may be considered. It is difficult, in fact, to imagine how Galatians can be understood apart from the conflict which it addresses. For better or for worse, we possess only the text itself as a source of data concerning this conflict, and so this investigation is text-centered. Second, the more general social world inhabited by Paul and the Galatians is open to investigation, though it might not contribute much to understanding the text. In fact, Galatians might reveal more about Paul's social world than that social world reveals about Galatians – a prospect which some will find stimulating. This second approach naturally welcomes data from sources outside the text as it attempts to recreate Paul's microcosm" (Kern, *Rhetoric and Galatians*, p. 76).

[255] Most scholars agree that Jesus of Nazareth called for the destruction of the Jewish Temple in Jerusalem. Howard Clark Kee describes: "Jesus, however, announces the temple's destruction without regret, and with no promise of its renewal, such as the Essenes expected to occur. The gospel tradition reports as his clear declaration that God has a new structure 'not made with hands' (Mark 14:58) in which he will dwell" (Howard

Galatians as Examined by Diverse Academics

Paul utilizes manner of triggering collective memory that can be described as "rhetorical violence." Thus, both the manner of triggering the collective memory and the Sitz im Leben of the audience functioned in the first trigger[256] and the second trigger. The first trigger is the triggering of the collective memory/understanding of early Christians that Abraham was saved by faith in Jesus Christ who is divine. The idea or phrase that Abraham is saved by faith was the key signifier that effectuated the first trigger. In the Sitz im Leben of St. Paul and the Galatian Christian communities, the phrase or idea that "Abraham was saved by faith" would trigger the collective memory of the sayings of Jesus which stated the same thing along with the explanation that he existed before Abraham. The idea that Jesus Christ is God and is pre-existent was already accepted and assumed, and thus this was already in the collective consciousness of the early Christians. And the sayings of Jesus that Abraham was saved by faith in Jesus who is God were already common among the early Christians.

In other words, the concept that is attested in the Gospel of John was ubiquitous in early Christian communities, although it was more fully explained in the Gospel of John. That is why St. Paul could assume that his listeners/readers understood that faith was faith in Jesus Christ who is God because that idea had become commonly accepted idea by the time

---

Clark Kee, *Knowing the Truth: A Sociological Approach to New Testament Interpretation* {Minneapolis: Fortress Press, 1989}, p. 86). Jesus of Nazareth attacked the Jewish Temple in Jerusalem and the Jewish Law vociferously, and this was in the collective consciousness of early Christians.

[256] Wayne Meeks explains that St. Paul intentionally modified the extant system of belief to include Jesus Christ as the Messiah; thus, Paul's theology cannot be separated from his Christology. Meeks writes: "For Paul, the paradox of the crucified Messiah became the key to a paradoxical relation between the movement of Jesus' followers and the established structures of Judaism in the Roman world. The Christians identify the 'one God' of Jewish worship, the God of the Fathers, as 'he who raised Jesus from the dead' (Rom. 4:24; 8:11; 2 Cor. 4:14; Gal. 1:1; Col. 2:12; 1 Thess. 1:10; cf. 2 Cor. 1:9). The result is a structural shift of the whole pattern of beliefs, so that Pauline theology, in the narrow sense, cannot be separated from Christology. The belief in the crucified Messiah introduces a new and controlling paradigm of God's mode of action" (Meeks, *The First Urban Christians*, p. 180). The position that Jews of St. Paul's time tolerated such a paradigm does not jive with ancient Jewish history and the characteristics of early Judaism(s).

Galatians as Examined by Diverse Academics

that St. Paul penned his epistle to the churches of Galatia. St. Paul was aware of the commonality of the idea that he can use it in his rhetoric to persuade the churches of Galatia to oppose his attackers, who emphasized the Jewish law.[257] If there had not been collective memory to draw from, the rhetorical attack would not have worked.[258] Because it was already assumed to be fact that Jesus Christ is the pre-existent God and because the sayings of Jesus of Nazareth that Abraham was saved by faith was ubiquitous that St. Paul could use the idea that Abraham was saved by faith as a rhetorical device. The very important point is that St. Paul does not focus on explaining what it meant for Abraham to be saved by faith; he merely uses this concept as a peg in his argument. This could not have been effective as a rhetorical tool, unless there was common acceptance of the idea. St. Paul was aware of his audience, and as an individual living in his own Sitz im Leben, he understood the power of his rhetoric, which appealed to collective consciousness. This is why identifying key signifiers is significant for understanding of the Sitz im Leben.

Key Signifiers and their double trigger could only work when there is collective consciousness/memory.[259] Thus, correctly identifying the key

---

[257] Jacques Derrida states: "If one is not to lose the enemy, one must know who he is, and what, in the past, the word 'enemy' always designated – more precisely, what it must have designated. No, what it *should have* designated" (Jacques Derrida, *Politics of Friendship*, trans. George Collins {London: Verso, 1997}, p. 88). The Judaizers fit Derrida's definition of "enemy" for St. Paul and for early Christians (Johannine community; sayings of Jesus). St. Paul is saying that salvation was always by faith, even in the Old Testament. Galatians, thus, describes the "enemy" relationship between early Christians on the one hand and Judaizers/Judaism on the other. That is why St. Paul could say, "Go to Hell!" to the Judaizers in early Christian churches' public contexts.

[258] Derrida makes a helpful assessment of historically engrained friend/enemy dialectics, which shed light on what happened in Galatia. Derrida describes why Europe will always fight against Islam. Islam represents the enemy of the political, that is the European. This structural assessment sheds equally valid light on why St. Paul and early Christianity fought against Judaizers/Judaism. Derrida states: "Although it can never be reduced to a question of language or discourse, the differentiated rooting of this friend/enemy opposition in certain idioms could never be considered accidental or extrinsic. It recalls the too-evident fact that this semantics belongs to a culture, to structures of ethnic, social and political organization in which language is irreducible" (Derrida, *Politics of Friendship*, p. 89).

[259] Group identity cannot be severed from group experience and memory of that experience. Mark van Vugt and Tatsuya Kameda explain in their own way: "Many

signifier necessarily involves understanding the socio-cultural environment of the microcosm of the group/audience and the larger context in which they found themselves that the text is addressing. St. Paul was effective at using his rhetorical tools. Thus, St. Paul used the key signifier of Abraham being justified by faith to trigger [260] his audience's collective consciousness/memory of the sayings of Jesus of Nazareth that Abraham was justified by faith and the common idea among Christians that Jesus Christ is pre-existent God. Once the first trigger was triggered by the key signifier, the second trigger was quickly triggered.

What was the second trigger? The answer can be found in the rhetorical violence of St. Paul. In a manner that would not be described as

---

groupish traits are likely to be domain-specific decision rules. They exist in the form they do because they solved a particular, recurrent group problem in our ancestral environment, such as understanding how to defend the group or climb the group status hierarchy. The primary aim of an evolutionary psychology approach to group dynamics is to identify, analyse, and understand specific adaptive group problems as well as the psychological mechanisms that have evolved to solve them" (Mark van Vugt and Tatsuya Kameda, "Evolution and Groups," in *Group Processes*, ed. John M. Levine {New York: Psychology Press, 2013, pp. 297-322}, p. 302). Collective experience builds group identity and collective consciousness.

[260] In a sense, this process can be languaged in terms of "negotiation," since St. Paul wanted to bring his audience, whom he considered a part of his own group, to his own side. This "negotiation" was necessary for St. Paul to stave off the attack of his opponents, the Judaizers. Leigh L. Thompson, Jiunwen Wang, and Brian C. Gunia define "negotiation" this way: "Anytime a people cannot achieve their goal without the cooperation of others, they are negotiating. By this definition, negotiation is a ubiquitous social activity. Research on negotiation has been influenced by a wide variety of fields, including mathematics, management, organizational behavior, social psychology, cognitive psychology, economics, communication studies, sociology, and political science" (Leigh L. Thompson, Jiunwen Wang, and Brian C. Gunia, "Negotiation," in *Group Processes*, ed. John M. Levine {New York: Psychology Press, 2013, pp. 55-84}, p. 55). In terms of "negotiation", St. Paul's use of the key signifier for his audience can be explained in terms of "intrapersonal system." Thompson, Wang, and Gunia explain: "We use the term 'intrapersonal system' to signify the ways that negotiation behavior and outcomes depend upon the perceptions and inner experiences of the negotiator. For example, the intrapersonal system might include research on how an individual's sense of power influences his or her negotiation behavior, satisfaction, and outcomes" (Thompson, Wang, and Gunia, "Negotiation," p. 56).

gentle or kind or loving in any way, St. Paul flatly imposes God's curse[261] on so-called Christian leaders[262] who were disseminating the Jewish propaganda. St. Paul claims eternal damnation for so-called Christian leaders who argue that a person can be saved by observing the Jewish law, as the Pharisees had claimed during the time of Jesus of Nazareth and even during St. Paul's time. Not only that, St. Paul attacks angels who might offer the same Jewish propaganda. The rhetorical violence of St. Paul shows that the second trigger was to drive out pro-Judaism faction among early Christians.[263] In effect, the second trigger is forcing early Christians toward an anti-Judaism direction.

Like the first trigger, the scholar needs to understand the socio-cultural environment of the audience/reader of the text to identify the second trigger. The second trigger would not work otherwise. That is why the literary device of the key signifier is a very complex literary device. One needs to understand not only the historical setting but also the socio-cultural[264] content, experience and identity of the group.[265] Perhaps,

---

[261] St. Paul curses the most in the New Testament. Kjell Arne Morland writes: "Paul is the author who uses curse terms most frequently. In three of his main letters he uses curse terms twelve times, nearly half of the occurrences in the New Testament. Therefore, a concentration on Paul seems natural" (Morland, *The Rhetoric of Curse in Galatians*, p 3).

[262] It was an "either or" proposition. The audience had to accept either St. Paul and his message or those of his opponents. Choosing one meant rejection of the other. Morland states: "He even amplifies the conflict to such extent that he *cursed his opponents*. There is no compromise; the Galatians have to choose one of the positions and reject the other. Message and preachers were regarded as a unity. When one of the teachings was rejected, also its defender had to leave the scene in Galatia" (Morland, *The Rhetoric of Curse in Galatians*, p. 241).

[263] Esler writes: "We have now reached a point, therefore, where our interest in the historical dimension of Galatians, its meaning for its original audience, has been shown to require an investigation of the text as a discourse written in a particular rhetorical situation with the aim of dissuading its audience from various types of inappropriate behavior or attitude" (Esler, *Galatians*, p. 18). Esler does not go far enough in terms of what St. Paul was trying to accomplish with the second trigger of the key signifier.

[264] Research on negotiation has illustrated that culture can impact understanding of causality; thus, groups of people experiencing the same history can act in diametrically oppositional ways based on their cultural background. Thompson, Wang, and Gunia illustrate this in describing culture-driven conflict in the same historical context: "Culture also has important effects on how individuals perceive causality. Psychological research has demonstrated that members of Western cultures tend to make the

this example can illustrate the point. In the United States, there are Jews who call themselves "culturally Jewish."[266] What does this mean? In contexts in which the term is not used, it may be very difficult to

---

fundamental attribution error more often than do members of non-Western cultures .... That is, they underestimate the impact of situational factors and overestimate the impact of others' dispositional factors in causing events ... The result for negotiation is that U.S. negotiators tend to make dispositional attributions for their counterpart's behavior and discount potential situational attributions .... Dispositional attributions for negative behaviors lead to negative consequences in negotiations. Specifically, dispositional attributions led to competitive perceptions of the situation and counterpart, resulting in a preference for adversarial instead of collaborative procedures" (Thompson, Wang, and Gunia, "Negotiation," p. 71).

[265] Group often becomes the primarily reference points for an individual. Kenneth Jerold Comfort states: "Consequently the human organism begins life in a group context, and spends the whole of life in one primary group or another and often in many groups simultaneously, and knows no other context in which to deal with the total array of tension-producing stimuli which envelops it. Even the socially isolated individual behaves in terms of reference groups such as the family in which he spent his formative years or later groups to which he transferred his gamily group relatedness before becoming socially isolated" (Kenneth Jerold Comfort, *The Ego and the Social Order* {Cohoes: The Public Administration Institute of New York State, inc., 2000}, p. 110).

[266] Creation of the identity, "culturally Jewish," can be seen as "irrational" cooperative choice in the social dilemma of Jewish group identity in the American context. Norbert L. Kerr explains this dynamics in a general way: "In a social dilemma, the personal rewards for competitive (usually termed *defecting*) choices are higher than for a cooperative choice, regardless of what choices others in the group make. In that narrow sense, it is personally rational to compete in social dilemmas. However, the collective and personal rewards of universal cooperation are higher than those for universal defection, So, if everyone in the group makes the 'rational,' defecting choice, they're all worse off than if they made the 'irrational,' cooperative choice. In a social dilemma, a personally rational choice is collectively irrational" (Norbert L. Kerr, "Social Dilemmas," in in *Group Processes*, ed. John M. Levine {New York: Psychology Press, 2013, pp. 85-110}, p. 85). In other words, an individual Jew who does not believe in a Jewish god or want to keep kosher, may personally find "freedom" as he leaves Jewish group identity, but such decisions by other individual Jews in similar situations may result in the weakening of the Jewish group in the groups-competitive environment of the American society which has over one hundred different ethnic groups competing for the same resources and advantages. Thus, secular individual Jews act "irrationally" in terms of personal satisfaction on a personal level to preserve the group which provides group protection for him and assist in his competition in the American society context for resources and advantages. Thus, the personally irrational decision to remain in the Jewish group with an identity called "culturally Jewish" is rational on a collective, or group, level.

understand what "culturally Jewish" means. There is the question of what the people who say, "I am culturally Jewish," mean when they use the term "culturally Jewish." And what complicates the understanding is that not all Jews agree on what it means to be "culturally Jewish." For instance, if you brought one hundred Jews in a room and asked them to explain what it means to be "culturally Jewish," you may have very different responses, or rather, what appear to be very different responses.

Obviously, you will need to group similar responses, together, for the sake of analysis. But even after such a grouping, it would be possible to identify several differing groups of responses. Some who may not be from the United States and lack the cultural experience of the United States or collective consciousness of Americans, may not be able to understand the grouping at all without a very detailed explanation. And still, there may be points of misunderstanding because someone from a largely homogeneous country like England and France has completely differing reference points for every word, such as "culture," "identity," "individual," and "freedom,"[267] as an American participating in collective

---

[267] Values are culturally conditioned and determined by the group. In the same way "freedom" or "social justice" is not an absolute value, but a relative "interpretation" by a group. Thus, values from one group to the next could be vastly different. Tom R. Tyler explains: "Justice is a social judgment. It is created by groups to manage social interactions by preventing conflict and promoting cooperation. As such 'justice' involves a set of socially shared rules whose function is to facilitate people's efforts to more efficiently and effectively achieve mutually beneficial goals. Rules of social justice define what is reasonable in social group settings, both in terms of how to divide resources and how to make decisions and behave when dealing with others. By so doing justice makes social life more viable. This is true with principles of distributive justice, which indicate who should receive what; with principles of procedural justice, which defines how groups should make decisions; and with principles of retributive justice, which indicate how norm violators should be treated" (Tom R. Tyler, "Justice," in *Group Processes*, ed. John M. Levine {New York: Psychology Press, 2013, pp. 111-134}, p. 111). Unfortunately, Tyler is simplifying the problem of determining justice. There is always inter-group conflicts and competition at play; this is nowhere more poignant than in the context of the United States, in which over one hundred ethnic group compete for the same recourses and advantages in every area of the American society. For instance, the Fugitive Slave Act, officially endorsed by the US government and the US Court of Justice, was "justice" for slave-owning farmers who had paid a price for their slaves, but it was not "justice" for African-American slaves who had been abducted and inducted into the slavery system. "Justice" is never the same for different groups in most

experience and collective consciousness of Americans (and to an extent in collective memory of Americans) has.[268] "Freedom"[269] does not mean the same when it is uttered in the United States and in China. There are vastly different understanding of the concept of "freedom" even between Europeans and Americans. For example, Americans believe that illegalizing anything, even Hitler's *Mein Kampf*, is morally wrong and infringes on personal and democratic freedom, but Germany disagrees and illegalizes it. Germans cannot understand why the FBI and US Government spend millions of dollars protecting Neo-Nazi groups and allowing them freedom of marches, association, and political activism. Germans cannot understand how American Civil Liberties Union and its Jewish lawyers could defend the "freedom" of Nazis and Neo-Nazis, spending millions of dollars of donations ACLU collected, because Germany is not America. The United States has its own constitution which is a sacred document for the American people which grants freedom of expression as a fundamental human right, but Germany does not. American historical experience has been against government

---

situations. Thus, like all values, "justice" has to be seen as relatively contingent on (different) group identity.

[268] It is important to remember knowledge of an individual in the group informs and directs that individual's response. And that individual's knowledge base is directed by the experience, often shared in the group. Franz From states: "In most of the above examples we find that the qualities which do not possess the imprint of sense qualities have to do with a knowledge in the observer, so that they can in some way be said to have a mental aspect. If, for example I see a cup, then my experience of it as intended for drinking may be intrinsic to the sight of the cup. This 'determination' of utility' may in some cases be immediately present as a property of the cup. A short consideration will easily persuade me that the immediately experienced quality is dependent on the knowledge I have of the object, i.e., on something mental" (From, *Perception of Other People*, p. 15). Obviously, knowledge influenced by socio-political group of the individual guides the psychoid entities of that individual on much complex levels.

[269] Nira Yuval-Davis states: "Using a common set of values, such as 'democracy' or 'human rights', as the signifiers of belonging can be seen as having the most permeable boundaries of all. However, these different discourses of belonging can be collapsed together or reduced down to each other in specific historical cases. Moreover, some political projects of belonging can present themselves as promoting more open boundaries than they actually do" (Nira Yuval-Davis, *The Politics of Belonging: Intersectional Contestations* {Los Angeles: Sage, 2011}, p. 21). The same can be said of "freedom."

censorship of all kinds, whether it is censoring pro-emancipation actions, 1960's marches, or pro-Union activities, whereas Germans have been largely docile to their Government in the history of Germany. Thus, "freedom" is understood differently in the United States and Germany, so that even in academia, the freedom of expression and the freedom of the press are limited in Germany and the rest of Europe. "Freedom" is therefore understood very differently by Americans and Europeans.

This is the case even on the level of the masses. This explains to a large extent why the English surrendered their guns to their government when ordered to do so, but many Americans in Pierce Morgan show in CNN vowed publicly to fight the US government if they are ordered to surrender their guns. The English do not understand that for Americans, the right to own guns is a fundamental human rights issue and a "God-given" right as Americans. Owning guns is also protected by the US Constitution, whereas such a clause does not exist in England or the rest of Europe. Thus, "freedom" as understood by Americans cannot be comprehended by an Englishman. And there are popular expressions of understanding this reality, such as Sting's song, "I am an Englishman in New York." And the two cultures – American and English – will always be fundamentally different, especially in terms of understanding what "freedom" means. That is why Pierce Morgan in CNN has many fights with famous Americans who support gun control and that is why many American actors, like Rob Lowe, who like Pierce Morgan smile at him and try to placate him when he keeps trying to impress his English-oriented value system by trying to corner them to agree with him. Just like every Catholic Priest assumes Gay Marriage is wrong and believes nations should illegalize it, every American expects their "God-given" freedom to own guns not violated. Of course, as in anything, there are a few exceptions. But it is the exceptions that prove the fundamental rule.

Thus, terms are understood differently based on group identity, both at the microcosm and the macrocosm levels. This is best illustrated by looking at "murder," which is criminal killing. Most of the Americans would not consider a soldier killing an enemy soldier as murder. It is seen as a justifiable killing. This is the macrocosm understanding of "murder" in the American context. But there are disagreements based on microcosm group identity.²⁷⁰ For instance, the Amish believe that soldier-killing in a war is "murder," and thus they refused to go to war as soldiers. For the Amish, all killing is "murder." They are willing to break national laws for their belief and go to jail for it.²⁷¹ Even if the enemy side is clearly "evil," however defined, the Amish believe that killing another human being is "murder."²⁷² Understanding the term, "murder," is clearly different based

---

²⁷⁰ Such a reality exists in terms of perception of St. Paul. Daniel Boyarin states: "Before World War II, and in certain circles until this day, Paul's oeuvre has been interpreted as a sustained attack on the Jewish religion. This is particularly the case in what has been (with some exaggeration) termed the 'Lutheran' reading of Paul. .... According to this interpretation, Paul became violently disillusioned with 'Judaism' because of its commitment to 'works-righteousness.' ....From the very beginning of any kind of scholarly dialogue, Jewish scholars had protested that this view of Judaism simply was not a fair representation of the religion" (Boyarin, *A Radical Jew*, p. 41). Was the Jewish "scholarly" response based on Jewish scholars' personal loyalties to modern Judaism or was it conditioned by historical analysis of ancient Judaism during the time of Jesus of Nazareth? Catholics no longer sell indulgences like during the time of Martin Luther. It is important for Jewish "scholars" not to be anachronistic and read *a priori* prejudices back into ancient history for the sake of their personal loyalties in the present. Boyarin shows that such a danger could exist in modern academic circles in terms of discourse on ancient Jewish history or ancient religions. In a sense, Boyarin is (perhaps unintentionally) signaling a need for caution for "Lutheran" scholars to question the prejudices of Jewish scholars in "any kind of scholarly dialogue."

²⁷¹ John M. Levine and Radmila Prislin state: "Disagreement between majorities and minorities can be problematical for several reasons. According to Festinger (1950), such disagreement interferes with group members' motives to validate opinions that are not anchored in physical reality and to move toward collective goals" (John M. Levine and Radmila Prislin, "Majority and Minority Influence," in *Group Processes*, ed. John M. Levine {New York: Psychology Press, 2013, pp. 135-163}, p. 136). The problem for the "majority" is that the Amish do not want to move toward collective goals, set by the US government, but the Amish are not alone in this type of minority dissent.

²⁷² Group identity determines values, especially against other groups and even the dominant majority group. John M. Levine and Radmila Prislin argue that this is to be presumed based on the relationship between individual identity and group identity. Levin and Prislin state: "The primary role of group membership in understanding social influence is a core assumption of *self-categorization theory* (Abrams et al., 1990; Turner, 1991). As discussed previously, this theory postulates shared group membership as a condition *sine qua non* for any influence, including that by minority sources. According to this perspective, disparate group membership between sources and targets of influence precludes influence because disagreement with different (outgroup) others is expected and hence does not create uncertainty regarding the validity of one's position. In contrast, disagreement with similar (ingroup) others is unexpected and hence creates uncertainty

on the microcosm context, even though the Amish are a part of the macrocosm group identity of being Americans. It is important to understand that Amish are willing to die for their microcosm group understanding of "murder," so that the difference cannot be slighted as being inconsequential.

Although less highly charged than the understanding of "murder" by the Amish in the macrocosm of the American society, Jewish use of the term "culturally Jewish" can be understood in a similar way. Just like all Amish understand "murder" in similar ways, those who are a part of the "Jewish experience" understand "culturally Jewish" in a similar way.[273] Obviously, "the Jewish experience" is placed in quotes, because it can be vastly different. There are some Jews who live in religious communities which observe all the rules of ritual observance and the Jewish law as enumerated in the Talmud, or at least strive to. And there are Jewish religious communities which have differing level of commitment to traditional religious observance. Then, there are assimilated Jews of differing levels. But despite these differences, all Jews in the United

---

that must be resolved" (Levine and Prislin, "Majority and Minority Influence," p. 150). In other words, a person's decision to be a part of a group makes it normal for him to be loyal to that group, even if that is a minority group. This explains the loyalty of the Amish to their group, even at the point of imprisonment for refusing to serve in the US Military (in cases of conscription).

[273] Nira Yuval-Davis argues that it is important to raise the question of identity especially in light of the fact that it was British nationals who carried out terrorist attacks on other British citizens on July 7, 2005. But Yuval-Davis questions why the journalists assumed that it was strange for those carrying British passports to attack other British citizens in a terrorist attack. Yuval-Davis encourages raising questions of identity to understand the dynamics in modern times. Yuval-Davis states: "The question of who is 'a stranger' and who 'does not belong', however, is also continuously being modified and contested, with growing ethnic, cultural, and religious tensions within as well as between societies and states" (Yuval-Davis, *The Politics of* Belonging, p. 2). Although our study is not focused on identifying potential terrorists, Yuval-Davis's comments on the complexity of identity politics are apropos. Whether in the twenty-first century United States or in the first century Galatia, the question of micro-identity vis-à-vis the larger national identity is an important issue. Since there were no passports during the time of St. Paul, we cannot really talk about which passport St. Paul carried, but no scholar will deny the similarities of identity politics in the twenty-first century and in the first century. The players are different, but the central theme is the same.

States understand "culturally Jewish"[274] in similar ways because of collective experiences,[275] collective consciousness, and collective memory. Thus, within the microcosm of "the Jewish experience" or Jewish group identity in the United States, the "masses" understand "culturally Jewish" in similar ways. This is done on mostly unconscious and uncritical levels. When a Jew refers to herself as "culturally Jewish" in the USA, she is basically saying that she is not religiously observant and does not believe in God or Judaism (with differing degrees of doubt and laxity in practice), but she identifies herself as "Jewish" because she is practicing Jewish "culture." Since many "cultural Jews" do not critically define themselves, when you press them to explain what they mean by "culturally Jewish,"

---

[274] Daniel Boyarin seems to imply that Jews could never become "non-Jews." Boyarin states: "On the other hand, Jews do not sense of themselves that their association is confessional, that it is based on common religion, for many people whom both religious and secular Jews call Jewish neither believe nor practice the religion at all. This kid of 'radicalism' is built into the formal cultural system itself. While you can convert *in* to Judaism, you cannot convert *out*, and anyone born of Jewish parents is Jewish, even if she doesn't know it. Jewishness is thus certainly not contiguous with modern notions of race, which have been, furthermore discredited empirically. …. Jews in general feel not that Jewishness is something they have freely chosen but rather that it is an essence – an essence often nearly empty of any content other than itself – which has been inscribed – sometimes even imposed – on them by birth" (Boyarin, *A Radical Jew*, p. 241). This raises the question: Do Jews consider those who convert to Christianity still as Jews? How about assimilated or converted Jews who deny their Jewish background and join the Nazi Party? How about those who did not know that they had Jewish ancestors who joined the Nazi Party and killed Jews? Although these questions may be asked regarding modern times, there are some questions for the ancient time as well. What does the excommunication of heretics in the Eighteen Benedictions refer to? Boyarin's claim that Jews could never become non-Jews raises some serious questions about identity and also history, which records divergence from this purported reality.

[275] Yuval-Davis states: "It is important to differentiate between belonging and the politics of belonging. Belonging is about an emotional (or even ontological) attachment, about feeling 'at home'" (Yuval-Davis, *The Politics of Belonging*, p. 10). Collective experiences often have a strong hold on individual identity and self-perception. Yuval-Davis argues that belonging "becomes articulated, formally structured and politicized only when it is threatened in some way. The politics of belonging comprise specific political projects aimed at constructing belonging to particular collectivity/ies which are themselves being constructed in these projects in very specific ways and in very specific boundaries (i.e. whether or not, according to specific political projects of belonging, Jews can be considered to be German, for example, or abortion advocates can be considered Catholic)" (Yuval-Davis, *The Politics of Belonging*, p. 10).

they struggle to define the term. But perhaps, that is the best evidence that she is "culturally Jewish." She lives it rather than analyzes it. Thus, "culturally Jewish" individuals may give a gift on Hannukah during Christmas time, with some refusing to celebrate Christmas as being a Christian holiday and with more assimilated Jews celebrating Christmas along with Hannukah. Often, "culturally Jewish" individuals will have Bar Mitzvah or Bat Mitzvah for their children, but invite Gentiles and have a mostly secular or non-religious celebration.

In a sense, "culturally Jewish" individuals often deprive traditionally religious Jewish celebration of the religious content, but retain the celebratory or commemorative nature of the namesake. Thus, "culturally Jewish" individuals generally do not keep kosher or observe the Sabbath or other distinctively religious rules of Judaism. Thus, in the diachronic development of Jewish history in the United States, "culturally Jewish" has been formulated as a term to oppose "religiously Jewish."[276] In other words, someone who is defining herself as "culturally Jewish" is in fact excluding herself[277] from the Jewish religious identity and even from the Jewish religion. Because this self-definition of "cultural Jewish" has more or less come to define the culturally Jewish "group," no religiously Jewish individual in the USA would explicitly refer to himself as "culturally Jewish." Thus, "culturally Jewish" and "religiously Jewish" have become mutually exclusive terms. The "masses" within the "Jewish experience" understand this phenomenon implicitly, and they do not have

---

[276] Comfort argues: "Because religion is effective as a tension-reducer only when the ego is able to sustain faith in religious belief, the ego is continually confronted by doubt which the impinging stimuli of reality impose. The mechanism most often applied to religious doubt by the ego is that of denial. The ego simply denies reality, and faith is the means by which denial is sustained in the face of impinging reality" (Comfort, *The Ego and the Social Order*, p. 210).

[277] Comfort states: "Tradition is comprised of customs, usage, manners and mores passed down through succeeding generations. They greatly influence religion and are influenced by religion. They reside in the superego where they are passed along from parent to child and thus from one generation to the next. But tradition is not immutable because change may be imposed upon it by the filial rebellion of the individuating adolescent when the latter's rebellion is supported by aggrieved members of society in sufficient number to modify tradition" (Comfort, *The Ego and the Social Order*, p. 215). This adequately describes the socio-psychological phenomena of "culturally Jewish" identity in the United States.

to explicitly define it. However, academics have to define the terms because of the nature of the academic study of religion and of the Jewish experience (history, sociology, etc.).

However, it is important to understand the difference between a controlled academic[278] analysis and experience as lived by the people without much critical thinking or analysis. Academics define in concrete terms and, in essence, minimize a complex reality.[279] A summary can be

---

[278] Michel Foucault is highly critical of academic analysis. Foucault argues that academics create categories and then fit people into it. Foucault gives the example of "monomania" in his "The Dangerous Individual" (1978). "Monomania" is a term crated by academics to describe a crime without any apparent cause or reason. James D. Marshall describes: "By inserting this concept into the medical field psychiatry was to define its specificity in the field of medicine, to ensure its recognition among other medical practices, claiming people as 'its own' in denouncing medical and legal practices and decision in courts, and publishing studies and reports on monomania. Only the trained expert could identify monomania and thereby through the effects of observation by the trained eye, *produce* monomaniac patients" (James D. Marshall, *Michel Foucault: Personal Autonomy and Education* {Dordrecht: Kluwer Academic Publishers, 1996}, p. 113). Thus, Foucault blames academics for creating and sustaining a fictitious entity that misled different fields, such as criminal law. Similar critique can be levied against charges of anti-Semitism in New Testament studies. The difference is that in New Testament studies, there is a form of witch-hunting of other academics ("anti-Semites"), which does not exist in psychiatry or other academic disciplines.

[279] Such simplistic minimization in academia is clear in the use of Rabbinic materials to discuss New Testament documents. Rabbinic materials were codified after AD 200; this means that the Rabbinic materials cannot be really used as historical sources that accurately represent the position of the Jews (even Pharisees, who are seen as proto-Rabbinics) at the time of the New Testament. For one, AD 70 and the destruction of the Jerusalem Temple represent a paradigm shift in Jewish history, which can be described as a great trauma for the Jewish people. Jonathan Klawans describes the monumental nature of AD 70 on the Jewish people: "It is, of course, widely accepted that the destruction of Jerusalem and its sacred shrine in 70 CE was a cataclysmic event in the history of the Jewish people. Indeed, it remains quite common, despite some objections, for scholars of ancient Judaism and teachers of religion to view 70 CE as a turning point for the purposes of periodization, marking the time when the second temple period comes to an end and the rabbinic period begins" (Klawans, *Josephus and the Theologies of Ancient Judaism*, pp. 180-181). In all histories, traumatic events in history have a way of imprinting new or revised realities onto a people or shifting the direction of the historical flow. This was certainly the case for the Jewish people.

accurate, but it could be misleading.[280] In the same way, academic minimization for the purpose of proving a thesis does not often explain the whole complexity of experience or identity. The nature of academics being what it is (that is, minimizing for the purpose of proving a thesis) can miss, either intentionally or unintentionally, the content or the object (a term which is radically limiting) of analysis.[281] But given the limitation of humanity, which is not all-knowing or infinite, and the diachronic development of academia, such limiting and sometimes misleading minimization is the norm of academic inquiry. But as postmodernists have shown, academics can provide often misleading and inaccurate picture of the reality due to their minimization and the essentially biased nature of the human individual. Postmodernists have shown that no scholar can escape such a prejudice.

And perhaps, that is why there is a radical difference between the analysis of academics and the reality of lived experience of the "masses" (for a lack of a better term). Geophysically, academics are often separated from the masses, as academics live, work, and socialize mostly in their ivory towers. The "masses" live, work, and socialize in the larger, broader

---

[280] Academics can have an agenda, based on their background. And this agenda could guide their scholarship. This reality is shown in Jonathan Klawans' confession: "Jewish scholarship, since the days of *Wissenschaft des Judentums*, has endeavored with some success to rehabilitate the reputation of the Pharisees. Yet in many cases, the reevaluation of the Pharisees came at the expense of the Sadducees" (Klawans, *Josephus and the Theologies of Ancient Judaism*, p. 24). Because modern Judaism is Rabbinic Judaism and the Pharisees were the proto-Rabbincs at the time of Jesus of Nazareth (Rabbinc Judaism was created only after the destruction of the Jerusalem Temple in AD 70), modern Jewish scholars pursue an apologetic "rehabilitation" of the Pharisees in academic discussions and university teaching and scholarly publications. Sometimes, this happens at the expense of demonizing the dissent as "anti-Semitic" because they perceive personal or group interests as being at stake. Such prejudiced agenda-driven scholarship is highly problematic, especially if it seeks to witch-hunt and burn at the stake the voices of dissent in academia (and society). In other words, agenda-driven Jewish scholarship can destroy freedom of speech and the freedom of open/free academic discourse.

[281] Foucault was opposed to simplification in academia. Marshall describes Foucault's ideas: "However, in typical Canguilhelm fashion he does argue that truth is not so obvious, or as straightforward, or as simplistic, as positivistic accounts would have it to be. Nevertheless Foucault maintained that there was no universal form that reason must take" (Marshall, *Michel Foucault*, p. 184).

contexts. Academics try to minimize the experience of the "masses" in formulas for the sake of analysis, examination, and understanding. Since there may be diverging experiences and social experiences, such a project may be doomed from the start. But obviously, some study may be more helpful than none, and the business of academia must continue and there is the need for some kind of understanding at the level of government ruling, business practices, social control, and desire for explanations; thus, the labors of minimization studies go on. But academics must not fool themselves. Minimized academic analysis sometimes captures a portion of the reality through minimization, but it certainly does not capture the whole of complex reality. Furthermore, even academics bring with them a prejudice[282] or bias for reading the text; the postmodernists showed that this is impossible to escape.[283] And this is certainly true in modern cultural studies, political science, international relations, religious studies, and sociology as it is true with more traditional disciplines, such as history, theology, philosophy, and classics. The experiences of the "masses" are often misunderstood or misrepresented.

---

[282] There are honest scholars who admit to being shaped by personal or historical trauma, such as Professor Jacob Neusner, a legend in Jewish studies. Klawans describes: "Lurking behind Bokser's views in particular may well be the views of his teacher, Jacob Neusner, who linked the events in a number of publications, including some produced during the time that Bokser was studying with him at Brown University. Neusner has also disclosed, in an autobiographical essay, that his personal grappling with the Holocaust shaped his life in general and his academic work on ancient Judaism in particular. Of course, it bears remembering that both Jacob Neusner and Baruch Bokser – along with practically two full generations of Jewish academics – studied with Shoah survivors and refugees at the Jewish Theological Seminary and other institutions. For these and perhaps other reasons as well, explicit comparisons between the Jewish responses to 70 CE and 1945 are not uncommon" (Klawans, *Josephus and the Theologies of Ancient Judaism*, pp. 182-183). Often, New Testament scholars do not respect this dimension of what is happening to American and British scholarly discourses; in essence, therefore, they deny the important historical phenomena. But it is very real.

[283] Daniel Boyarin's honest confession is refreshing. Boyarin writes: "Here, then, you have a talmudist and postmodern Jewish cultural critic reading Paul. I think that my particular perspective as a practicing Jewish, non-Christian, critical but sympathetic reader of Paul conduces me to ways of understanding his work that are necessarily different from the ways of readers of other cultural stances" (Boyarin, *A Radical Jew*, p. 1). No scholar of St. Paul can hide behind pretentious claim of objectivity; all come with some bias and prejudice based on their identity, experience, training, and preference.

Galatians as Examined by Diverse Academics

It is the need to understand thoroughly the socio-cultural identity of the "masses" who receive the text and the larger socio-historical context that the literary device of the key signifier is difficult to identify and explain. A superficial reader of ancient history may be able to identify a simile by looking for the equivalent of "like" or "as," which is relatively easy to do, but she cannot identify the literary device of the key signifier without a deep and thorough understanding of the complexities of microcosm and the macrocosm of the group identity in which the individual identities are enmeshed in the particular experience of the audience (or readers) of a text. However, it is this complexity that makes the literary device of the key signifier rewarding. If a scholar is able to identify the literary device of the key signifier, then she can open up wealth of understanding that spans collective memory to collective consciousness to a group's value system to the hopes and aspirations (and fears) of a people, or various peoples involved. In essence, the literary device of the key signifier is the most complex literary device in existence that helps to identify not only the form (which most literary devices focus on) but the content and the function of the literary device.

That is why identifying the literary device of key signifier in the phrase, "Abraham is justified by faith," is so significant. It not only identifies the first trigger, but also helps to identify the second trigger. And with the hindsight of history, we can ascertain whether the literary device of the key signifier worked. And history seems to show that St. Paul's employment of the key signifier worked as he intended it to. The history shows that the second trigger was successful. It is difficult to find Jewish converts to Christianity[284] holding any major leadership position in

---

[284] St. Paul shows that he was at conflict with Jewish converts to Christianity who held onto Jewish traditions as leaders of Christianity. In a sense, therefore, St. Paul set up an us-versus-them conflict between anti-Jewish faction and pro-Jewish faction in early Christianity in a way that one had to be eliminated and the other had to become dominant. Ronald Y. K. Kung writes: (p. 36) – "The emphatic contrast with which Paul describes his apostleship is intended to underline its divine origin: he asserts that his apostolic commission, with regard to both its source and its mediation, was from God and Christ, just as a little later on he will categorically declare that his gospel, with regard to both its source and the manner in which it was communicated to him, was a direct revelation from God (1:12, 16). Appearing at the very outset of the epistle, and read in the light of the great stress which Paul subsequently places on his independence of the Jerusalem church (1:18-2:10), his assertion reflects a polemical situation in which the dignity,

Galatians as Examined by Diverse Academics

the Christian Church that was becoming institutionalized after the time of St. Paul.[285] Most of the Church Fathers, thus, were Gentiles or Gentile converts to Christianity.[286] And throughout the 2,000 years of the history of Christianity, it is difficult to identify any major leaders of Christianity as a convert from Judaism or having discernible Jewish background. The second trigger of the key signifier as found in Galatians was completely successful in the way that St. Paul envisioned it.

St. Paul was careful to emphasize that he understood the Jewish propaganda that some so-called Christian leaders were trying to force down on early Christian converts.[287] St. Paul claims that he was very rigorous in the religion of the Jews. Not only did St. Paul understand Judaism[288], St. Paul, before his conversion[289] to Christianity, was

---

indeed the validity, of his apostolic status is being challenged" (Fung, *The Epistle to the Galatians*, p. 36).

[285] St. Paul's conflict with the Judaizers and even Jerusalem's Christian leadership harbingered the end of Christian leadership filled by those who would identify themselves ethnically, socially, or culturally as Jewish. Howard writes: "The presence of judaizers in Galatia in this sense was thus ominous. If left unchecked, it would destroy the foundations of the gospel of Christ. Paul had faced judaizers earlier, and had even been to Jerusalem before the 'pillars' to set forth the gospel he preached with its implications for unity. To his delight he saw them extend their right hands in fellowship in recognition of his Gentile apostleship. But his joy was short-lived for at Antioch Peter wavered" (Howard, *Paul*, p. 81). St. Paul's view that Jewish Law and the espousers of it posed a real threat to Christianity is historically significant in understanding the socio-historical development of the history of Christianity.

[286] George Howard states: (p. 53) – "Paul's prohibition of the law is so absolute and irrevocable that he leaves open no conceivable occasion when Gentiles might submit to circumcision and be saved" (George Howard, *Paul: Crisis in Galatia: A Study in Early Christian Theology* {Cambridge: Cambridge University Press, 1979}, p. 53). Logically, such a conclusive prohibition of the Jewish Law would preclude any possibility of pro-Jewish Law leadership.

[287] Van Os shows that Jewish Christians, including Peter, were afraid of Jewish persecution that would result if they allowed Jewish Christians not to be circumcised (Van Os, "The Jewish Recipients of Galatians," p. 62). Such fear could have driven Jewish Christians to extremes of Judaizing converts to Christianity.

[288] Josephus is a Jewish historian who was a contemporary of St. Paul, and Josephus argues that what unifies Jews of all differing groups is their commitment to the Jewish law. Jonathan Klawans writes: "There are further common denominators among *Antiquities* and *Apion* – and even *War* – that deserve mention here. We have reviewed many instances where Josephus opposed changes in custom or law introduced by

dedicated to protecting[290] the purity of Judaism.[291] In other words, before his conversion to Christianity, St. Paul fought with zeal to propagate the

---

wayward teachers, rebels, or royals. The various details we have reviewed find their most general expression in *Apion*, where Josephus takes pride that the Jewish people lack 'innovators' (2.182-83). Unlike other nations, who alter their ancestral customs at will (2.182), the Jews steadfastly oppose whatever their ancient law prohibits (2.183)" (Klawans, *Josephus and the Theologies of Ancient Judaism*, pp. 174-175). Obviously, the brunt of Josephus' witness about Jewish groups must be seen as somewhat reliable. Taking Josephus seriously, it is impossible to argue that St. Paul's ideas would be considered "Jewish" by any Jewish group at the time. Some New Testament scholars may be ideologically committed in a post-Holocaust setting to imprison St. Paul into a Jewish matrix out of some kind of psychological guilt at the Holocaust or desire to be politically correct, rather than due to serious, objective historical analysis. Contemporary representative writers within Judaism(s) during the time of St. Paul would seriously object to including St. Paul within Judaism(s) of the first century AD.

[289] Martin Hengel dates St. Paul's conversion to Christianity within 31 AD (one year after the crucifixion of Jesus of Nazareth) to 34 AD time frame (Martin Hengel, *The Pre-Christian Paul* {London: SCM Press, 1991}, p. 63).

[290] Martin Hengel notes that St. Paul before his conversion persecuted Christians out of his own firm personal conviction as a Pharisee at his own initiative (Hengel, *The Pre-Christian Paul*, p. 65). But obviously, if there were someone like Saul of the Pharisees, there would have been others like him among the Pharisees. Furthermore, a Pharisee acting on his own without the group's endorsement is difficult to fathom in the context of first century Palestine, in which group identity reigned supreme. See Bruce Malina, *The New Testament World: Insights from Cultural Anthropology* (Louisville: John Knox Press, 1981), particularly pages 51-70. Stanley B. Marrow recognizes as "bare fact that Paul persecuted the Church violently, with fanatic zeal, and that he even tried to destroy it" (Stanley B. Marrow, *Paul: His Letters and His Theology* {New York: Paulist Press, 1981}, p. 25). F. F. Bruce explains that the idea that a messiah could be someone who is crucified was odious to Judaism. Bruce states: "A crucified Messiah was a contradiction in terms. Whether his death by crucifixion was deserved or resulted from a miscarriage of justice was beside the point: the point was that he was crucified, and therefore came within the meaning of the pronouncement in Deuteronomy 21:23, 'a hanged man is accursed by God.' A crucified Messiah was worse than a contradiction in terms; the very idea was an outrageous blasphemy" (F. F. Bruce, *Paul: Apostle of the Heart Set Free* {Grand Rapids: William B. Eerdmans Publishing Company, 1977}, pp. 70-71). The reality of St. Paul's persecution of Christians before his conversion to Christianity is universally accepted as a fact.

[291] Martin Hengel argues that persecution of Christians by Jews must be seen as natural from the point of view of sociology. Hengel explains: "A synagogue community formed a fixed social group which depended for its existence on the social cohesion of its members and their readiness to support it. If 'enthusiastic sectarians' had invaded such a

idea that salvation[292] was by keeping the Jewish law. In essence, St. Paul claims that he was one of the greatest propagators of the Jewish propaganda in his time period. St. Paul's zeal for the Jewish law and for Judaism led him to persecute Jewish converts to Christianity.[293] In fact, St. Paul had dispensation from the top echelons of Judaism to persecute and even imprison Jewish converts to Christianity. F. F. Bruce states:

---

relatively closed group and sought to alter the old, sound order, there must have been bad blood" (Hengel, *The New Testament World*, p. 80). In other words, Jews in synagogues would have been threatened by Jewish Christians who believed in salvation through faith in Jesus Christ and they would have acted violently towards them. This means, obviously, that violence by Jews against Jesus and his followers can be traced to the earliest strata of the Jesus movement, even before the crucifixion of Jesus of Nazareth.

[292] George W. E. Nickelsburg makes an important statement about using the term, "salvation." Nickelsburg states that it is a distinctively Christian terminology based on the death and resurrection of Jesus of Nazareth and is "foreign to many of the texts in the corpus of ancient Jewish literature" (George W. E. Nickelsburg, "Salvation among the Jews: Some Comments and Observations," in *This World and the World to Come: Soteriology in Early Judaism*, ed. Daniel M. Gurtner {London: T. & T. Clark, 2011, pp. 299-314}, p. 299). Daniel M. Gurtner agrees (Daniel M. Gurtner, "Introduction," in *This World and the World to Come: Soteriology in Early Judaism*, ed. Daniel M. Gurtner {London: T. & T. Clark, 2011, pp. 1-11}, p. 4). Nickelsburg's analysis can be applied to St. Paul as well. Before his radical conversion to Christianity, St. Paul probably did not talk in terms of being saved through the law. But as he began to follow Christianity's Christological emphasis of salvation through faith in Jesus Christ that he came to use the same kind of terminology to exclude Judaism and its ability to "save." Furthermore, as Christianity developed its language of salvation, opponents of Christianity began to use the framework terminology to negate the Christianity's emphasis by offering an opposing or a diverging concept. Thus, in the first two centuries of the common era, both Christians and Jews began to use distinctively Christian terminology to define themselves against the other.

[293] Hansen, in fact, argues that devotion to Judaism necessarily causes persecution of Christianity, as evidenced in St. Paul before his conversion. Hansen writes: "Paul draws attention to two characteristics of his previous way of life in Judaism: his intense persecution of the church (1:13) and his zealous devotion to Jewish traditions (1:14). The two are connected. The message of the church, that a crucified Messiah provides salvation for all, contradicted the traditions of Judaism. Certainly a Messiah on a Roman cross contradicted the Jewish expectation of a Messiah on David's throne. And Jews believed that salvation was to be found only in the law-observant Jewish nation. No wonder then that Paul's zeal for the Jewish traditions made him a fanatical persecutor of the church" (Hansen, *Galatians*, pp. 43-44). In other words, there is a direct correlation between being religiously Jewish and being a persecutor of Christians.

> The law and the customs, the ancestral traditions, and everything that was of value in Judaism, were imperiled by the disciples' activity and teaching. Here was a malignant growth which called for drastic surgery. The defence of all that made life worth living for Paul was a cause which engaged all the zeal and energy of which he was capable. When the chief priests [of the Jerusalem Temple] and their associates launched their attack on the disciples, Paul came forward as their eager lieutenant. Their motives may have been partly political, while his were entirely religious, but their action provided him with the occasion to protect the interests of the law.[294]

Thus, St. Paul can be described as having been the Jewish Inquisition for Judaism, before his conversion to Christianity. He had official authority of Judaism to persecute Jews who left Judaism. Thus, the conversion of St. Paul can be likened to an individual in the Catholic Inquisition with official authority of the Vatican to persecute those who became Protestant, who himself becomes a Protestant after many years of persecuting Catholics who became Protestant. This is to say that St. Paul had been an authority in Judaism, for which he had persecuting those who converted to Christianity. This past experience of St. Paul before his conversion to Christianity gave St. Paul the legitimacy in his mind to anathematize Judaizers as eternally damned to Hell.[295]

St. Paul was explicitly mentioning his role within Judaism and the Jewish propaganda machine in order to show the audience that he

---

[294] Bruce, *Paul*, p. 71. Bruce recognizes that Jewish synagogues actively participated in the persecution of Christians (p. 70). Thus, what emerges is a picture of targeted Jewish conspiracy and systematic persecution against Christians not only in Jerusalem but throughout the known world through Jewish associations and Jewish houses of worship, such as synagogues in the Diaspora. The Jewish conspiracy was aiming at debunking innately Christian ideas, smearing Christian leaders as illegitimate, and even arresting Christian leaders (and Christian laity) as a threat to the Jewish people and Judaism.

[295] This can be described as one of the earliest apostolic excommunications on record.

understood the message of the Judaizers, who were so-called Christians[296] who were pushing the Jewish propaganda that salvation was through observing the Jewish law.[297] St. Paul calls the Jewish propaganda,

---

[296] Gerd Luedemann states: "There is no doubt that the opponents of Paul are Christian preachers. ...they were Jewish Christians" (Gerd Luedemann, *Opposition to Paul in Jewish Christianity*, trans. M. Eugene Boring {Minneapolis: Fortress Press, 1989}, p. 99). Luedemann identifies them more specifically with the "false brethren" who failed to force Titus to be circumcised at the Jerusalem Conference. But Luedemann is not sure if they had the backing of the Jerusalem church or not (p. 101). It is important to note that inner Jewish discussions were relevant to how so-called Jewish Christians acted. Clearly, many Jewish Christians were influenced or even compelled by Jews who were not Christians at all.

[297] Daniel Boyarin states that Prof. E. P. Sanders of Duke University effectively defended Judaism from Christian "slander" that Judaism is focused on the law for salvation, so that on English-speaking soil, no Christian can say that Judaism is about salvation through the law. Boyarin states: "Sanders has forever changed the way that Paul will be read by scholars and interpreters of his work. In his masterwork, he finally achieved what several Christian and Jewish scholars (including Davies) had tried for decades to achieve – to demonstrate that the slander of early Judaism promulgated by interpreters of Paul was simply and finally just that, a slander. Pauline studies will never be the same, at least on English-speaking soil" (Boyarin, *A Radical Jew*, pp. 46-47). What is troubling about this statement is the characterization of all Christians who describe Judaism as focused on the law for salvation as "slanderers of Judaism." Since the Talmud, the chief religious text for Rabbinic Judaism, is basically a legal text (no Jewish scholar would object to that), describing Rabbinic Judaism as being focused on the law should not be characterized as "slander." Furthermore, Torah (often called the "Mosaic Law") emphasize observation of the law, and Second Temple Judaism focused a lot on the observation of the law (see Qumran documents, which every scholar accepts as written by Jews of Judaism for Jews of Judaism, for example), it would not be "slander" to discuss Second Temple Judaism as focused on the law. Such loaded language does not breed an atmosphere of academic freedom and freedom of expression in American universities and British universities "on English-speaking soil." If Boyarin is correct, then his statement casts doubt on the objectivity of St. Paul studies conducted "on English-speaking soil" both at the university level and at the seminary level. This means that the preachers in American and British pulpits in Christian churches may represent a post-Holocaust biased representation of St. Paul that has been sanitized of "slander" that existed in the Christian church for 2,000 years. The question, then, rises: is modern "slander"-free interpretation of St. Paul the truth and all who came before were just "slanderers"? Boyarin's praise of Duke University's Prof. E. P. Sanders and Boyarin's argument that English Christian commentaries that came after his "victory over slander" tended toward the "slander"-free position (Boyarin mentions commentaries of Galatians by Professor James D. G. Dunn and Professor John Barclay – both of whom are highly "respected" even by evangelical

"another Gospel."[298] Thus, another Gospel can be described as the teachings of the leaders of Judaism[299], including the Pharisees, that the

---

theologians at evangelical seminaries like Dallas Theological Seminary, Talbot School of Theology, Trinity Evangelical Divinity School, Westminster Theological Seminary, Calvin Seminary, Gordon-Conwell Seminary, and Fuller Theological Seminary – as surrendering to "the new paradigm" {p. 47}) may ironically indict Pauline studies "on English-speaking soil" as a whole, including the commentaries on Galatians by evangelical seminary professors and the evangelical Christian churches in the United States and England. Can Pauline studies "on English-speaking soil" ever be free to conduct research on St. Paul apart from the "new paradigm"? Or are church-goers in the USA and the United Kingdom to submit to the "new paradigm" as well and free themselves of being "slanderers" like the Christians of past two thousand years? Boyarin's description of the current status of studies on St. Paul "on English-speaking soil" is deeply troubling on many levels. But if Professor Boyarin is correct, then difficult questions about American evangelical preachers preaching on St. Paul and Christian theology regarding St. Paul in the United Kingdom may have to be raised. Have they been herded into the "new paradigm" and see St. Paul and Galatians from that biased position? Or would Professor Boyarin of the University of California at Berkeley and Professor E. P. Sanders of Duke University object to even raising a question against the "new paradigm" and bully the questioners as "slanderers"?

[298] Dunn writes: "Paul is making several points to the Galatians here. One is that he himself knew from inside the life-style and commitment which they were finding so attractive; if Judaism was so enticing, particularly Jewish customs and traditions, then he himself had been more committed to this Judaism and more successful in it than many (=most?) of his contemporaries. When he would subsequently seek to dissuade the Galatians from making such commitment and embracing such traditions, it was not because he was ignorant of their appeal. Another is the clear indication that it was this same commitment which had made him an enemy of the church: it was as an expression of his way of life within Judaism that he persecuted the church in excessive measure and tried to destroy it. Again the implication is obvious: there was something antipatheical between typical and traditional life-style practiced within Judaism and the church of God" (Dunn, *The Theology of Paul's Letter to the Galatians*, pp. 66-67).

[299] Often, scholars are afraid to discuss the possibility that St. Paul actually did attack Judaism as a religion, because of the historical experiences of the Jews, particularly in the twentieth century. Some feel that such discourse contributes to violence against Jews, and they do not want to bear the responsibility that such a scholarly discourse could contribute to violence against Jews. Other scholars, often Jewish, are reactionary against past scholarship and blame it for violence against Jews, so they go to the opposite side of the pendulum. For instance, Daniel Boyarin writes: "Since World War II, the study of Paul's letters has taken on a new sense of urgency and importance. Much of the horror inflicted on the Jews in this century can be traced at least partially to theologically informed attitudes of contempt for the Jews. These attitudes of contempt are partially

Galatians as Examined by Diverse Academics

salvation was through the Jewish law.[300] Obviously, the motivation of the Judaizers can be questioned. It is possible that some of them were like St. Paul before his conversion; namely, being zealous for the Jewish law and trying to bring people back into Judaism.[301] In other words, just as St. Paul had been entrusted with bringing Jewish converts to Christianity back to Judaism by Jewish authorities themselves, some Judaizers were really working for Jewish authorities.[302] This explains the anathema uttered by

---

produced in the context of a particular reading of Paul's texts, a reading which depicts him attacking Judaism as inferior, mechanistic, commercialized religion, exactly paralleling portrayals of the Jewish People current in anti-Semitic Europe – witness even so relatively mild and nuanced a case as *The Merchant of Venice*. This reading of Paul's attitude toward Judaism usually goes along with two corollary propositions: that Paul converted to Christianity owing to his disgust with ancestral religion, and that God had rejected the Jews because of their inferior religious stance" (Boyarin, *A Radical Jew*, pp. 40-41). Although such a perspective may not be characterized as paranoia, certainly such a moralizing voice can become tyrannical if it curbs freedom of research and freedom of expression. Pursuit of the truth and accurate history is a moral value in and of itself, and academia has no place for bully pulpits preventing propounding of divergent ideas, no matter how much a prejudiced person (in regards to that idea) may find it offensive. In other words, scholars should not be herded in a particular direction to avoid the possibility of someone or some nation using that research for their own interests. For accurate understanding of the past and of history is important in and of itself. In a sense, Muslims who deny the existence of the Holocaust, because they feel that the acknowledgement of its existence might spur their young ones toward philo-Semitism are qualitatively the same as those who deny that St. Paul attacked Judaism as an entity because they fear a growth of anti-Semitism. When tyranny on intellectual freedom and freedom of expression proliferates, academic research degenerates and academic integrity atrophies to the extent that the value of academia as a whole can be questioned. There must be freedom to research and freedom to express that research without tyrannical censorship or despotic oppression.

[300] Dunn writes: "This presumably throws light on the puzzle still left in 1.6-7; whether what the other Christian Jewish missionaries preached to the Galatians was in fact also the gospel" (Dunn, *The Theology of Paul's Letter to the Galatians*, p. 27).

[301] Daniel Boyarin states: "Paul ... railed once again against his Jewish Christian opponents for insisting that the Galatians must become Jews in order to be Christians" (Boyarin, *A Radical Jew*, p. 32). It is possible to question the motive of the Judaizers who wanted Christians to become Jews.

[302] Such a socio-political structure was definitely in place. Esler states: "To be effective, the threat of persecution ... mentioned by Paul in 6.12 would need to involve recourse to the disciplinary procedures available in the synagogue or to other means whereby Israelite authority was enforced. This is in keeping with what Paul says elsewhere in the

St. Paul.[303] St. Paul would not have used such a rhetorical violence against those whom he considered to be truly saved, as being true members of the Body of Christ.[304] St. Paul assumed that these Judaizers were not really Christians,[305] or truly born again.[306] This is consistent with the message of St. Paul. If Abraham was justified by faith in Jesus Christ, then everyone is justified by faith in Christ.[307] Judaizers were

---

letter" (Esler, *Galatians*, p. 74). The historical context of the time certainly included proactive persecution of Jewish converts to Christianity by leaders of Judaism and their deputized agents.

[303] Yuval-Davis states: "The boundaries the politics of belonging are concerned with are the boundaries of the political community of belonging, the boundaries which, sometimes physically, but always symbolically, separate the world population into 'us' and 'them'" (Yuval-Davis, *The Politics of Belonging*, p. 20).

[304] Fung writes: "The twice-repeated 'let him be accursed' (AV, RSV), coupled with the indication that this was not the first time such an anathema had been invoked, shows that it cannot be explained as 'a careless utterance, expressing more accurately his immediate feelings than his general theory,' but must be taken with all seriousness as indicating Paul's attitude toward any teaching that is at variance with the gospel. The fearful verdict, 'let him be anathema' (RV), can hardly mean being 'held outcast,' that is, excommunicated, since it envisages an angel as a possible object. It thus more likely means being delivered up and devoted to the judicial wrath of God: 'the kind of zeal which Israel directed against apostates to preserve her own salvation, and which Paul himself had formerly exercised against Christians, he now directs against the Judaizers to protect the church" (Fung, *The Epistle to the Galatians*, p. 47). But fallen angels do go to Hell.

[305] Yuval-Davis states: "The politics of belonging involves not only constructions of boundaries but also the inclusion or exclusion of particular people, social categories and groupings within these boundaries by those who have the power to do this" (Yuval-Davis, *The Politics of Belonging*, p. 18). St. Paul's power was in his apostleship.

[306] Howard denigrates Judaism and Jewish Law to the level of Paganism, thereby driving a conclusive wedge between Christianity and Judaism as affinity religions. Howard writes: "Indeed it may be said that a distinctive characteristic of the word 'law' in the history of the interpretation of this passage is the concept of enslavement to legalism. This concept is used to explain Paul's apparent equation between Judaism and paganism. Since both are legal systems, to be under one is tantamount to being under the other and to be under either is to be under the 'elements'" (Howard, *Paul*, p. 71). Thus, St. Paul grouped Paganism with Judaism as similar on the qualitative level (See also Morland, p. 146).

[307] Yuval-Davis states: "The politics of belonging also include struggles around the determination of what is involved in belonging, in being a member of such a community" (Yuval-Davis, *The Politics of Belonging*, p. 20).

emphasizing that salvation was through Jewish law. If these leaders based their salvation primarily on observance of the Jewish law, then they were not really saved, or regenerated.[308] Those who preached another Gospel believed in another Gospel.

Another Gospel is the claim that one can be saved by keeping the Jewish law. Perverted Gospel is analogous to another Gospel, but the focus is placed more on the perverter,[309] who is depicted as a traitor to the Gospel. Whereas the Jews and Judaism preach another Gospel, the perverted Gospel is preached by those who know the true Gospel, but has rejected it or modified it. The Perverters of the Gospel can be seen specifically as so-called Christian leaders, who used their knowledge of Christianity to lead the Christian faithful astray. But obviously, another Gospel and perverted Gospel are synonymous since they share the same premise that salvation is through the Jewish law. In essence, they both privilege Judaism in ways that offends St. Paul. The difference is the identity of the propagator; the perverter of the Gospel disseminates the false message, pretending to be a true servant of Christ, but is actually a traitor, like Judas Iscariot.

Obviously, St. Paul's attack of another Gospel is not new. In the Gospels, Jesus of Nazareth attacked the Jewish law and leaders of Judaism, frequently. However, what is new is the terminology. In the Gospels,

---

[308] The emphasis on faith as an antithesis of the law can be seen as anti-Semitic, according to Daniel Boyarin. Boyarin states: "One of the crucial passages in Paul for determining (or rather, constructing) his posture vis-à-vis the Jewish religion – the Law – is Galatians 3:10-4:7. Many interpreters, especially of the 'Lutheran' school, have read this passage as if the 'curse of the Law' consists of the inability of human beings to ever meet its demands fully and therefore the irreparable curse that it places on all. The whole purpose of the Law, on this account, is to *increase* sin in the world, so that the saving grace of the cross will be even more abundant. As can be imagined, such an interpretation of Paul leads easily to charges that he was rabidly anti-Jewish. Moreover, if such views are asserted as a theologically correct view of Judaism and its historical role, then the theology is anti-Judaic (and later anti-Semitic)" (Boyarin, *A Radical Jews*, p. 136). *Ad hominem* attacks on those who analyze a text in a particular way or draw a different conclusion with terms like "anti-Semitism" do not encourage open academic discourse; rather, it creates an atmosphere of witch-hunting in academia and universities.

[309] Morland writes: "In 1:8-9 Paul cursed those who perverted the Gospel as preached by him. This makes it necessary not only to establish the *ethos* of Paul as in 1:10, but also to underscore the authority of the Gospel" (Morland, *The Rhetoric of Curse in Galatians*, p. 155).

Jesus of Nazareth did not call the idea that keeping the Jewish law would bring salvation as another Gospel. But this difference can be due to the fact that the Jesus movement was mostly a populist movement, and the institutionalization of the Jesus movement had not occurred at the stage in which the Gospels were depicting. Thus, Jesus of Nazareth writes off Judaism wholesale and attacks leaders of Judaism constantly.[310] In a sense, Jesus of Nazareth created an us-versus-them mentality against Judaism among his followers. For example, Jesus of Nazareth calls the Pharisees and the Sadducees, "brood of vipers." Pharisees and Sadducees are different branches of Judaism, as Protestantism and Catholicism are different branches of Christianity.

Jesus of Nazareth, in essence, opposes all denominations of Judaism.[311] Not only does Jesus of Nazareth oppose the Pharisees and the Sadducees, Jesus of Nazareth opposes Jerusalem Temple priests. In fact, the High Priest of the Jerusalem Temple says that it is better to kill one man, Jesus Christ, rather than endanger the whole Jewish nation. The High Priest of the Jerusalem Temple saw Jesus of Nazareth as a threat to the Jewish State, because Jesus of Nazareth opposed Judaism in all its

---

[310] Jerry L. Sumney argues that developing self-identity requires drawing up of boundaries that often results in identifying and attacking enemies. This was particularly important for self-identity of the early Christian communities (Sumney, *'Servants of Satan', 'False Brothers' and Other Opponents of Paul*, p. 18).

[311] Although the Pharisees can be seen as proto-Rabbinic, the Pharisees cannot be equated with the Rabbinic. Daniel Boyarin makes this important point: "I would like to make this absolutely clear. It is proper to speak of 'rabbinic' Judaism only with regard to the second century and onward, because we have no direct evidence for such a movement prior to the Mishna formed in the late second century. The Rabbis see the first-century Pharisees as their spiritual ancestors, and there is no reason to doubt that sensibility, but, on the other hand, neither is there reason to assume that the later rabbinic reports about those Pharisees have not been substantially re-formed in the light of rabbinic Judaism itself" (Boyarin, *A Radical Jew*, p. 2). Often in New Testament studies, there is a tendency toward uncritical use of rabbinic materials to apply to the first century of the common era, and this is just shoddy scholarship and certainly not in line with critical analysis. Such uncritical analysis ignores the trauma of Jewish history in AD 70, in which the Jerusalem Temple was completely destroyed by the Roman Empire and all Jews expelled from Jerusalem. Such traumatic experiences imprints on history realities that are often reactionary or paradigmatically different from before the trauma. Thus, the divide between the Pharisees and Rabbinic Judaism has to be upheld for the sake of historical accuracy and academic integrity.

different manifestations, from the Pharisees to the Jerusalem Temple leaders. The Gospels describe leaders of different denominations of Judaism all united against Jesus of Nazareth. Not only that, the Gospels describe Jewish leaders as successful in galvanizing support of the Jewish masses against Jesus of Nazareth. Thus, Jesus of Nazareth dies with the hatred of the Jewish people against him and the order of capital punishment by the Sanhedrin, the Supreme Court of the Jewish State. It is irony that he was called "The King of the Jews" in his capital punishment on the cross.

After the death of Jesus of Nazareth, Christianity began to be institutionalized with committee meetings, regular places for converts to congregate and worship, and a network.[312] As the teachings of Jesus of Nazareth propagated throughout nascent Christian communities, which were becoming institutionalized, subversive elements to the new institution were identified. St. Paul identifies these subversives as those who preached another Gospel or a perverted Gospel that Jewish law is necessary for salvation. Thus, it is understandable why the term "another

---

[312] Gerd Theissen actually argues that early Christianity was marked by itinerant preachers spreading a new propaganda; thus, Theissen presents a picture of anti-establishment/anti-institutionalization. Theissen states: "As nobody could suspect that the primitive Christian movement would one day transform and shape our entire culture, its missionaries were not the esteemed founders of Christianity, but homeless, roving propagandists without roots or a means of livelihood. They embodied a form of socially divergent behavior which was estranged from society's fundamental norms and necessities. One need only recall the demands on the disciples to forsake home, possessions, security, and family. By doing so they preached and lived a freedom from basic social responsibilities of a sort which could be put into practice only by those who had removed themselves from the stabilizing and domesticating effects of a continuing life of work – not by virtue of privilege of possessions, but by means of the ascetic poverty of an insecure marginal existence comparable to the life of the itinerant Cynic philosopher" (Gerd Thessen, *The Social Setting of Pauline Christianity*, trans. John H. Schütz {Philadelphia: Fortress Press, 1982}, p. 27). Like St. Francis of Assisi, early Christian missionaries were considered socially deviant and overtly propagandistic, who were marked by lack of money and a steady job. Although I would agree with Professor Theissen that early Christian missionaries were social-rejects and that early Christian communities were not organized or socialized in the way that churches are today, I would argue that there had been a kind of "institutionalization" at the level of idea or practices of the group, such as acceptance of the idea that Jesus Christ is God and the practice of the Lord's Supper to remember the death and resurrection of Jesus of Nazareth.

Gospel" is coined by St. Paul. Early Christianity reached a level of institutionalization that would allow for the identification of the "correct Gospel" as a term and phenomenon. Obviously, one cannot have an "another Gospel" without a "correct Gospel."

But it is important to recognize that St. Paul's position is consistent with the Jesus movement. Jesus of Nazareth chose to set himself and his followers in an us-versus-them position against Judaism in all different manifestations. Jesus of Nazareth chose to attack the leaders of Judaism, such as the Pharisees, Sadducees, the High Priest of the Jerusalem Temple, both explicitly and publicly. Jesus of Nazareth pro-actively taught his followers to hate Jewish leaders by calling them names, such as "brood of vipers." Thus, hatred of Judaism and the Jewish Law can be dated to the earliest strata of the Sitz im Leben of the early Christian movements. Therefore, St. Paul merely represents continuity with the wishes of the founder of what is now known as the Christian church; namely, that of the position of Jesus Christ Himself.

Galatians as Examined by Diverse Academics

Bibliography

Boyarin, Daniel. *A Radical Jew: Paul and the Politics of Identity*. Berkeley: University of California Press, 1994.

Bruce, F. F. *New Testament History*. New York: Doubleday, 1969.

----. *Paul: Apostle of the Heart Set Free*. Grand Rapids: William B. Eerdmans Publishing Company, 1977.

Comfort, Kenneth Jerold. *The Ego and the Social Order*. Cohoes: The Public Administration Institute of New York State, Inc., 2000.

De Boer, Martinus C. (Editor). *From Jesus to John: Essays on Jesus and New Testament Christology in Honour of Marinus de Jonge*. Sheffield: Sheffield Academic Press, 1993.

De Jonge, Marinus. *Jesus, The Servant-Messiah*. New Haven: Yale University Press, 1991.

Derrida, Jacques. *Politics of Friendship*. Translated by George Collins. London: Verso, 1997.

Dunn, James D. G. *The Theology of Paul's Letter to the Galatians*. Cambridge: Cambridge University Press, 1993.

Esler, Philip F. *Galatians*. London: Routledge, 1998.

From, Franz. *Perception of Other People*. Translated by Erik Kvan and Brendan Maher. New York: Columbia University Press, 1971.

Foucault, Michel. *The Hermeneutics of the Subject: Lectures at the College de France, 1981-82*. Translated by Graham Burchell. New York: Palgrave Macmillan, 2005.

Fung, Ronald Y. K. *The Epistle to the Galatians*. Grand Rapids: William B. Eerdmans Publishing Company, 1988.

Gunter, John J. *St. Paul's Opponents and Their Background: A Study of Apocalyptic and Jewish Sectarian Teachings*. Leiden: E. J. Brill, 1973.

Gurtner, Daniel M. *This World and the World to Come: Soteriology in Early Judaism*. London: T. & T. Clark, 2011.

Hansen, G. Walter. *Galatians*. Downers Grove, IL: InterVarsity Press, 1994.

Hengle, Martin. *The 'Hellenization' of Judaea in the First Century after Christ*. London: SCM Press, 1989.

----. *The Pre-Christian Paul*. London: SCM Press, 1991.

Howard, George. *Paul: Crisis in Galatia: A Study in Early Christian Theology*. Cambridge: Cambridge University Press, 1979.

Kee, Howard Clark. *Knowing the Truth: A Sociological Approach to New Testament Interpretation*. Minneapolis: Fortress Press, 1989.

Kern, Philip H. *Rhetoric and Galatians: Assessing an Approach to Paul's Epistles*. Cambridge: Cambridge University Press, 1998.

Kim, Heerak Christian. *Key Signifier As Literary Device: Its Definition and Function in Literature and Media*. Lewiston: Edwin Mellen Press, 2006.

----. *The Jerusalem Tradition in the Late Second Temple Period: Diachronic and Synchronic Developments Surrounding Psalms of Solomon 11*. Lanham: University Press of America, 2007.

Galatians as Examined by Diverse Academics

Kim, Seyoon Kim. *Paul and the New Perspective: Second Thoughts on the Origin of Paul's Gospel.* Grand Rapids: William B. Eerdmans Publishing Company, 2002.

Klawans, Jonathan. *Josephus and the Theologies of Ancient Judaism.* Oxford: Oxford University Press, 2012.

Levin, John M. (Editor). *Group Processes.* New York: Psychology Press, 2013.

Lohse, Eduard. *The New Testament Environment.* Translated by John E. Steely. Nashville: Abingdon Press, 1976.

Luedemann, Gerd. *Opposition to Paul in Jewish Christianity.* Translated by M. Eugene Boring. Minneapolis: Fortress Press, 1989.

Machen, J. Gresham. *The Origin of Paul's Religion.* Grand Rapids: Wm. B. Eerdmans Publishing Company, 1925.

Malina, Bruce. *The New Testament World: Insights from Cultural Anthropology.* Louisville: John Knox Press, 1981.

Marrow, Stanley B. *Paul: His Letters and His Theology.* New York: Paulist Press, 1986.

Marshall, James D. *Michel Foucault: Personal Autonomy and Education.* Dordrecht: Kluwer Academic Publishers, 1996.

Meeks, Wayne A. *The First Urban Christians: The Social World of the Apostle Paul.* New Haven: Yale University Press, 1983.

Morland, Kjell Arne. *The Rhetoric of Curse in Galatians: Paul Confronts Another Gospel.* Atlanta: Scholars Press, 1995.

Parente, Fausto, and Joseph Sievers (Editors). *Josephus and the History of the Greco-Roman Period: Essays in Memory of Morton Smith.* Leiden: E. J. Brill, 1994.

Porter, Stanley E. (Editor). *Paul: Jew, Greek, and Roman*. Leiden: Brill, 2008.

Poythress, Vern S. *The Shadow of Christ in the Law of Moses*. Phillipsburg: P. & R. Publishing, 1991.

Sumney, Jerry L. *'Servants of Satan', 'False Brothers' and Other Opponents of Paul*. Sheffield: Sheffield Academic Press, 1999.

Theissen, Gerd. *The Social Setting of Pauline Christianity*. Translated by John H. Schütz. Philadelphia: Fortress Press, 1982.

Vanhoye, A. (Editor). *L'apôtre Paul: Personnalité, style, et conception du ministère*. Leuven: Leuven University Press, 1986.

Wilder, William N. *Echoes of the Exodus Narrative in the Context and Background of Galatians 5:18*. New York: Peter Lang, 2001.

Yuval-Davis, Nira. *The Politics of Belonging: Intersectional Contestations*. Los Angeles: Sage, 2011.

www.ingramcontent.com/pod-product-compliance
Lightning Source LLC
Chambersburg PA
CBHW020732240426
43665CB00052B/453